Centering the Margins of
Anthropology's History

Histories of Anthropology Annual

EDITORS

Regna Darnell
Frederic W. Gleach

Centering the Margins of Anthropology's History

Histories of Anthropology Annual, Volume 14

EDITED BY REGNA DARNELL AND
FREDERIC W. GLEACH

University of Nebraska Press | *Lincoln*

Publication of this work was assisted by the Murray-Hong Family Trust, to honor and sustain the distinguished legacy of Stephen O. Murray in the History of Anthropology at the University of Nebraska Press.

Library of Congress Control Number: 2020945633

Set in Arno Pro by Mikala R. Kolander.

CONTENTS

EDITORS' INTRODUCTION

Each volume of *Histories of Anthropology Annual* presents a stand-alone collection of papers roughly assembled around a theme or set of themes of concern to contemporary anthropologists, historians, and multiple disciplinary and community-based others. The juxtapositions invite comparative perspectives across time and space as well as disciplinary and theoretical traditions. At the same time, we aspire to build a critical mass of scholarship in which each volume extends the definition of what anthropology's history might encompass and expands the audience for this body of work. The choice of histories in the plural is a self-conscious claim that history exists only when interpretations are imposed upon primary data of various kinds.

Volume 14 circles around the conscious recognition of margins and suggests that it is time, in terms of both a changing theoretical openness and a supporting body of scholarship, to bring the margins to the center, if not to problematize the very dichotomy of center and margin itself. Over recent decades, much has been made of voices from the margins. Standpoint-based approaches have named and challenged the de facto exclusion of the voices of women, Native Americans, Afro-Americans, Asian Americans, Latinx, immigrants, and others. Class barriers to mobility have been considered, along with limitations and marginalizations due to homelessness, poverty, and lack of access to resources for education and employment. Regional studies clusters have emerged alongside the institutionalization of global capitalism despite globalization's surface appearance of increasing homogeneity. This emphasis on the margins is not a perfect solution, but at least takes a step toward more inclusion and awareness and the crossings of various margins. Yet there has often been a strident undertone, a fear that no one is listening, an implicit victimology.

This volume explores two major strands of redefining the relationship of center and margins: On the one hand, anthropologists and historians have sought out marginalized and forgotten ancestors, arguing for their present-day relevance and offering explanations for the lack of attention to their contributions to theory, analysis, methods, and findings. We will return below to a second strand of margins to center relationship dealing with experiments in genres of writing that explore the nature of ethnographic enterprise. The implicit limitation of biography to a single subject can be overcome when several figures from the same period or intellectual tradition are juxtaposed so that their contrasts and connections can be brought into the historian's spotlight. The diverse reasons for choosing a biographical subject reflect the interests, experience, and institutional location of the historian arguing for a reassessment of the subject's reputation and importance. Although the method is historicist, the historian cannot be neutral; nor will their research attract an audience unless it is seen by readers as relevant. Many scholars who focus on biographical reclamation dabble in such projects when a particular ancestor comes to their attention. Collectively, these scholars contribute significantly to a growing database for the history of anthropology. Exemplars included in this volume explore the institutional and social contexts, and what the late Raymond D. Fogelson has called "epitomizing events," within which individual scholarship is framed. These contexts rapidly become unintelligible to successive generations without reflexive retrospective reassessment.

No adequate disciplinary history can afford to emphasize only the major figures, the public intellectuals, the great theorists and organizational leaders. Such icons as Franz Boas, Bronislaw Malinowski, Margret Mead, A. R. Radcliffe-Brown, Claude Lévi-Strauss, or Clifford Geertz did not and do not operate in a vacuum but were and are supported by many who are too often dismissed as minor figures, when remembered at all. Collectively they constitute a social and interactional network relative to one another within a professional generation or national tradition. Understanding those networks of individuals injects personal agency into the debates and events of the past. Changes over an individual's professional lifetime reveal how their thinking evolved over a career, and lead back to the contexts in which their goals are embedded. Biography, then, far from being solely the history of an individual, becomes a potential window into how individual lives and careers move the discipline forward with some degree of synchronicity across individuals, events, and paradigm shifts. The papers included in this volume explore some of the ways in which a biographical starting point can draw on the historian's other archival research or ethnographic experience to frame an individual biography in a nuanced manner.

Herbert Lewis identifies H. Scudder Mekeel as a "forgotten pioneer" who came to his attention as he explored the history of his own Department of Anthropology at the University of Wisconsin. Many of the figures he followed through different phases of departmental history have been key participants in the larger discipline. Lewis situates Mekeel at the transition from Boasian historicism to the study of contemporary living tribes, then called acculturation. Mekeel's symbolic and psychological approach did not resonate in the latter days of Boasian hegemony precisely because it straddled the old and the new, emphasizing process but retaining perspectives seemingly at odds with the future of "action anthropology." Contemporary dismissal of Mekeel's work in Thomas Biolsi's "harsh" review reflects his failure of historicism as he rewrites the past in response to Vine Deloria Jr.'s wholesale critique of anthropology as a discipline. Although Mekeel was ahead of his time, he has been ignored since.

David Posthumus documents the Lakota and their Indigenous anthropologists with a more charitable eye, focusing on Deloria Jr.'s niece Ella Deloria, whose collaboration with Franz Boas supported her research into the language and ritual culture of her people. Boas encouraged both her fictional and ethnographic and linguistic writing, as well as providing modest funds, mentorship, and reciprocal respect. To dismiss Boas's failure to obtain an academic position for her—a position incompatible with her many community obligations in any case—as exploitative of her gender or stature as an Indigenous intellectual is again a failure to consider the context of the collaboration in its time. Boas highly valued Deloria's culturally embedded judgments of other work on the Sioux—for example, her skepticism about the "idiosyncratic" legends and interpretations recorded by James R.

Walker. (Deloria systematically attempted to verify Walker's claims with other Lakota cultural experts and was unable to do so.)

In another welcome chapter in Joshua Smith's meticulous documentation of the action anthropology initiated by Sol Tax and associates at the University of Chicago, Smith describes the personal experience, politics, and "spirit of anthropology" consistently reflected in the career of Robert Rietz. Smith carefully interweaves intersecting academic and applied scholarship by Marc Pinkoski, Michael Asch, and others now identifying themselves as action anthropologists. That Rietz was not Indigenous is not made explicit until well into the paper; for the post–World War II generation of action anthropologists, this did not preclude participation in the political process of working to achieve community goals through collaboration, nor did it render him ineffective in his role as director of the Chicago American Indian Center from 1958 until his death in 1971.

Ian Puppe, with coauthors North De Pencier and Gerald McKinley, draws on an ongoing study of the medical records of the Sioux Lookout Zone Hospital in Ontario, Canada. The discovery of these archives enables a longitudinal study of the standpoints of medical practitioners and community members accessing services, especially their cultural values surrounding mental illness. Puppe deploys an unpublished 1971 paper by Adrian Tanner, included here as exemplary of the context in which it was prepared, to argue that Tanner's work foreshadowed the development of medical anthropology a generation later. Puppe also shows how interpretive frameworks have changed by recovering an Indigenous ontological perspective from A. Irving Hallowell's work with nearby Objibwa communities in the 1930s and 1940s. Tanner's political ecology of health care delivery urged physicians to acknowledge the need for social science in northern health care; he emphasized environmental stressors and equated mental illness with assimilation and "becoming white." Puppe's analysis, in contrast, aspires to collaboration between the different but not necessarily incompatible Indigenous and biomedical health specialists in service of effective community care. The two kinds of knowledge must be seen by both sides as equal in value and coherence for such a convergence to occur.

Nicholas Barron focuses on an event rather than a single individual: an international symposium in 1981 sponsored by the prestigious Wenner-Gren Foundation for Anthropological Research (W-G) and held partly on the Pascua Yacqui Reservation near Tucson, Arizona. The planned reenactment of a deer dance that had fallen into disuse permitted the Yacqui community, which had only recently obtained federal recognition as an Indian tribe, to seize the opportunity to perform their identity in contemporary and innovative terms. A single enterprising individual was able to deploy the event in service to his personal political agenda because the scholars sponsored by the W-G had no context for the performance and uncritically accepted it as representing a timeless Yacqui culture shared by the entire community. Cross-cultural miscommunication arose in large part because anthropologists who had worked extensively with the Yacqui, particularly Edward and Rosamond Spicer, were not considered experts in the W-G context and were invited as an afterthought. Ethnography and local knowledge were not recognized as relevant expertise. Barron highlights the irony of artificial distinctions that fail to center margins being recognized in today's anthropological histories as significant.

Geoffrey Gray traces F. G. G. Rose's journey to oblivion in the history of anthropology as the inevitable result of the outmoded evolutionary models he acquired from his training with A. C. Haddon and the absence of relationships between Cambridge and the Australian anthropological establishment. Gray's extensive writings on the personnel and institutional development of the discipline in Australia focus here on the curtailment of academic freedom resulting from (inaccurate) accusations of Rose's Communist Party sympathies and possibly membership. Gatekeepers in academic institutions colluded with security services to marginalize his persistent efforts to carry out ethnographic research in Australia in the late 1930s. Rose does not seem to have been aware of the behind-the-scenes enmity of A. R. Elkin and was forced to return to his native Germany, where he made an academic career but remained peripheral to the larger discipline. His return to Australia in the 1960s still found him barred from funding and research permits, and his Australian kinship work remains a minor footnote in disciplinary history. Biography in this case is subsumed to, but clarifies the nature of, institutional dominance and the potential of collegial networks to exclude even the most determined.

On the other hand, consideration of marginalized and forgotten ancestors contextualizes a second strand of margin to center relations in the histories of anthropology that is found in the range of genres through which anthropologists and their historians have attempted to present their results in provocative and open-ended formats. The chapters here by Charles Laughlin and Regna Darnell explore the attraction anthropologists have long felt toward science fiction, although they approach the subject in very different ways. Science fiction calls into play the methodologies anthropologists use to describe and interpret their subject matter.

Laughlin's extraterrestrial anthropology focuses on the relationship between science and technology and outlines the range of subjects for his discipline's speculation, from the stresses of space travel to the modes of first contact and the effects of anthropological musings on the imagination that fuels science and exploration. He emphasizes the adoption by seti of cultural anthropologists' certainty that an authoritarian, military model of planetary settlement and conquest is doomed to failure. Not all reviewers of science fiction have acknowledged the formative presence of anthropologists and anthropological thinking at the core of the genre, and Laughlin's chapter provides a welcome corrective.

Darnell explores Ursula K. Le Guin's explicitly ethnographic novel *Always Coming Home* (1985) as a reflection on the continuity of the California Indians that she knew as a child, as the daughter of anthropologist Alfred Kroeber and folklorist and writer Theodora Kroeber, and a vision of a postapocalyptic future through the continuity of the land that brought alive what archaeology could not access. Her alter ego Pandora worries about the Kesh lack of interest in history beyond personal memory or in preserving written records beyond what matters for oral tradition. Her perspective is one Pandora had never considered, and this challenges her unreflexive assumption that preservation of data is neutral and accessible to all. The alternative evokes contemporary Indigenous uses of oral tradition to transmit ties of land; kinship (including with nonhuman relatives); and ongoing, continuous, and dynamic reformation and adaptation of continuities from the past to contemporary realities. The Kesh alternative may indeed foreshadow a possible non-polarized conversation between a living history and contemporary political activism. Darnell, like Le Guin, applies an ethnographic methodology to disentangling oral and written strands and imagines a past that flows into the present through generations. Such a model retains the possibility of nonbinary conversation across what first appeared to be irreconcilable divides.

The late Vintilă Mihăilescu bends the genre conventions of writing anthropology's history in a different way, using personal reflections to explore how he experienced the post-communist transition to capitalism in Romania after the Soviet collapse of 1989. As a cultural anthropologist and public intellectual—a combination largely unfamiliar to North American audiences—he distills two decades of writing monthly magazine articles in Bucharest. He compares the ongoing thread from anecdote to interpretation to the never-complete continuities of the Arabic *1001 Nights* but goes on to frame them as representative of larger perspectives—that is, as generalizable. This chapter derives from the introductory section of a longer manuscript that was in progress at the time of Mihăilescu's death. Continuity is provided by the author's well-honed ethnographic eye, moving from the ground up to grander issues of social and political change on a global scale while remaining firmly grounded in the local. Structure is provided by a dialectic moving from *thesis* (food in an oral society and the changing role of the pig in Romanian cuisine) to *antithesis* (communist ruptures allowing economic development for some in the cities but poverty in the villages left behind) to *parenthesis* (the ethnographic importance of the everyday) to *synthesis* (reflections on postmodernity). These are the processes of historicist reflexivity and its centrality to the history of anthropology. The epilogue muses on understanding what is hard for the author to accept in a rapidly and irreversibly changing world. Readers will find the ethnography of Romania and its position in the post-Soviet realignment of Eastern Europe fascinating for its own sake, but there is also a superimposed challenge to tailor our histories—disciplinary or otherwise—to the local experiences of real people in specific times and places. The anthropologist's view aspires to capture the essence of a society in transition and place it in a general human framework. The European Association of Social Anthropology obituary (Heintz 2020, at the association's website) notes the implicit paradox of a reputation more local than Mihăilescu's stature as a public intellectual merited precisely because the contributions it made to social anthropology were so deeply grounded in the "specific, singular but comparable, linkable historical configuration" of his ethnography of Romanian society and the changes in it that he documented.

The final chapter did not begin as an experiment in genre. The editors of *Histories of Anthropology Annual* envisioned a feature highlighting the work of a senior historian of anthropology reflecting on the trajectory of their career. This is a well-established genre, drawing on conventions of interview, but one that rarely finds a home in scholarly publications. In this case, however, the interview came to have a flavor perhaps more reminiscent of European public intellectual debates, in which a peer interviewer discusses their work and ideas with the subject without aiming at neutrality. Stephen O. Murray served on the HOAA editorial board and as coeditor of the University of Nebraska's Critical Studies in History of Anthropology series from the planning stages preceding first publication to his death in August 2019. His health precluded completion of the envisioned interview, which was a collaborative enterprise from its inception. The resulting chapter has four coauthors, each exploring aspects of Steve's life and work as related to their own. We hope that this experimental format offers a dynamic, multifaceted perspective that captures one of the dominant (if sometimes marginalized) voices in the history of anthropology. Steve's career developed at the institutional margins of several academic disciplines and activist discourses but his distinctive voice has been, and will remain, at the center of our history. He was also a dear friend, to these projects and to us personally, so we are happy to be able to share these last conversations with a broader audience.

REGNA DARNELL

FREDERIC W. GLEACH

*Centering the Margins of
Anthropology's History*

1

A Forgotten Pioneer

Haviland Scudder Mekeel and the
Expansion of Anthropology

Haviland Scudder Mekeel had begun to play an important role in the expanding world of American anthropology in the 1940s when he died suddenly in 1947 at the age of forty-five. Perhaps he would not have remained on the margins had he lived, as his intellectual direction, psychological anthropology, grew in prominence in the next decades, but this is idle speculation. My attention was drawn to Mekeel through a fortunate accident, but I discovered that his was not a simple and predictable career as an anthropologist raised in the late 1920s. This was a lesson to me: don't assume that you know a person by their age, era, and beginnings. I was also prompted to do the research and write this article because of my concern about the treatment and understanding of the history of anthropology in the era of the "posts."

The editors of this volume remark that, "although the method is historicist, the historian cannot be neutral; nor will their research attract an audience unless it is seen by readers as relevant." This author is not neutral. I have not infrequently expressed my concern that the understanding of American anthropology's past has been grievously distorted as a result of the upheavals and turmoil of the late 1960s. From then until now, many popular approaches (including deconstructionist, Marxist, postcolonial, and decolonizing) have contended that most of what came before their own revolutions was shameful and often harmful to the people whom anthropologists claimed to be understanding and whose cultures they were recording and supposedly saving. I write against these tropes, this discourse. I hope that this research is relevant and contributes to a clearer understanding of not only the motivations but also the contributions of these individuals from an earlier era. These ancestors from other social, cultural, and political contexts were struggling with the same problems that we have today. I hope that this representation of one particular earlier anthropologist will contribute to the "reflexive retrospective reassessment" that the editors call for.

Haviland Scudder Mekeel (1902–1947) began his education in anthropology in the second decade of the Boasian era, when the historicist and diffusionist approach to ethnography was dominant. But he was a pioneer in the study of change among living American Indian and Euro-American populations, and in applied and psychological anthropology. By the 1940s, Mekeel was engaged with the social psychology of prejudice and "devoted to the causes of understanding the social and psychological problems of minority groups and of furthering their rights to participate fully in a democratic nation" (Macgregor 1948, 95). Mekeel's career mirrored important developments in the growth and expansion of American anthropology in the late 1930s and 1940s, and his life and work shed light on an unappreciated period in our history.[1]

Mekeel's name would have been far better known had he not died suddenly of a heart attack when he was forty-five years old. To my knowledge there are only two published pieces dealing specifically with Haviland Scudder Mekeel: one is the obituary in the *American Anthropologist* by Gordon Macgregor, a friend and fellow applied anthropologist; the other is a critical evaluation by Thomas Biolsi in the volume *Indians and Anthropologists: Vine Deloria, Jr., and the Critique of Anthropology* (Biolsi and Zimmerman 1997). The sources for this article are mostly limited to those two pieces, Mekeel's published writings, and his correspondence from 1940 to 1942.[2]

Scudder Mekeel was born in St. Louis but began his peripatetic college career at the California Institute of Technology, which he attended from 1920 to 1921. He continued at Princeton University from 1921 to 1924, and next tried his luck in France at the University of Strasbourg from 1925 to 1926. According to Macgregor it was Mekeel's wife who convinced him to return to the United States to get a degree; he in turn convinced a reluctant Harvard to admit him, and he finally received his BS there in 1928. Mekeel then studied at the University of Chicago, receiving an MA degree in 1929, then followed Edward Sapir to Yale, where he and the linguistic anthropologist Stanley Newman received Yale's first two anthropology PhDs in 1932. It was Sapir's cultural and psychological work, not his linguistics, that primarily interested Mekeel.

While a graduate student at Yale he was appointed assistant anthropologist at the Yale Institute of Human Relations, where Clark Wissler, who was teaching there, interested him in "American Indian culture under the influence of white civilization" (Macgregor 1948, 96). He carried out his doctoral research on acculturation among the Teton-Dakota and produced "one of the first intensive acculturation studies among the American Indians" (Macgregor 1958, 96). Having developed an interest in problems of "personality in cultural disintegration" and other aspects of psychology in culture, Mekeel then spent 1933 through 1935 in training in Boston as a fellow of the Social Science Research Council, and at Harvard as a fellow in psychology with Harry Murray, contributing to his *Explorations in Personality* (1938).[3]

Mekeel's early positions involved him in applied anthropology on New Deal projects, first for the newly reorganized Office of Indian Affairs under John Collier, where he served as a field representative and director of the Applied Anthropology Unit in 1935, and briefly as the head of a "special socio-economic unit of the Soil Conservation Service of the Department of Agriculture" (Hartshorne et al, n.d.). He became director of the Laboratory of Anthropology in Santa Fe in 1937, and in 1940 he accepted a position as associate professor in the Department of Anthropology and Sociology at the University of Wisconsin.

Macgregor writes that Mekeel's sudden death "has taken from the ranks of younger anthropologists a leader in the integration of cultural anthropology and psychoanalysis, a teacher highly stimulating and deeply human, and a mind of great pioneering capacity. It has also taken from this country a man devoted to the causes of understanding the social and psychological problems of minority groups and of furthering their rights to participate fully in a democratic nation" (1948, 95). Allowing for some hyperbole in the cause of *de mortuis nil nisi bonum*, this is still an impressive tribute. What lay behind it?

Mekeel's first field experience came in 1929, when he received a fellowship from the new Laboratory of Anthropology in Santa Fe and joined the field-training party of five advanced students who spent eight weeks interviewing informants from the Walapai tribe in Arizona. This work was directed by A. L. Kroeber at a time when he and his colleagues were producing ethnographic accounts on the basis of memory culture and searching for traits to fill out trait lists for the historical and ecological study of culture areas, development, and diffusion. Their joint research resulted in a volume edited by Kroeber and others, *Walapai Ethnography* (1935), with Mekeel writing eleven of the thirty-seven sections, including those on plant foods and preparations, death, law, and the Ghost Dance. Kroeber apparently had his suspicions of this new boy, however; Macgregor writes that "Dr. Kroeber predicted at this time that Mekeel would probably pursue fields 'on the fringes of anthropology'" (1948, 96). Presumably he suspected that Mekeel was more inclined to the social science approach that the natural historian Kroeber feared would take over anthropology (Kroeber 1963).

Mekeel soon bore out this prophecy with his dissertation, in which he turned his attention to contemporary conditions and cultural change among the Lakota (Teton-Dakota) of the White Clay District of the Pine Ridge Reservation, as it was in 1930. "A Modern Indian Community in the Light of Its Past: A Study of Cultural Change" (Mekeel 1932) was one of the earliest studies of North American Indians to focus on acculturation rather than the memories of informants. Mekeel's approach to culture in this work was strikingly different from that of the Walapai study. As Elizabeth Colson put it (pers. comm., April 7, 2010), "He was writing about things as they then were rather than things of the nineteenth century." (The groundbreaking "Memorandum for the Study of Acculturation" by Robert Redfield, Ralph Linton, and Melville Herskovits did not appear until 1936.)

Mekeel published three papers from his dissertation dealing with contemporary conditions and predicaments. In the first, "A Discussion of Cultural Change as Illustrated by Material from a Teton-Dakota Community" (1932), he recommends a new approach to studying cultural change "in the hope that there may develop a deeper understanding of culture forces—and, possibly, of human nature as well" (1932, 275).

When culture comes to be studied more intimately in terms of processes, the need will be increasingly felt for gathering more complete data on the subjective aspects of culture products within definite ethnographic areas. A study of change as a process of culture, for instance, inevitably leads to a consideration of the transformations in concepts, attitudes, values—in short, the complete psychological *aurae*—surrounding those culture traits which are in flux. For people react not to object-in-itself reality, but to its symbolic derivatives. Therefore only by an investigation of meanings current within a group can one approach an etiology of alterations in specific culture products; an etiology necessary for understanding the nature of culture change in whatever form—invention, diffusion, or modification. (1932, 274)

In writing of the three sources of change, "invention, diffusion, or modification," Mekeel is connected to the central cultural historical debates within American anthropology, but he was a pioneer in the manner in which he stressed the symbolic and psychological aspects of process.[4]

The ethnographic material for the paper comes from his observation of the summer nomadic travels and encampments of groups of Oglala Teton-Dakota in 1930. Mekeel suggested that the contemporary pattern of extended visiting of relatives spread far and wide, and encampment for long periods at the sites of fairs and rodeos, was a replacement for, or even a continuation of, earlier social and cultural patterns. He compares the nineteenth-century political organization of the Oglala at their great summer encampments, with their ceremonies and buffalo hunts, as reconstructed by Clark Wissler, with the patterns of activity and leadership that he witnessed at rodeos and fairs in 1930.

Mekeel uses this case study as the basis for asking more fundamental questions about the study and understanding of cultural change. He wonders how one can tell whether "this nomadic, restless tendency" can be considered a "cultural trait which has been passed on from generation to generation" (younger Indians would say it was "in the blood") or if it is better explained by contemporary stimuli. He asks, "What forces are at work for and against the continuance of this nomadic summer life?" (1932, 283) and wonders about future changes in organization and about approaches to predicting a future that depends partly on government action. "If techniques be devised for answering [these types] of problem for the whole cultural content of a people, and be applied to many ethnographical areas, what would be the possibility of formulating laws of culture processes?" (1932, 284). In this, the earliest of his papers, he declares his hope for "the study of social laws" for modern man to "direct the formation of the cultural or social meanings" in light of the great rate of "increase in new material products. Control involves a knowledge of process as well as of objective—whether in the physical or social sciences. May not something at least be learned about culture processes through a study of change in civilizations alien to our own?" (1932, 285).

The second paper, "The Economy of a Modern Teton Dakota Community" (1936a), is a study of the economic activities of the White Clay community of the Pine Ridge Reservation. Mekeel begins by declaring that "the values and attitudes behind the concrete patterns of a culture have been too often neglected by the ethnographer and, with unfortunate results, by administrator and missionary" (1936a, 3). After a discussion of key values among the Teton, above all bravery and generosity, Mekeel outlines some of the dilemmas facing the different generations on the reservation. He points out that hunting buffalo was more than merely a way of getting food. It was the center of a great complex of exciting activity, social and political organization, and sacred rituals; "[practically] every part of its body entered into some part of the culture. . . . Its spirit was deified. It was the mainstay of the economy and the warp of religion. The loss of this animal proved to be a death-blow to the culture" (1936a, 5). With the end of the buffalo hunt and of warfare against both Euro-Americans and other Indian tribes, "the Teton men lost their traditional activities and with them their chief paths to glory and prestige" (1936a, 5). But there remained the value of generosity, which still played a powerful role in the 1930s.

Mekeel divides the population into three age categories based on their varying historical experiences. The oldest could still remember "the days of the buffalo-hide tipi." The men had counted coup, hunted buffalo, sought visions, and witnessed the Sun Dance. "They and their fathers were lords of the prairie and made treaties as the white man's equal" (1936a, 5). Even though "the cessation of intertribal warfare is regarded as a boon by the women," Mekeel concludes that those of that oldest generation "live in the past and think of the future only with despair" (1936a, 6). It does not get better, in his telling. "The second group knows itself only as a defeated tribe which is entitled to support," robbed of the good life they had heard about in their childhoods and dependent on government rations. He sees them as living a "parasitic life" (1936a, 6). "The third stratum, those thirty years old or younger, know from experience neither the old life nor the full-ration days," but, as they are better educated, they resent the leadership of the old men and think they are more qualified to deal with Washington officials (1936a, 6). But they do not see a bright future either.

Mekeel details the severe economic problems faced by these people during the Great Depression—long after the loss of the buffalo econ-omy. He concludes that agriculture, the subsistence base that govern-ment planners expected—even demanded—that the Teton-Dakotas adopt, failed for three main reasons. First, it is very difficult and gen-erally unrewarding in their environment: it offers no prestige to the farmer and it has no cultural resonance for them, in sharp contrast to the people of the pueblos, such as the Hopi. Secondly, the central value of generosity, the culturally cherished value that could still be practiced, had the effect of socially and economically levelling the population. (Mekeel presents a detailed discussion of the various ways the value of generosity was constantly being displayed and the stingy person shunned.) And finally, they know that if and when they are truly des-titute the government will step in to feed them (1936, 14). "Agriculture then is apparently not securely rooted [a deliberate pun?]. . . . It is not an integral part of the social whole, coalesced by sentiment, reinforced by value, and maintained by prestige" (1936, 14).

The third paper based on his doctoral research involved Indian edu-cation and appeared in the journal *Progressive Education* in 1936. *Progres-sive Education* was a publication of the Progressive Education Associa-tion, several of whose leaders were particularly interested in reforming Indian education. Mekeel's piece is a heartfelt plea for those undertak-ing the education of Indian children (or adults) to try to understand and take into account their cultures. Drawing on his experience of twenty months among Teton-Dakotas, Mekeel presents a fundamental argument of cultural anthropology (supplemented by his work in psychology): that "human drives come from sources other than that of formal education. By a process as unconscious as breathing, certain attitudes and values are absorbed from one's family and from one's other human contacts, all of whom are representatives of many social institutions, a home, a city or rural community, a trade, a business or profession, or perhaps a club. Mere acquirement of knowledge is not sufficient to break down a set of emotionally coalesced sentiments and to replace them with a new set" (1936b, 158). His critical evaluation of Indian education includes a presentation of what he considers to be the core values of Teton-Dakotas that have not been taken into account, as well as a plea to "understand and utilize the native culture in the educational system" (1936, 159).[5]

His concern about the conditions of Indians and his timely publications led to his first full-time professional employment. In 1934 Congress passed the Indian Reorganization Act (the Wheeler-Howard Bill), which proposed major changes in government policy. It was intended to "(1) restore to the Indian management of his own affairs; (2) prevent further depletion of his material resources; (3) build up an economically sound basis for livelihood" (Mekeel 1944, 209). According to Macgregor, "[Mekeel's] report and interpretation of the effect of Government programs upon the Sioux greatly impressed the Washington staff" (1948, 96) of John Collier, President Roosevelt's new commissioner of Indian Affairs, and from 1935 through 1937 Mekeel served as director of the Applied Anthropology Unit in the Office of Indian Affairs, as well as "the personal representative of the Commissioner, acting as his anthropological consultant" (Mekeel 1944, 210). Mekeel's explanation of why he was asked to take this position was that "it was just because I was one of the few who had actually studied the modern Indians. . . . Mostly, scientists had been studying them as they were when Columbus landed."

John Collier was a reformer, a visionary, a quasi anthropologist, and a man who saw himself as one appointed to undo the wrongs of the previous century in Indian affairs. His administration truly did oversee a "New Deal" for America's Indian tribes, at least in intention, although the successes were spotty and mixed. "Mekeel's major contribution to Indian Service administration was . . . advising on immediate problems and pointing out cultural difficulties and Indian attitudes. It was a lack of appreciation of these that frequently lay at the bottom of administration frustrations" (Macgregor 1948, 96–97). Mekeel quickly grew disenchanted with the Indian Service, and many of those working with Indians, because of their lack of knowledge and their insensitivity to the culture, interests, and expectations of the people they were supposed to serve. He resigned from Collier's organization in 1938 and in 1944 published an article detailing his criticisms of the Indian Reorganization Act. Another article, "Comparative Notes on the 'Social Role of the Settlement House' as Contrasted with that of the United States Indian Service" (1943), was more generally critical of the bureaucracy dealing with Indians.

Mekeel remained in contact with Willard W. Beatty, however, supporting his efforts to reform Indian education. Beatty, an early proponent of the Progressive Education movement with Carson Ryan, was brought into Collier's Indian New Deal project. Among their innovations were "the recognition of anthropology as an aid in understanding Indian cultures" and the idea that "the Indian child would learn through the medium of his own cultural values while also becoming aware of the values of white civilization" (Szasz 1999, 50). They stressed the appreciation of Indian cultures, attempted to introduce texts in Indian languages, and tried to shape educational and vocational education to the needs of particular communities. Mekeel served as an informal advisor.

By the early 1940s, Scudder Mekeel had become a center of communication for people concerned about social science and social and psychological issues as anthropology expanded its horizons (Kehoe and Doughty 2012). During those years he was in contact with many anthropologists, social scientists, editors, and publishers dealing with many subjects, including Japanese-American relocation and internment, the training of administrators of areas liberated during World War II, and, above all, the problems of racism, antisemitism, and equality in American society.

By the time Mekeel joined the Department of Sociology and Anthropology at the University of Wisconsin, he had chosen his direction as an activist foremost concerned about social science in social action and human rights, with major interests in personality and culture and the social psychology of prejudice. His correspondence in those years, as well as his publications—usually short and problem-oriented— were directed that way. "The American Indian as a Minority Group Problem" (1944) presents an overview of the situation of Indians in the early 1940s. "The present World War has considerably expanded our horizons. We are beginning to realize that our treatment of racial and minority groups is now of world significance. There is a certain similarity in our attitude toward all such groups. Thus we may be able to gain some insight into our treatment of some of the other minority peoples by examining the history of our contacts with the American Indian" (1944, 3).

In 1943 and 1944 he was on leave from the university as a consultant to the Julius Rosenwald Foundation working on what Macgregor called the problem of Negro-White race relations (Macgregor 1948, 97).[6] "At the same time he had been working to formulate more clearly his particular field of research interest, still a new and little ploughed one, that of the determination of social behavior through the effect upon the developing child of the particular patterns of culture to which it is exposed" (Hartshorne et al, n.d., 1). He was particularly interested in socialization and the problem of racism; he had just begun a year of studying child development at the New York Academy of Medicine when he died. His careful but engaged involvement in the developing field can be seen in his critical but respectful review of Abram Kardiner's pioneering work (written in collaboration with Ralph Linton), *The Individual and His Society: The Psychodynamics of Primitive Social Organization*. The review was anthologized by George Stocking in *Selected Papers from the American Anthropologist, 1921–1945* (Mekeel 1940).

In words calculated to delight social and cultural anthropologists, an article in the *Milwaukee Journal* of March 10, 1946, led its story this way: "As an anthropologist, Prof. H. Scudder Mekeel of the University of Wisconsin is more concerned with what goes on inside the skulls of people today than he is with the now empty skulls of earlier ages" (Smith 1946). The headline read "Race Prejudice Linked to Other 'Hates'; U.W. Professor Trying to Find Out Why." The article reported that he "is concerned with what causes racial prejudices, and how to avert them in the United States." His "immediate program to combat race prejudice includes: . . . Doing everything we can to work toward economic security, thereby lessening the tensions of race prejudice. Working for child training, the goal of which is a more complete and plastic personality. Publicizing the *dangers of hate organizations operating behind a mask of nationalism*" (italics mine). The article notes that, according to *Fortune Magazine*, Mekeel suggested an Elmo Roper poll surveying antisemitism in the nation.[7] Mekeel had previously done a study of antisemitism in the Chicago area with support from the Rosenwald foundation. He was working on a book tentatively titled *Americans and Their Prejudices* in his last years.

His activities, published works, and professional correspondence during his years in Madison offer evidence of a sincere and serious man dedicated to the alleviation of human problems through anthropological and psychological knowledge. Macgregor writes of his "intellectual and emotional concern for the underprivileged" (1948, 97). H. Scudder Mekeel had become more radical through the Depression and World War II. He published a striking piece in 1944 in the *American Journal of Sociology* calling for a fundamental transformation of American political economy in order to control the forces of rampant capitalism and big business! It is a passionate and radical cri de coeur filled with some interesting statements that have distinct resonance with our current situation. Here are two passages from that short but intense manifesto.

> Capitalism in its pre-war form has been a historic, but not an inevitable, accompaniment of democracy. The doctrine that morality and economic self-interest necessarily coincide must be abandoned. Not organized business, but the people as consumers and citizens, can solve the problems of unemployment and inequality and determine the economic and hence the moral basis of reconstructed society. (1944, 208)

> The new faith will have to revive and renew the ideal of equality which, however imperfectly realized, lies at the root both of Christianity and of Communism, and which was deliberately rejected by the capitalist system.[8] Of the vitality of the modern demand for

equality there is no doubt whatever. . . . It is specifically a demand for economic equality-for equality of economic resources or equality of economic opportunity. This problem too requires, in the first instance, a positive and constructive rather than a purely negative and destructive *programme* [*sic*]. Our deliberate purpose should be to build up equality rather than to break down inequality. (1944, 212)

Other than the obituary in *American Anthropologist*, there seems to be only one piece of writing devoted to H. Scudder Mekeel: Thomas Biolsi's article "The Anthropological Construction of 'Indians': Haviland Scudder Mekeel and the Search for the Primitive in Lakota Country." Biolsi offers up young Scudder as a cautionary example of the harmful consequences to Indians of "anthropological cultural relativism and its intellectual construction of the primitive and of authentic and inauthentic Indians" (1997, 150). The thrust of Biolsi's article is this: Mekeel may have had "humane concerns for the 'underprivileged,' 'minority groups,' and ending racism," and may have had "a career dedicated to the welfare of the disempowered and struggle against racism" (134), but "his intellectual vision was systematically *disciplined* [italics mine] by anthropology and by the wider intellectual climate of the period" (135)—in very unfortunate ways. According to Biolsi, Mekeel was conditioned by "his search for the primitive," which was the outgrowth of a discursive formation that "undergirded an ethnographic worldview and determined what anthropologists saw on Indian reservations" (136). This worldview was one of radical cultural relativism and Sapirian and Benedictine romanticism that directed Mekeel to see the Lakota people as "the alien primitive Other, separated from him by a chasm of race and culture" (138). This intellectual framework is *not* guiltless or neutral, says Biolsi, but "had, and has, direct, concrete [negative— HSL] ramifications in the lives of Indian people" (150).

Biolsi's article presents several examples of what the author sees as Mekeel's "primitivism" and destructive relativism, particularly the distaste Mekeel expressed in his field notes from his first days on Pine Ridge Reservation for those he called "the in-betweens—loafers, criminals, delinquents . . . all bums" (Biolsi 1997, 134). (Elsewhere in his fieldnotes he compared such individuals to "riff-raff—about the same type one sees among whites hanging around street corners" [Biolsi 1997, 138]). On the other hand, Mekeel expressed his admiration for those he saw as either "pagan and living as near as possible in old way, and perhaps succeeding *spiritually* to some extent," or "Christian and trying to be acculturated" (134). Although these private notes were based on first impressions and were never published by Mekeel in any form, Biolsi builds them into a complex yet predictable post-1968 critique of Western civilization, American culture, and, especially, anthropological cultural relativism as he imagines it based on Sapir's article "Culture, Genuine and Spurious," Ruth Benedict's writings of the period, and a long list of post-1968 authors.

In keeping with this construction of Mekeel, Biolsi interprets two of our subject's published writings as harshly as possible. For example, Mekeel accounted for the remarkable degree to which Teton-Dakotas valued hospitality, generosity, sharing, and "giveaways" as a vital part of their culture, still basic to their lives under changed circumstances. In contrast to "American society," writes Mekeel, "Teton-Dakota society... has founded its cardinal values on the release of wealth—the amount released by an individual at any one time and the number of times so released" (1936, 11). Biolsi considers this an unworthy and outmoded essentialist search for "survivals" and instead attributes the undeniable significance of generosity to that favorite Marxist interpretation of a reaction to class situation and poverty (1997, 148).[9]

With the wisdom of having begun fieldwork fifty years later than Mekeel and writing AVD (after Vine Deloria), Thomas Biolsi must invent an essentialized cultural relativist version of Scudder Mekeel who can't get any wiser after his initial impressions and couldn't get anything right. In fact, as his writings on culture and change show, Mekeel's approaches to culture and the individual were nowhere near the stereotype that Biolsi depicts. In the words of Nancy O. Lurie, an activist and a devoted student of American Indian life, "Biolsi's chapter is a particularly striking example in taking some naïve unpublished musings on the Teton Sioux by Mekeel at the start of his first field trip in 1930 as the full measure of the man and of anthropology. . . . I can attest that he outgrew, if he had ever embraced, the kind of anthropology and attitudes toward Indians that Biolsi attributes to him; he was my first anthropology teacher" at the University of Wisconsin (Lurie 1998, 573).[10]

It seems that it is Biolsi who is "in search of the alien primitive"—anthropologist! With this mindset, this idée fixe, Biolsi has invented, constructed, and imagined an anthropologist not as he was but as Biolsi and his discourse want him to be. Although there are lines in Mekeel's writings from the 1930s and even the 1940s that make us, modern and much wiser people of the twenty-first century, do a double take, Mekeel was in many respects a pioneer in the study of cultural change and acculturation, one who did *not* look for "primitives" but for the variations in behavior, attitudes, and values among people undergoing losses and changes.

Mekeel was a cultural relativist in the sense that he believed that one should try to study, appreciate, and take into consideration the understandings, interests, values, attitudes, contexts, personalities, preferences, and points of view of people of all sorts, especially those who are underprivileged and in need of help. I hope there is nothing so wrong with this—although I am painfully aware that several generations of "critical" anthropology and literary theory have been trying to tell us that there is.

NOTES

1. My interest in Scudder Mekeel began when a secretary brought me a carton containing five old-fashioned ledger boxes filled with his correspondence from the 1930s and 1940s. After his sudden death the contents of his office were relegated to the department storeroom, where they languished for five decades. The cache included letters, some film from the field in the 1930s, nineteenth-century volumes containing missionary Bible translations into Indian languages, and the 165 stenographers' notebooks and other materials from the Oneida Ethnological Project (Lewis 2005). A collection of Mekeel's photographs is housed in the National Anthropological Archives.

2. A number of works dealing with Indian education and the Indian Reorganization Act refer to Mekeel's ideas and activities but do not discuss the person himself. These include Szasz (1999) and Taylor (1975, 1980).

3. Mekeel influenced Erik Erikson's decision to conduct studies with American Indians, and his name was linked with other pioneers in the

psychology of personality such as Abram Kardiner, Karen Horney, and Franz Alexander (Macgregor 1948, 98).

4. This emphasis on the psychological aspects of processes of change associates him with one of the perspectives of Franz Boas as expressed in his paper "The Methods of Ethnology" (1920).

5. It is not surprising that Franz Boas was concerned about this same problem. See his letter to Natalie Burlin/Curtis of 1903 expressing similar concerns (BP / Burlin, Natalie Curtis: From Boas. 1903 Aug. 20).

6. Sears president Julius Rosenwald established his foundation for the "well being of mankind" in 1917 and took particular interest in the plight of African Americans in the South. The foundation gave large sums of money for the construction of schools in poor, rural, largely Black school districts. His funds built thousands of school buildings and several industrial high schools. He gave millions of dollars to Black colleges and scholarships to their students. Franz Boas was closely connected to the foundation—which at one time gave a fellowship to Zora Neale Hurston for graduate work in anthropology at Columbia.

7. The poll in 1946 indicated that antisemitism correlated with some other "hates," according to the newspaper account. Of interest for our situation in 2018 is the finding that "anti-Semitism runs parallel with hostility to a. Great Britain, b. Russia" [on temporary hold in 2018, apparently] and "anti-Semitism runs parallel with disapproval of a. Large scale government work projects to help prevent unemployment. b. Labor unions" (*Milwaukee Journal*, March 10, 1946).

8. These words are a striking echo of those of Lewis Henry Morgan at the end of *Ancient Society* (which Friedrich Engels quoted to end his own rewrite of Morgan!): "It will be a revival, in a higher form, of the liberty, equality, and fraternity of the ancient gentes" (Morgan 1877, 562).

9. Apparently for Biolsi it couldn't have been some combination of the two, though in a footnote he grudgingly admits that, "in fact, Mekeel did leave open the possibility that the value of generosity survives among the Lakotas because it is adaptive, but the thrust of his paper is that generosity is an ancient vestige"—two terms Mekeel didn't use. Apropos Mekeel's observation that there were "many more 'longhairs' and quantities of horses" at White Clay District, Biolsi stoops to citing Gerald Sider's claim that "the fascination of anthropologists with Plains Indians' horses as opposed to mules . . . [is] because mules 'make Native Americans seem more like us'" (Sider quoted in Biolsi 1997, 151).

10. Lurie was referring to the papers in the Biolsi and Zimmerman volume that credit Vine Deloria with reforming anthropology. She claims that the book presents a "self-serving caricature of the work of early anthropologists" rather than a serious documentation of the work of anthropologists before 1969 (Lurie 1998, 573).

REFERENCES

Biolsi, Thomas. 1997. "The Anthropological Construction of 'Indians': Haviland Scudder Mekeel and the Search for the Primitive in Lakota Country." In *Indians and Anthropologists: Vine Deloria and the Critique of Anthropology*, edited by Thomas Biolsi and Larry Zimmerman, (133–59). Tucson: University of Arizona Press.

Boas, Franz. 1920. "The Methods of Ethnology." *American Anthropologist* 22: 311–21.

Engels, Friedrich. 1902. *The Origin of the Family, Private Property, and the State*. First English language ed. Chicago: Charles Kerr.

Hartshorne, Richard, John Useem, and W. W. Howells. n.d. "Memorial Resolution for Haviland Scudder Mekeel, 1902–1947."

Kardiner, Abram. 1939. *The Individual and His Society: The Psychodynamics of Primitive Social Organization*. New York: Columbia University Press.

Kehoe, Alice Beck, and Paul L. Doughty. 2012. *Expanding American Anthropology, 1945–1980: A Generation Reflects*. Tuscaloosa: University of Alabama Press.

Kroeber, A. L., ed. 1935. *Walapai Ethnography*. Memoirs of the American Anthropological Association no. 42.

———. 1963. *An Anthropologist Looks at History*. Berkeley: University of California Press.

Lewis, Herbert S., ed. 2005. *Oneida Lives: Long-Lost Voices of the Wisconsin Oneidas*. Lincoln: University of Nebraska Press.

Lurie, Nancy Oestreich. 1998. "Selective Recollections on Anthropology and Indians." *Current Anthropology* 39: 572–74.

Macgregor, Gordon. 1948. "H. Scudder Mekeel, 1902–1947." *American Anthropologist* 50: 95–100.

Mekeel, Haviland Scudder. 1932. "A Discussion of Cultural Change as Illustrated by Material from a Teton-Dakota Community." *American Anthropologist* 34: 274–85.

———. 1936a. "The Economy of a Modern Teton-Dakota Community." *Yale University Publications in Anthropology* 6: 3–14.

———. 1936b. "An Anthropologist's Observation on Indian Education." *Progressive Education* 13: 151–59.

———. 1940. "Review of Abram Kardiner, *The Individual and His Society: The Psychodynamics of Primitive Social Organization.*" *American Anthropologist* 42: 526–30.

———. 1943. "Comparative Notes on the Social Role of the Settlement House as Constrasted with that of the United States Indian Service." *Applied Anthropology* 3: 5–8.

———. 1944a. "An Appraisal of the Indian Reorganization Act." *American Anthropologist* 46: 209–17.

———. 1944b. "The American Indian as a Minority Group Problem." *American Indian* 2: 3–11.

———. 1944c. "Citizenship, Education, and Culture." *American Journal of Sociology* 50: 208–13.

Morgan, Lewis Henry. 1877. *Ancient Society or Researches in the Lines of Human Progress from Savagery through Barbarism to Civilization.* New York: Henry Holt.

Murray, Henry A. 1938. *Explorations in Personality.* New York: Oxford University Press.

Redfield, Robert, Ralph Linton, and Melville J. Herskovits. 1936. "Memorandum for the Study of Acculturation." *American Anthropologist* 38: 149–52.

Smith, Willard R. 1946. "Race Prejudice Linked to Other 'Hates'; U.W. Professor Trying to Find Out Why." *Milwaukee Journal*, March 10, 1946.

Szasz, Margaret C. 1999. *Education and the American Indian: The Road to Self-Determination Since 1928.* 3rd ed. Albuquerque: University of New Mexico Press.

Taylor, Graham D. 1975. "Anthropologists, Reformers, and the Indian New Deal." *Prologue* 7, no. 3: 151–62.

———. 1980. *The New Deal and American Indian Tribalism: The Administration of the Indian Reorganziation Act, 1934–45.* Lincoln: University of Nebraska Press.

2

Dear Dr. Boas

*The Collaboration and Contribution of
Ella Cara Deloria and Franz Boas*

For those of us interested in traditional Sioux culture, history, and language, the legacy of Yankton Sioux ethnographer, linguist, and educator Ella Cara Deloria is enormous.[1] This chapter explores Deloria's immense contribution to ethnographic studies of the Sioux; her mutually beneficial and productive relationship with Franz Boas, the father of Americanist anthropology; and the significance of Deloria's critique of the James R. Walker collection.

Trained and guided by Boas, Deloria was a Boasian par excellence. The quality of her work and its continuing relevance speak to the enduring value of the Americanist tradition as discussed by Regna Darnell in her classic book *Invisible Genealogies: A History of Americanist Anthropology* (2001). Deloria's interests, like the distinctive features of the Americanist tradition, focused on the intersections of cultural anthropology, history, and linguistics among American Indians. Boas's undeniable influence is reflected in Deloria's theory, method, and practice, particularly her lifelong commitments to participant-observation fieldwork and the Boasian text tradition. Ella Deloria epitomizes the very best of the Americanist tradition in anthropology.

Some recent works (Cotera 2008; Finn 1995; Gardner 2009) have attempted to paint Deloria's relationship with Boas in a negative light, claiming that it was based on an exploitative, colonialist, gendered power dynamic. These authors interpret the Deloria-Boas relationship from a presentist perspective based on ideological premises and political theories. While there was certainly an unequal power dynamic based on the fact that Franz Boas was an established and successful scholar in his field with more access to various resources, this same power dynamic operates in every mentor-mentee relationship. In her collected works, Beatrice Medicine (2001), a Standing Rock Sioux anthropologist who knew and worked with Deloria and who was often unabashedly critical of anthropology and anthropologists, never mentions the exploitative, negative dynamic that recent authors claim dominated Deloria's relationship with Boas. Even more telling is that, in Vine Deloria Jr.'s selected essays (1999), published late in his illustrious career, he never characterizes Boas's relationship with his aunt Ella as exploitative. If neither Bea Medicine nor Vine Deloria Jr., both Native academics known for their critiques of anthropology, mention this supposedly significant aspect of the Boas-Deloria collaboration as advanced in recent revisionist histories, it seems that, in the words of Herbert S. Lewis, these versions of history, "although fashionable, are probably untrue" (2001, 460). This chapter explores Ella Deloria's life and contributions, reflects on biography and the increasing need for balance and context in much scholarly work today, and frames Deloria's story in relation to other contemporaries in this volume.

Ella Cara Deloria was born on January 31, 1889, among her mother's people in the White Swan district on the Yankton Sioux Indian Reservation in southeastern South Dakota.[2] Her Indian name was Beautiful Day Woman (*Aŋpétu Wašté Wíŋ*). Her father was Reverend Philip Deloria, one of the first Sioux Episcopal priests, and her mother was Mary Sully Bordeaux. Both of her parents were enrolled members of the Yankton Sioux Tribe and descended from Dakota (Eastern Sioux) and Euro-American ancestors. Ella was the firstborn daughter of a prominent mixed-blood Episcopal family, and her status as an *iyéska* (a mixed-blood interpreter, intermediary, or "insider/outsider" [Gardner in Deloria 2009, x] and culture broker), continued into her professional career as a Native anthropologist (Murray 1974, 22–62; Picotte biographical sketch included in Deloria 2009, 229).

The lives of Ella's grandfathers vividly illustrate the conflicting worlds in which she moved, the two roads she walked. Her Dakota grandfather was François (Saswe) des Lauriers, a Yankton chief and powerful medicine man. Her white grandfather was Brigadier General Alfred Sully, a career Indian fighter perhaps best known for his role in the harsh reprisals following the Dakota Conflict in Minnesota in 1862, which culminated in the Battle of Whitestone Hill in September 1863, in which U.S. troops under Sully's command utterly destroyed a village of some five hundred lodges of Dakota, Yankton, and Lakota people, including many women and children. These people were Sully's own affinal relatives and, later, Ella's people (Gardner 2009, vii; DeMallie 2005; Vine Deloria Jr. 1998, ix–xi; Olden 1918; Deloria 2000).

A year after Ella's birth her family moved to Wakpala on the Standing Rock Reservation in northcentral South Dakota. The Lakota people there were speakers of the L dialect of the Sioux language rather than the D dialect spoken by the Yanktons. Thus Ella, although Yankton by birth, grew up speaking Lakota. As the eldest child whose brothers came much later, Ella became the inheritor of many family traditions and was treated as if she were the son to whom Philip could pass down the family's stories. Apparently an ethnographer from a very young age, she was acquainted with many of the elders at both Standing Rock and Yankton reservations, learning firsthand from them the old Sioux ways (DeMallie 2005; Deloria 1998, ix–xii). In his important introduction to the reprint edition of Ella's *Speaking of Indians*, first published in 1944, her nephew Vine Deloria Jr. recalls, "In her belongings I found a picture of the people at Wakpala sitting on the hillside watching a fast train speed through the reservation. It is dated 1903, when Ella was just reaching adolescence, and I suspect she was the photographer, recording behavior even at that early age" (Deloria 1998, xix).

Ella was schooled at St. Elizabeth's Mission in Wakpala until 1902, when she began attending Bishop Hare's All Saints School, an Episcopal boarding school in Sioux Falls, South Dakota. Ella attended the University of Chicago, then Oberlin College in Ohio, before transferring to Columbia Teachers College in New York City in 1913, where she earned her BS in 1915. Although Deloria was pursuing a degree in physical education, without coursework in ethnology or linguistics, she met Franz Boas and Ruth Benedict in her senior year at Columbia. This fortuitous twist of fate led her to attend classes taught by Boas and Benedict in anthropology, folklore, linguistics, and research methods, which eventually blossomed into a productive relationship between Deloria and Boas that led to Deloria's reputation today as the most prolific Native scholar of the Lakotas (Gardner 2009, x; DeMallie 2005; Deloria Jr. 1998, xii).

When Boas met Deloria at Columbia he was immediately intrigued by her fluency in the Sioux language. According to Vine Deloria Jr., "Contrary to the contentions of some modern scholars, Ella spoke all three dialects of the Sioux language, although she was most familiar with the 'd' dialect. She had picked up great fluency in the 'l' dialect from her late childhood years at Wakpala among the Hunkpapas and Blackfeet Sioux" (Vine Deloria Jr. 1998, xiv). In 1915 Boas hired Deloria to work with him and his students translating Sioux language texts in one of his courses at Columbia. As Ella would later remind Boas, it was her first paying job (Lewis 2001, 460).

Deloria was the answer to Boas's long search for a native speaker who could help him in his study of the Sioux language. Boas proceeded to train her in the formal study of American Indian languages and cultures, which set in motion the course of much of the rest of Deloria's life. In 1927, after losing touch for a number of years while Deloria pursued various Indian education positions, Boas contacted Deloria (Gardner 2009; DeMallie 2009, 234–35; 2005; Vine Deloria Jr. 1998, xiii–xiv). Herbert S. Lewis writes, "Their collaboration and correspondence continued from that time until he died. He encouraged her, he found money for her, and he supported her work in the field and for her stays in New York" (2001, 460).

After learning of Deloria's whereabouts, Boas visited her at the Haskell Institute in Lawrence, Kansas, to propose that she resume her studies of Lakota language and culture. Deloria readily agreed, writing to Boas on December 25, 1927, "[I] want you to know that I would rather do this work on the Dakota than anything else" (Gardner 2009, xiii). Thus began the rest of Ella's life as an ethnographer and linguist, a recorder, translator, and sender of words, as well as the productive, influential, and mutually beneficial and respectful collaboration and genuine friendship between Boas and Deloria that lasted until Boas's death in 1942.

As Raymond DeMallie (2009, 234) points out in his afterword to the new edition of Ella's classic novel *Waterlily*, in order to understand Deloria's work it is important to appreciate the intellectual context in which it was born and nourished: Boasian or Americanist anthropology in the 1930s and 1940s. Deloria's close associations with Franz Boas, Ruth Benedict, Alexander Lesser, and Margaret Mead shaped and directed her studies of the Sioux. Her early work with Boas focused on the Sioux language, checking the accuracy and translations of George Bushotter's texts and the Dakota dictionary prepared by the missionary Stephen R. Riggs (Deloria Jr. 1998, xiii–xiv; Whitten and Zimmerman 1982, 162).[3] Among the fundamental tenets of the Americanist tradition are the related ideas that native-language texts are the appropriate database for anthropological interpretation, ethnology, and linguistics, and that the study of Native American language is the ideal entrée into Native thought and worldview (Darnell 2001, 13–15).

It should come as no surprise that Deloria's exemplary anthropology was a reflection of Boas and the fundamental tenets of the Americanist tradition. This is meant in no way to detract from Ella's sharp intellect and unique gifts and abilities as an ethnographer and linguist. In addition to training her, Boas also directed much of Ella's research, proposing that she record "all the details of everyday life as well as of religious attitudes and habits of thought of the people" (Boas in DeMallie 2009, 235–36). Although Boas planned to work collaboratively with Deloria on the Sioux language, the initial project for which she was hired was psychological in nature: the creation of a culture-free IQ test to dispel myths about the correlation of race and IQ.

Boas facilitated his students' research by finding funds to support it and helping to design many of the projects carried out by his students (DeMallie 2009, 234–36; Whitten and Zimmerman 1982, 162–63). Ella's initial research design was no exception. In a letter dated January 26, 1928, Boas outlined the research design of the project to Deloria: "The primary objective of the investigation is a critical study of the psychological tests by which it has been claimed racial differences can be established. In our opinion, it seems not unlikely that the cultural conditions under which the individual grows up and lives have a far reaching effect upon any kind of test that may be made" (Boas to Deloria, January 26, 1928; Whitten and Zimmerman 1982, 163). Working with psychologist Otto Klineberg, Deloria developed a special Sioux IQ test involving beadwork and administered it to Sioux and white children in South Dakota. Sure enough, the Sioux children fared much better on the test than did their white counterparts (Whitten and Zimmerman 1982, 163).

From 1928 to 1938, with support from Boas and Columbia University, Deloria studied the Sioux language, recorded stories and ethnographic material from Lakota elders throughout South Dakota, and translated historical texts written by tribal members. From 1939 until Benedict's unexpected death in 1948, Deloria continued to work, as time and finances allowed, on the materials she had collected. Throughout her life, Ella's work was often compromised by family responsibilities and financial hardship (Deloria Jr. 1998; DeMallie 2005).

Deloria's life as an anthropologist was largely nomadic and often *úŋšika*, an important Lakota cultural symbol meaning pitiful or humble. At one point she was living in her car and carried with her only a handful of alienable possessions that were dear to her. Among these precious belongings were two photographs: one of her father, the Reverend Philip Deloria, and the other of her mentor and friend Franz Boas (Murray 1974, 4). Deloria respected and admired the charismatic Boas for his integrity and scholarship. In a letter congratulating him on his eighty-first birthday, Deloria wrote, "I would not trade the privilege of having known you, for anything I can think of" (Deloria to Boas, July 17, 1939).

Vine Deloria Jr. and Bea Medicine both mention a tragic episode in Deloria's life as a scholar. Deloria had two steamer trunks full of linguistic and ethnographic notes recorded throughout her career as an ethnographer. According to her brother Vine Deloria Sr., these trunks contained a large portion of her collection. When Ella and her sister Susan travelled west in 1944, she stored the two steamer trunks in Fort Lee, New Jersey, but unfortunately ran out of money to pay the storage bill. The space she had was soon closed and her things sold, probably for no more than the value of two used steamer trunks. Her invaluable notes and writings on Sioux language, culture, and history were lost forever (Deloria Jr. 1998, xvi–xvii; Medicine 2001, 281).

Ella looked to Boas as a father figure, as did the rest of Boas's students, many of whom affectionately referred to him as "Papa Franz." As a sign of her deep respect for him, Deloria referred to Boas as "Father

Franz," acknowledging the closeness of their relationship but marking her respect, much as she would have in addressing her Sioux elders and respect relatives.[4] Indeed, Boas's intellectual genealogy was and continues to be based on kinship, as was the fabric of the societies typically studied by the Americanist anthropologists he trained (DeMallie 2005; Murray 1974, 4). When Ella addressed Boas, the prototypical Jewish scholar, as Father Franz, he responded by saying, "Ella, you make me feel like a Catholic priest!" Deloria replied, "Next to my own father, you are the most truly Christian man I ever met" (DeMallie 2009, 234).

Toward the end of her life, when she was living in poverty in Vermillion, South Dakota, Deloria spoke to a group of women about her career in anthropology. When the topic of her late mentor came up, Deloria said, "Dr. Boas is a great anthropologist. He's dead now, and he was at Columbia, and he really started the general interest in anthropology. And he was a great man" (Deloria and Medicine 1969). According to Bea Medicine, the picture of Boas continued to be a fixture in Ella's motel room in Vermillion, and she treasured it until her death in 1971. Medicine writes, "When I drove to her motel to take her to lunch, she would scan the motel room, humming and looking for something to give to me. There was little but stained coffee cups, a picture of Franz Boas, a typewriter, and several boxes. Her humor and her pleasure at 'going out to lunch' were sufficient" (Medicine 2001, 280).

The relationship between Boas and Deloria was warm and in many ways mutually beneficial and dependent. In a letter of recommendation written in July 1937, Boas comments that Ella's "knowledge of the Sioux is unique" (Boas to Deloria, July 7, 1937). In a letter to Deloria biographer Janette K. Murray, Margaret Mead recalls that Boas had a deep respect for and dependence upon Ella (Murray, personal interview, 2016). In a letter from Boas to Ruth Benedict in November 1930, Boas discusses funding Deloria's "Dakota work." He states frankly, "I cannot afford to lose her services just now" (Benedict 1959, 406). In 1934 Boas wrote a flattering letter for Ella to John Collier, commissioner of Indian Affairs, recommending her as a qualified person who could help implement the Indian Reorganization Act.

The mutual respect between Boas and Deloria was also reflected in Deloria's relationships with many of Boas's students. As mentioned above, Ella was especially close to Ruth Benedict, Alexander Lesser, and Margaret Mead. According to Bea Medicine, Mead told her that "Ella was an asset at Columbia" (Medicine 2001, 282). In a 1973 publication Mead refers to Deloria as a "colleague" (Mead 1973). Esther Goldfrank, Jeanette Mirsky, and Ethel Nurge depended heavily on Deloria's expertise and ethnographic materials in their own work (Medicine 2001, 282, 286n4), as have Bea Medicine, Raymond DeMallie, Vine Deloria Jr., Julian Rice, and many other scholars since, including myself. So many of us owe an enormous debt to Ella Deloria.

Deloria, in turn, genuinely liked and admired Boas, who gave her the financial support she needed to do what she truly loved: recording and writing ethnographic materials (Medicine 2001, 281). Aside from keeping a picture of Boas as one of her most prized possessions, there are many examples in Ella's work and in her correspondence with Boas and others that clearly demonstrate her positive feelings. Speaking of the grammar she wrote with Boas (Boas and Deloria 1941), which some linguists consider to be the finest grammar of an American Indian language, Ella wrote, "So many people are asking about our grammar, I feel very proud to be your co-author" (Deloria to Boas, July 15, 1941; Lewis 2001, 461). In 1939 Deloria wrote to Boas commenting on a tribute to him that had appeared in the *New York Times*. "It is beautiful, isn't it," she writes, "but not a whit more than you deserve. Please allow me to add my feeble bit to the well merited praise, who have really known you rather better than many, through many years of profitable association with you. I would not trade the privilege of having known you, for anything I can think of" (Deloria to Boas, July 17, 1939). In a letter written a year before his death Deloria poignantly summed up her appreciation for Boas, writing, "You have always been my best friend and have helped me to do what I wanted to do" (Deloria to Boas, June 17, 1941; see Lewis 2001, 461). Writing of Deloria's correspondence with Boas, Herbert Lewis reasonably concludes that "perhaps we can deconstruct these texts and see her words as mere flattery and a sign of her dependence upon him, but this would probably do a grave injustice to Ella Deloria, her feelings, and the realities of her life story. In the absence of any other evidence, in the light of their long, mutually respectful and profitable collaboration, why search for hidden motives and misunderstandings that diminish both or either of them?" (Lewis 2001, 461).

As mentioned above, at Columbia in the spring of 1915 Boas provided Deloria with the first paycheck she ever received. Although Ella's work with Boas was steady, it hardly offered a stable salary with any sense of security. Boas did his best to encourage and support Ella financially, occasionally paying her at his own expense and opening his home to her on at least one occasion. Boas raised funds from an array of sources to support Ella's work with few gaps from 1928 until his death in 1942. Deloria earned between $100 and $200 per month (equivalent to between roughly $1,900 and $3,800 by 2020 standards). Out of this salary Deloria was expected to pay for all of her transportation and field expenses. According to those who knew her best, Ella was always short of funds to support herself and her sister Susan (Deloria 1998, xiv; Gardner 2009, xiv; DeMallie 2009, 235; Murray 1974, 94; Whitten and Zimmerman 1982, 162).

According to her nephew Vine Deloria Jr., throughout her life Ella took on much of the burden of family leadership. She was trapped by family responsibilities, caught between two conflicting worlds, one focused on traditional kinship and generosity and the other on individual achievement and the accumulation of wealth. Ella was like a mother to her younger siblings, and throughout her life she cared for her sister Susan, who needed help and support throughout her life. Susan was Ella's closest companion but also hampered her ability to pursue her career goals and financial stability (Deloria 1998, xi–xiv). As Bea Medicine put it, "Ella's letters to Boas reflected the conflict between her professional commitments and deeply felt kinship obligations. She cared for her father during his long illness and helped to support her sister Susie" (Medicine 2001, 280).

In addition to Deloria's own work and correspondence and the writings of Bea Medicine, none of which mention the exploitative relationship described by some contemporary authors, the writings of Vine Deloria Jr. on the subject are telling and significant. In his selected works (Deloria 1999), published later in his career, there is some criticism of Boas and anthropology, to be sure, but no mention whatsoever of an exploitative relationship between Boas and his aunt Ella. In terms of assessing their relationship, perhaps the most important document not written by Boas or Deloria is Vine Deloria Jr.'s introduction to the paperback edition of Ella's *Speaking of Indians* (Deloria Jr. 1998).[5] In the introduction he frequently mentions Boas, but never in an openly critical or hostile way. Vine humanizes Boas in a way that he might not have in a different venue or context. While a clear sense of frustration is evident over Ella's financial hardships, Vine does not seem to blame Boas personally. "Boas apparently raised funds to support Ella's work on an ad-hoc basis," he writes, "and she was always short of funds to support herself and Susan" (Deloria Jr. 1998, xiv). In addition to describing the productive scholarly collaboration between Boas and Deloria, Vine also shares a number of anecdotes in which Boas provided much-needed support at crucial moments. He writes, "Ella and Susan visited our home several times during the mid-1930s, staying until Boas could send some money or Ella could get paying speaking assignments" (Deloria Jr. 1998, xv). Vine also notes that Boas was able to find additional funds to help Ella continue her language work in the late 1930s. Finally, in reference to the 1940s and Ella's reliance on her mentor, Vine writes, "Boas had died the previous year [1942] and her only continuing source of support had vanished with him" (Deloria Jr. 1998, xvii). If indeed the relationship between his aunt Ella and Franz Boas was exploitative or negative, why would Vine Deloria Jr., perhaps the greatest critic of anthropology, not make it known publicly when he had the opportunity?

Ella spent the last years of her life at the University of South Dakota in Vermillion, where she served as assistant director of the W. H. Over Museum doing work on the Sioux dialects and compiling a Santee Sioux dictionary.[6] Ella's work with her people continued until her death in Wagner, South Dakota on February 12, 1971. Like Boas, she felt a great urgency to record and document Sioux language and culture in the face of unparalleled cultural change. Up until her last days Ella continued to make trips to the reservations to work collaboratively with elders who still remembered the old language and culture (Whitten and Zimmerman 1982, 163; Deloria 1998, xviii–xix; cf. Darnell 2001, 15–16). After a particularly exhausting trip to Pine Ridge Reservation, she confided to her nephew Vine, "Research is getting so hard to do—there are hardly any elders around nowadays" (Deloria 1998, xviii–xix).

Ella Deloria's contribution is enormous and can be measured in various ways. Here I will focus on her contributions as they line up with the fundamental distinctive features of the Americanist tradition as discussed by Darnell (2001, 11–20). Ella inherited a cognitivist, symbolic approach to culture from Boas and a focus on the collaborative interpretation of meaning based on both observed behavior and its explications in words. Her lifelong commitment to participant-observation fieldwork led to the production of several ethnographic and ethnohistorical manuscripts, many of which remain in unpublished manuscript form in the Library of the American Philosophical Society in Philadelphia and the Dakota Indian Foundation in Chamberlain, South Dakota. These include *The Dakota Way of Life* (1995), which DeMallie describes as "a cultural description in a Boasian sense: an idealized and generalized synthesis of the past, a testament to the old and valued customs of the Sioux" (2009, 237); *Speaking of Indians* (1998), a popular book first published in 1944 to promote cross-cultural understanding of Indian people; a large corpus of unpublished ethnographic materials relating to all aspects of traditional Sioux life and culture; and the classic *Waterlily* (1988), a historical novel published posthumously that has become a best seller for the University of Nebraska Press. *Waterlily* is a truly masterful work, unique in its presentation of traditional nineteenth-century Lakota culture and life from female perspectives. It is also an essential read for anyone interested in Sioux kinship.

In terms of the Boasian text tradition and Americanist emphasis on language as symbolic form, Deloria was no less prolific. Darnell writes, "Boas was particularly adamant about the urgent need of linguistic description for the scholarly record as well as for use in the communities where languages were spoken. The Boasian program committed the student, at least in principle, to produce a grammar, a dictionary, and texts for each language and culture studied" (2001, 14). In this respect, Deloria went above and beyond the call of duty, recording, transcribing, and translating a vast corpus of Sioux language texts, including commentaries on dictionaries and translations of large text collections by George Bushotter, George Sword, and Jack Frazier. Ella transcribed and translated an enormous body of texts on topics including traditional myths, anecdotes, autobiographies, political speeches, conversation, humorous stories, and aphorisms. According to DeMallie, "a written record of such magnitude and diversity does not exist for any other Plains Indian language" (2009, 236). Interestingly, Deloria was critical of the interlinear, line-by-line style of translation. According to Vine Deloria Jr., "Ella did not like this kind of translation, which suggested that words and ideas could be easily matched across complex linguistic traditions. She felt a better rendering of the nuances of the Sioux language could be achieved by translating whole phrases and speeches in a free form. Sometimes when she and Susan would visit us she would get to talking about how certain things that had been translated word for word missed the point altogether" (Deloria Jr. 1998, xiv).

Deloria's skepticism of the James R. Walker corpus is significant and underappreciated. James R. Walker was a physician with the Indian Service of the United States government who spent the years from 1896 to 1914 at Pine Ridge Reservation. According to DeMallie, "it was at Pine Ridge that Walker developed a lifelong interest in the Lakota (Oglala Sioux) Indians and ultimately became one of the foremost scholars of Lakota religion, preserving a multifaceted documentary record as important to the Lakota people themselves as to academic researchers" (2005, 9667). The Walker material is widely considered to be among the most influential sources documenting traditional Lakota beliefs and rituals. Yet Ella Deloria, asked by Boas in the 1930s to investigate Walker's findings, was skeptical. She found no evidence in her own ethnographic studies to support the scheme of fours pervasive in the Walker material, nor Walker's classification of the spirits or gods into hierarchies. Deloria was also skeptical of Walker's epic myth cycle and personification of natural phenomena (see Posthumus 2018, 127–28; Jahner in Walker 2006, 129–31). Ella wrote in a letter to Boas that she was unable to find any traces of the myths as they were recorded by Walker, noting that they were almost unrecognizable to her consultants, who were generally skeptical of their origins because certain aspects of them were contested. She wrote that the plots and style of the stories as presented by Walker seemed to her and her consultants to be the work of a clever and idiosyncratic Lakota storyteller, perhaps *Makhúla* or Left Heron, a famous Oglala storyteller known to have worked with both Walker and Deloria. Ella also recognized the "work of a systematic European mind" in the Walker materials (Deloria to Boas, June 28, 1938; May 12, 1939). While the potential implications of Deloria's criticism of the Walker texts are immense, I will not attempt to follow that thread here, but the issue certainly calls for further exploration.

Deloria published an article in the *Journal of American Folklore* titled "The Sun Dance of the Oglala Sioux" (1929), based on George Sword's Oglala Lakota Sun Dance account, which is still one of the very best sources on the Lakota Sun Dance. Boas and Deloria coauthored an article in the *International Journal of American Linguistics* titled "Notes on the Dakota, Teton Dialect" (1933) and the classic aforementioned *Dakota Grammar* (1941), to this day the best reference grammar of the Sioux language. Deloria also developed a Lakota lexicon and a Santee dictionary. In 1943 Ella received the Indian Achievement Award from the Indian Council Fire in Chicago, at that time the most prestigious award a Native American could receive (DeMallie 2005; 2009, 236; Deloria Jr. 1998, xiv–xvii). Further, countless scholars in anthropology, history, linguistics, Native American studies, women's and gender studies, literary studies, and beyond have benefitted from Ella's masterful fieldnotes and linguistic work, and a significant body of contemporary literary criticism and feminist scholarship has taken shape around her life and work (Gardner 2009, ix; Whitten and Zimmerman 1982, 162).

Indeed, Ella Deloria was much more than "an insightful and hardworking key informant," as she has been described (Whitten and Zimmerman 1982, 163). She was an anthropologist of the highest caliber in her own right, even though she humbly did not consider herself as such, as she confessed to Boas in 1935. While Ella was content to call herself a linguist, her reluctance to consider herself a full-fledged anthropologist in the same category as Boas, Benedict, and Mead may have been tied to her embeddedness in Lakota culture, which honors humility as a core value (Deloria to Boas, December 5, 1935; DeMallie 2009, 242–43).[7] Vine Deloria Jr. (1998, xix) notes that his aunt Ella was also reluctant to consider herself an elder.

In many ways Deloria was what we would today call an activist, a spokesperson for her people, a cultural mediator, and an interpreter between cultures. She campaigned and toiled tirelessly to increase visibility, understanding, and appreciation of Native peoples and cultures in mainstream American society. As Susan Gardner (2009, xi) points out, Ella wrote for the survival of her people that the people may live, as the Lakota expression goes. DeMallie (2009, 237) writes, "The dedication that is apparent in Ella Deloria's lifelong quest to preserve traditional Sioux language and culture was deeply rooted in her concern for the future of her people." It is my sincere hope that we as the inheritors of the Americanist tradition in anthropology will always acknowledge and appreciate Ella Cara Deloria and her contribution as a significant, unique, influential, and prolific member of our intellectual genealogies.

NOTES

1. Here I use Sioux as a convenient cover term to refer to the Dakota, Yankton, Yanktonai, and Lakota peoples collectively. The best general works on the Sioux are the relevant chapters in DeMallie (2001) and Gibbon (2003). *Očhéthi Šakówiŋ* (Seven Council Fires) is now sometimes used as an umbrella term referring to the Sioux tribes collectively, whereas Dakota was used in the past. On the Seven Council Fires see DeMallie (2006).

2. On the life of Ella Deloria see the biographical sketch by Agnes Picotte and afterword by Raymond DeMallie in Deloria (2009), Prater (1995), and Medicine (2001, 269–88). Murray (1974) remains the best work on Ella's life.

3. On Bushotter see DeMallie (1978).

4. On Sioux kinship see DeMallie (1994, 1998).

5. Vine's introduction, along with Bea Medicine's chapter on Ella (Medicine 2001, 269–88), is especially important for understanding Deloria family dynamics and history, as well as Ella's personal dignity and idiosyncrasies as a mixed-blood, Christian, Lakota woman and ethnographer-scholar.

6. According to Bea Medicine (2001, 285), in 1969 the Ella Deloria Scholarship for Indian Women at the University of South Dakota was established, but apparently this scholarship no longer exists.

7. Bea Medicine (2001, 284–85) refers to Ella as "vain," discussing her vanity and sense of superiority in relation to full-blood Lakotas, but this likely reflects the complicated internal politics often found in Native communities.

Benedict, Ruth. 1959. *An Anthropologist at Work: Writings of Ruth Benedict.* Edited by Margaret Mead. Boston MA: Houghton Mifflin.

Boas, Franz, and Ella Cara Deloria. 1933. "Notes on the Dakota, Teton Dialect." *International Journal of American Linguistics* 7, no. 3/4: 97–121.

———. 1941. "Dakota Grammar." National Academy of Sciences (U.S.) Memoirs. Vol. 33. Washington: U.S. Government Printing Office.

Cotera, María Eugenia. 2008. *Native Speakers: Ella Deloria, Zora Neale Hurston, Jovita González, and the Poetics of Culture.* Austin: University of Texas Press.

Darnell, Regna. 2001. *Invisible Genealogies: A History of Americanist Anthropology.* Vol. 1. Lincoln: University of Nebraska Press.

Deloria, Ella Cara. 1927. Correspondence with Franz Boas. MS 31, Boas Collection. American Philosophical Library, Philadelphia.

———. 1929. "The Sun Dance of the Oglala Sioux." *Journal of American Folklore* 42, no. 166: 354–413.

———. 1988. *Waterlily.* Lincoln: University of Nebraska Press.

———. 1995. *The Dakota Way of Life.* Bloomington: Indiana University Press.

———. 1998. *Speaking of Indians.* Lincoln: University of Nebraska Press.

———. 2009. *Waterlily,* New Edition. Lincoln: University of Nebraska Press.

Deloria, Ella, and Beatrice Medicine. 1969. Oral history interview with Ella Deloria conducted by Beatrice Medicine. American Indian Research Project, no. 386. Vermillion: South Dakota Oral History Center, University of South Dakota.

Deloria, Vine, Jr. 1998. "Introduction." In *Speaking of Indians* by Ella Deloria, ix–xix. Lincoln: University of Nebraska Press.

———. 1999. *Spirit and Reason: The Vine Deloria, Jr., Reader.* Edited by Barbara Deloria, Kristen Foehner, and Samuel Scinta. Golden CO: Fulcrum.

———. 2000. *Singing for a Spirit: A Portrait of the Dakota Sioux.* Santa Fe NM: Clear Light.

DeMallie, Raymond J. 1978. "George Bushotter: The First Lakota Ethnographer." In *American Indian Intellectuals,* edited by Margot Liberty, 91–102. 1976 American Ethnological Society Proceedings. St. Paul MN: West.

————. 1994. "Kinship and Biology in Sioux Culture." In *North American Indian Anthropology: Essays on Society and Culture*, edited by Raymond J. DeMallie and Alfonso Ortiz, 125–46. Norman: University of Oklahoma Press.

————. 1998. "Kinship: The Foundation for Native American Society". In *Studying Native America: Problems and Prospects*, edited by Russell Thornton, 306–56. Madison: University of Wisconsin Press.

————. 2001. *Handbook of North American Indians, Volume 13, Plains*. Edited by Raymond J. DeMallie. Washington DC: Smithsonian Institution.

————. 2005. "Deloria, Ella Cara." In *Encyclopedia of Religion*. 2nd ed. Edited by Lindsay Jones, 2264–65. Detroit MI: Gale Virtual Reference Library and Macmillan Reference USA.

————. 2005. "Walker, James R." In *Encyclopedia of Religion*. 2nd ed. Edited by Lindsay Jones, 9667–68. Detroit MI: Gale Virtual Reference Library and Macmillan Reference USA.

————. 2006. "The Sioux at the Time of European Contact: An Ethnohistorical Problem." In *New Perspectives on Native North America: Cultures, Histories, and Representations*, edited by Sergei A. Kan and Pauline T. Strong, 239–60. Lincoln: University of Nebraska Press.

————. 2009. "Afterword." In *Waterlily*. New ed. Lincoln: University of Nebraska Press.

Finn, Janet L. 1995. "Ella Cara Deloria and Mourning Dove: Writing for Cultures, Writing against the Grain." In *Women Writing Culture*, edited by Ruth Behar and Deborah A. Gordon, 131–47. Berkeley: University of California Press.

Gardner, Susan. 2009. "Introduction." In *Waterlily*. New ed. Lincoln: University of Nebraska Press.

Gibbon, Guy E. 2003. *The Sioux: The Dakota and Lakota Nation*. Malden MA: Blackwell.

Lewis, Herbert S. 2001. "The Passion of Franz Boas." *American Anthropologist* 103, no. 2: 447–67.

Mead, Margaret. 1973. "The American Indian as a Significant Determinant of Anthropological Style." In *Anthropology and the American Indian: A Symposium*, edited by Jeannette Henry, 68–74. San Francisco CA: Indian Historian Press.

Medicine, Beatrice. 2001. *Learning to Be an Anthropologist and Remaining "Native": Selected Writings*. Edited by Sue-Ellen Jacobs. Urbana: University of Illinois Press.

Murray, Janette K. 1974. "Ella Deloria: A Biographical Sketch and Literary Analysis." PhD diss., University of North Dakota.

Olden, Sarah Emilia. 1918. *The People of Tipi Sapa (The Dakotas): Tipi Sapa Mitaoyate Kin.* Milwaukee WI: Morehouse.

Posthumus, David C. 2018. *All My Relatives: Exploring Lakota Ontology, Belief, and Ritual.* New Visions in Native American and Indigenous Studies Series. Lincoln: University of Nebraska Press.

Prater, John. 1995. "Ella Deloria: Varied Intercourse: Ella Deloria's Life and Work." *Wicazo Sa Review* 11, no. 2: 40–46.

Walker, J. R. 2006. *Lakota Myth.* Edited by Elaine A. Jahner. Lincoln: University of Nebraska Press.

Whitten, Richard G., and Larry J. Zimmerman. 1982. "Directions for Miss Deloria: Boas on the Plains." *Plains Anthropologist* 27, no. 96: 161–64.

JOSHUA SMITH

3

Reckoning with Rietz

A Sketch of an Action Anthropologist

Stick with the little people. They all have names and faces even though
you never read about them in the newspapers. Big people are always
trying to step on little people. Every time they do it, bite their foot.

—Robert Rietz's memorial service program

This vignette or sketch of Robert W. Rietz (1914–1971) aspires to provide a starting point to recover the person, his politics, and, perhaps,
the contemporary need for his spirit of anthropology. Although he was
an exceptionally talented and radically caring action anthropologist,
according to the accounts of those who knew him, Rietz remains largely
unknown, without biographies or canonical works. For many of his
contemporaries, he personified the spirit of action anthropology. This
sketch brings together a few eclectic works to draw him forward into
the history of anthropology in the twenty-first century and to reckon
with his leadership as an early theorist of decolonizing research methods. I consider his method of leadership *radical caring*.

Robert Rietz, a veteran of World War II, worked with Indigenous
peoples in Iowa, North Dakota, and Illinois. He served as the director
of the American Indian Center in Chicago. He was one of the original
six graduate students to participate in the Chicago Project in Tama,
Iowa.[1] From 1950 to 1953 Rietz worked at the Indian Reservation at
Fort Berthold, North Dakota, with the mandate to assist members of
the Three Affiliated Tribes (Hidatsa, Mandan, and Arikara) in relocat-
ing from their lands following the construction of the Garrison Dam.
Rietz worked as both a community analyst and a relocation officer
for the Bureau of Indian Affairs, and led the Chicago Project in Tama

from 1954 to 1957. He was a cofounder of the Summer Workshops in American Indian Affairs in Colorado and Canada. In 1958 he returned to Chicago to direct the American Indian Center, which he continued to do until his death in 1971.

Rietz was part of a close-knit community of anthropologists who worked together to conceptualize and implement what they called action anthropology. In addition to Rietz, the core group included Sol Tax (1907–1995), Nancy Lurie (1924–2017), Samuel Stanley (1923–2011), and Robert K. Thomas (1925–1991). All contributed to the development of the theory and method of action anthropology through their projects and efforts. But Rietz was Tax's right-hand man and was often singled out as especially talented at articulating the goals of action anthropology. At a 2013 AAA panel that I organized to reflect on the legacies of action anthropology, Nancy Lurie referred to him in panel discussions and personal communication as "the sainted Bob Rietz."

Understanding what motivated Rietz's anthropology requires outlining the political context that necessitated what he, Tax, and others called action anthropology. Defining action anthropology is challenging, because it emerged in the context of post–World War II assimilation policies but continued to evolve as a counter to the applied anthropology of the 1950s. Action anthropology sparked an anti-colonial shift in social science in opposition to the reemergence of assimilationist policies in the United States that began in the mid-1940s and continue into the present (Smith 2010, 2012, 2015).

In 1944 Congress began a campaign to abolish the Bureau of Indian Affairs and terminate tribes. By 1947 Congress sought to move forward aggressively to terminate tribes it deemed ready to no longer exist legally; henceforth, they would no longer receive aid. Public justifications for these actions were based on some anthropologists' scientific support for assimilation, although private agendas based on finance, resources, and land were also in play. In 1946 the Indian Claims Commission (ICC) began the process of termination as it started to settle Indigenous legal claims against the United States. Congress passed the Indian Claims Commission Act in 1946. The commission was organized as a "tribunal for the hearing and determination of claims against the United States ... by any Indian tribe, band, or other identifiable group of Indians living in the United States" (Pinkoski 2006, 115). The commission's assumption that the "Indian Problem" could be dealt with by providing compensation for lands taken involved anthropology in its application in that "the U.S. Department of Justice questioned the level of social organization of the Indigenous peoples before the court, following a line of argument in the common law regarding the colonization of new territories by limiting the aboriginal interest in the land based on social evolutionism" (Pinkoski 2006, 171; see also Asch 1992).[2] The new connections between the Department of Justice, cultural evolutionism, and social science led to a dynamic whereby "the very nature of the ICC itself placed anthropologists in a position to legitimize the denial of Indigenous rights to collectively held land and to other collective rights guaranteed by treaty with the U.S. government" (Pinkoski 2006, 171).

Their powerful role in the ICC forced anthropologists to reckon with their anxieties over scientific versus professional identities. They began to draw disciplinary lines in the sand and debate the issue of scientific integrity. In 1947 the AAA issued a statement on human rights. Susan Trencher notes that "[Julian] Steward, again representing the argument for a more positivistic scientific practice, claimed that the AAA statement was inappropriate: In the absence of objective scientific evidence that human rights exist, 'as a scientific organization, the Association has no business dealing with the rights of man'" (Trencher 2002, 453). This callous opposition from a society of anthropologists, most of whom based their careers on studying Indigenous peoples, is remarkable for its failure to consider anthropologists' complicity in the destruction sustained by Indigenous peoples in the postwar era, not only from assimilationist shifts in policy and government, but also from direct physical violence in developmental projects. This had a direct impact on Tax and Rietz, who both committed their careers to fighting assimilation; their approach became action anthropology.

In April of 1946 the Army Corps of Engineers invaded Fort Berthold to start construction on the Garrison Dam. Built on the main stem of the Missouri River, it became the fifth largest dam in the United States at a cost of $299 million. It was built:

on tribal land resulted in the taking of 152,360 acres. Over 25 percent of the reservation's total land base was deluged by the dam's reservoir (known as Lake Sakakawea today). The remainder of the Mandan, Hidatsa, and [Sahnish] lands was segmented into five waterbound sections. The project required the relocation of 325 families, or approximately 80 percent of the tribal membership. For many successful years as ranchers and farmers, these industrious people lost 94 percent of their agricultural lands. (Lawson 1982, 59)

The devastating consequences of the construction of the Garrison dam came to test action anthropology in 1950 and eventually led action anthropologists to the conclusion that an action anthropologist can never have an institutional master (in this case the BIA).

In 1950 Rietz went to work in Fort Berthold with a mandate to help relocate members of the Three Affiliated Tribes whose land was being flooded by the construction of the Garrison Dam, but "the relationship was not an altogether happy one. As a community analyst for the BIA, Rietz expected to spend a lot of time learning about the social organization of the community and using that to encourage members of the tribes to take over running more reservation activities themselves. Instead, he found himself saddled with administrative responsibilities" (Daubenmier 2008, 175–76).

Tax and Rietz, working closely together, faced increasing challenges with the BIA, which sought to transfer Rietz from Fort Berthold to the Cheyenne River Sioux Reservation to assist with yet another devastating colonial relocation project. Rietz refused the transfer. This early experience made clear to him what the action anthropologists felt all along. Tax resolved that the project "must be unattached to any actual or potential exercise of coercion over the group" (Daubenmier 2008, 177).

Vine Deloria Jr.'s criticisms of anthropology justly accused the discipline of sitting idly by while Indigenous peoples faced challenges alone. "During the crucial days of 1954, when the Senate was pushing for termination of all Indian rights, not one single scholar, anthropologist, sociologist, historian, or economist came forward to support the tribes against the detrimental policy. How much had scholars learned about Indians from 1492 to 1954 that would have placed termination in a more rational light? Why didn't the academic community march to the side of the tribes?" (Daubenmier 2008, 187). Tax and Rietz are examples of anthropologists who turned their energies toward fighting government policy on several fronts. In 1995 Deloria Jr., speaking at Tax's memorial service, acknowledged the role action anthropology played in changing the discipline: "Between John Collier and the Indian move for self-determination, 1969, you look around and what do you find? You find Sol Tax liberating the whole discipline. Liberating them from the idea that they have to be objective scientists therefore can never be advocates" (Deloria Jr. 1995). Deloria Jr.'s eulogy also pointed out that Tax had a knack for recruiting talented anthropologists such as Rietz.

The nightmare of termination became reality in 1953, when Congress passed House Concurrent Resolution 108 (HCR 108) and Public Law 280 (PL 280).[3] Thus began an onslaught against tribal sovereignty. PL 280 gave certain states power of criminal and civil jurisdiction on reservations without tribal consent. Supporters of termination sought to liquidate tribal land bases and abandon the obligations and responsibilities that the United States had accepted when it entered into treaties with tribes. They claimed to be offering Indigenous peoples equal rights and U.S. citizenship in exchange for the end of tribal governments; that is, Indigenous polities would no longer exist. Treaties, already being ignored, became completely irrelevant. Indigenous nations would have no recourse as Congress tried to legislate away and erode their sovereignty by turning Indigenous nations into municipalities or communities with no distinctions from any other such entities in the United States.

In response, action anthropologists devised a method that they referred to as the non-use of power. This method is crucial to understanding Rietz's effectiveness in his role as director of the American Indian Center despite not being Indigenous himself. While remaining wholeheartedly committed to the goals and objectives of Chicago's diverse Indigenous community, he served the center's actual members and participants in a deeply troubled time worsened by aggressively assimilationist government policies. It could even be said that Rietz's leadership is best explained by what he did not do rather than what he did.

Although Rietz and Tax were rarely explicit in publications about the theories and methods of action anthropology, at some point during the late 1950s they coauthored the undated and unpublished *Action Anthropology Reader* (AAR).[4] They wrote about the significance of the non-use of power as it relates to action anthropology by making a distinction between applied and action anthropologies: "I often think therefore that it is better for emphasis and clarity to make a clean break by using the term action anthropology to denominate not simply a kind of applied anthropology, but to label a competing philosophy and method by which the anthropologist operates in community development programs" (AAR, 15).

The distinction has largely to do with the locus of power, that is, acknowledging power and divesting oneself of it so as to not to exercise it over others and to avoid denying or impeding people's abilities to determine their own destinies. Rietz and Tax maintained that such a position or approach was not possible in applied anthropology for several reasons, all of which have to do with the political and relational dynamics of power. The statement merits quoting at length. First, "it is not clear that, from the position of applied anthropologists, hired as expert advisors to administrators with power, it is possible to reject power over the community when the anthropologist works for an administrator, since his obligation . . . is to satisfy not only the ends of the community, but the ends of an administration which characteristically has its own problems." Second, "it is difficult to avoid having undue influence over the people. In order to reject power we must actually work. We find it necessary actively to convince the people that we have no goals of our own other than a desire to help them clarify, compromise, and achieve their own goals. That is still more difficult, if not impossible, if the anthropologist is placed structurally in a position of power" (AAR, 8).

These political and relational challenges led action anthropologists to conclude that "there is an essential difference between action and a few applied projects on the one hand and most applied projects on the other" (AAR, 3). Moreover, they did not underestimate the difficulties in taking this new path.

> Need I repeat that even under ideal circumstances where the anthropologist operates unconnected with administration and its power,

it is exceedingly difficult not to exercise undue influence. . . . He has power whether he wants it or not; to succeed in stripping himself of this power takes time, patience, luck, and a genuine desire to do so. . . . Insofar as we have succeeded, a major reason is that we are a group; a lone man could not, very probably, hold himself in adequate check. (AAR, 12)

Rietz and Tax saw action anthropology as a collective enterprise of anthropologists working on behalf of Indigenous peoples. Their example changed the discipline of anthropology itself but no single individual should take credit.

Drafted in the late 1950s, the *Action Anthropology Reader* provides an early perspective on the political conceptualization of action anthropology's value of self-determination. To Tax and Rietz this "means simultaneously two things. It is a check on what we will do and what we will not do in the field. In that sense its meaning is that we cause ourselves to be permissive in our dealings with the Indians. The logical extreme is the position that, *where the group studied faces a choice point, their decision is by definition the good decision*" (AAR, 5–6, emphasis mine; Smith 2015, 57). This was at the core of Rietz's approach as director of the American Indian Center. Moreover, action anthropologists operated on the assumption that "self-determination by a human group is not a thing that is ever achieved":

It is not a goal that can be "reached" in some definite sense-not even by a tribe in isolation leave alone a group in the modern one-world. Rather, it is a way of valuing one state of affairs relative to another in two groups or in one group at different times. But even relatively, self-determination is difficult to see or measure. . . . *If a human group is not self-determining in some large measure, it is recognized by common sense and by solid science to be sick.* (AAR, 6–7, emphasis mine; Smith 2015, 57)

Maintaining the "value position" of self-determination "requires the *absolute rejection of a position of power over the people and the community*" (AAR, 8, emphasis mine; Smith 2015, 57).

Although AAR theorizes action anthropology without the benefit of contemporary political philosophy and discourses on sovereignty, power, and colonialism, Rietz was working on and with the same concepts, problems and challenges.

When Tax and Rietz faced increasing challenges with the BIA, exemplified by Rietz's refusal to accept a transfer from Fort Berthold to the Cheyenne River Sioux Reservation, Rietz explained "that it is no part of my function or my interest to study situations or to influence Indian people with the goal of helping to implement policy of the Indian Office where this policy is in disagreement with my own beliefs, or is neglectful towards the types of action which I believe are called to redesign the role of Indian Service anthropologist to allow such leeway" (Daubenmier 2008, 175). The most compelling application of the theory of action anthropology came when Rietz became the executive director of the American Indian Center, which was founded in response to the growing population of Indigenous people in Chicago.

The center began as a BIA relocation center that provided welfare assistance and services to help people adjust to urban life. In the 1950s Sol Tax was able to secure funding from the Emil Schwarzhaupt Foundation to support the hiring of Rietz as director (Daubenmier 2008, 301). Indigenous people began to pour into Chicago due to both the relocation program promoted by the BIA and the lack of other opportunities for some forty thousand Indigenous veterans returning home from World War II. With an estimated population of fifty-six thousand in 1950, the Indigenous community in Chicago was beginning to swell, but few services were available to address their unique challenges and needs (Laukaitis 2009, 6).[5]

Although the BIA promoted relocation via false promises about the opportunities and economic stability it would bring, Indigenous people found neither opportunity nor stability. Even as the BIA misrepresented the conditions in Chicago, the funding for relocation tripled by 1956. Philleo Nash later commented that "[Indian Commissioner] Dillon Myer's relocation was an underfunded, ill-conceived program" (Laukaitis 2009, 9). The BIA created and articulated "an 'imagined landscape' to promote and advance their assimilation program, which is the real impetus for relocation: to see Indigenous peoples move off the reservation and vanish into the general population" (Arndt 1998b, 114, 121; Laukaitis 2009, 9): "The Chicago Relocation Office knew that the job market in the city was thinning, but did not communicate this information in publicizing relocation programs on reservations. Instead, the BIA persisted that 'splendid opportunities' existed in Chicago and, moreover, that 'Offices maintained by the government render unlimited services to people who are entering a different phase of life' (Laukaitis 2009, 12).

As this was happening in Tax's home city of Chicago, he "made it clear that the lack of employment, substandard housing, and deficient support by the BIA led to 'urgent and prominent problems.' In his view the relocation program was 'a one-way ticket situation where bureaucrats filled their quotas'" (Laukaitis 2009, 13). The All-Tribes American Indian Center (AIC) was established in 1953 and, with other organizations, asserted and sustained increasing Indigenous agency and cultural persistence, not to mention Indigenous community development in all areas of urban life. But the center struggled due to conflicts over its objectives and purpose. Much dissension was caused by the center's ongoing association with the assimilationist goals of the BIA. It also struggled to retain consistent leadership. The AIC had four directors in four years: Thomas Segundo (1953–1954), Ted White (1954–1955), Allen Seltzer (1955–1957), and Thomas Segundo (1957–1958). The AIC overcame this tumultuous beginning when Robert Rietz was hired as executive director on September 27, 1958.

Immediately following Rietz's appointment a new advisory board was established (Laukaitis 2009, 26–27). Rietz's leadership exemplified the action anthropology philosophy of the non-use of power as he worked to represent the interests of the Indigenous community and AIC membership he served. Shortly after Rietz started the AIC changed the bylaws to give "more power to members than they previously had" and, "while the bylaws of the AIC always mandated a simple majority of American Indians on its board of directors, the revised bylaws allowed only American Indian members the power to vote in elections, motions, and new policies" (Laukaitis 2009, 29). Moreover, the new advisory committee to the board of directors included Tax. Committee members served merely as support and held no voting powers on the board. According to Rietz, "We of the Center Staff are not preparing a Program for you.... Our program is to assist you in the program that comes about from your interests and the activities that you keep going" (Laukaitis 2009, 29). Looking back on the tumultuous early history of the center in 1988, Tax noted that Rietz was highly regarded by all who worked with him. In many ways, for Tax and other action anthropologists, Rietz set a high standard for working with communities selflessly as a "nondirective director" who has been "remembered long and well by the American Indian community for his role in helping to build the AIC" (Tax 1988, 12).

With funding from the Emil Schwarzhaupt Foundation and Rietz's committed leadership, the AIC was on solid ground within a few years. According to Laukaitis,

> the overall stability of the AIC led to a growth of 126 dues-paying members in July of 1958 to 540 in July of 1959. The AIC in 1959 averaged 1,000 participants in its activities each month with some regular events attracting as many as 500 people. According to a 1959 report to the Schwarzhaupt Foundation submitted by the AIC's Board of Directors, "The amount of participation in activities of the larger community has increased. This is a matter of deliberate policy on the part of the Executive Director." (Laukaitis 2009, 30–31)

The center grew into a major cultural, economic, educational, political, and social meeting place and resource for Chicago's Indigenous population. It offered "counseling, referral services, emergency assistance, casework, and educational programs" (Laukaitis 2009, 21). Additionally, it provided social services assisting with "problems with employment, health services, housing, alcoholism, and discrimination," but, most importantly, the AIC "emphasized the importance of Indian control in its pursuit of helping those in need" (Laukaitis 2009, 38). According to Laukaitis, services and programs included "childcare, employment services, vocational counseling, alcohol treatment, youth services, and family and personal counseling in addition to its ongoing social and recreational activities" (2009, 39). By the early 1970s, over 7500 people per year used the AIC, whose "social services addressed many problems including unemployment, poor housing, alcohol, and drug abuse, inadequate medical care, and legal issues" (Laukaitis 2009, 46).

Rietz's work with the center remains a critical aperture within the history of anthropology through which to explore enduring and apposite issues in the myriad approaches to the political challenges of community engagement. These methods or research identities vary and come with their own origin stories, epistemic foundations, and modi operandi.[6] Rietz's action anthropology rested on his commitment to the community he felt obligated to serve. For both Rietz and Tax, it was not so much a profound invention or shift in anthropology that they "discovered"; it was more what they deemed the point of anthropology. Rietz's selfless dedication to the non-use of power in his approach to ethnographic participant-observation best served a community's needs as they were articulated to him in ways both direct and indirect.

The unpublished AAR is the best source document from which to extrapolate the theory and method of action anthropology. Throughout the document Rietz's commitment and energy remain focused on his work with Chicago's Indigenous community. At no point does Rietz seem concerned or preoccupied with popularizing his philosophy or elaborating on it further, which ironically is an enormous loss to anthropology today.[7]

Rietz's personal papers record an anthropologist whose ethnographic sensibilities are deeply felt by anyone attempting to listen to his archive.[8] They echo his relational politics as both a person and an anthropologist who put his uncompromising concern for people first. Rietz exhibited patience while making sure to understand all perspectives on problems as they were articulated. Moreover, he approached action anthropology not merely as a new method or experimental innovation in social science, but infused it with a practice of what I have termed radical caring. A quote is attributed to Rietz on the cover of his memorial service program from 1971: "Stick with the little people. They all have names and faces even though you never read about them in the newspapers. Big people are always trying to step on little people. Every time they do it, bite their foot" (Robert Rietz memorial service program; RRP).

The remarkable success of the American Indian Center during Rietz's tenure as director is due in no small part to this sentiment. Ironically, such sentiments are too often deemed incongruous with the objectives of scientific research. When it comes to politics, power, and justice, "finding a place to stand" within the politics of research, in Asch's formulation, is too often disdainfully regarded as unscientific. Rietz, however, knew where he stood vis-à-vis the people he felt obligated to help.[9] Without imposing himself or leveraging his position to further his career, Rietz succeeded by actively listening and fostering relationships for their own sakes. One of action anthropology's goals is to become unnecessary and work itself out of a job. In this regard, at least, Rietz failed as an action anthropologist by rendering himself too valuable in his role as director.

The modus operandi of Rietz's action anthropology was relationality. He did not view people as subjects or informants. The notion of relationships being crucial to sound ethnographic and community engagement practices is nothing new in anthropology. Yet, as Rietz saw it, anthropology *is* relationality, and research is synonymous with relationships. As he forged relationships and undertook actions premised on what he heard and learned from those experiencing immense hardships due to oppressive policies and governance, Rietz succeeded in giving his power away in order to become an instrument of decolonization. Always eschewing credit, Rietz learned ethnographically to understand that the mechanics of the problems Indigenous people face are due to reified notions of who or what Indigenous individuals or polities must be. In this way, Rietz identified and evaded the trappings of both essentialism and "going native." He met people on their own terms and embraced their choices as the best choices for them. Yet Rietz was reflexive enough to understand the oppressive politics of settler society and to take a stand against it without judging, essentializing, or infantilizing Indigenous people for the choices any person or group might make in accordance with their own experiences and wisdom. He said as much in a letter to Tax in 1958 that encapsulates his position and stands as a manifesto to radical caring in action anthropology:

> We have thought of Indian communities as being more than just "Indian." We have pointed out that they are economically depressed communities and have explored, analyzed and presented some of

what we believe are major problems of their minority group status. For example, we have pointed out that the Indian community is too poor to provide for essential community services, and that it will be necessary to subsidize much services for some time to come. . . .

The necessarily subsidized community services involve much of the vital concerns, conceptions and role-relationships we refer to as community social organization. Where the roles of responsibility are pre-empted by outside administrators in the operation of such matters there can be no community of the sort that is expected to develop. The community itself is isolated, in terms of the larger social organization, which encompasses it. . . .

As Felix Cohen once pointed out, even the man who empties the ashes in the school is not responsible to the community in which he serves. In this situation, the relations between Indians with reference to something like a day school are largely in terms of their relationship to an administrator, to a government, to a "white man." A long backlog of developmental experiences and learning, and a longer backlog of developing community organization have been substituted for with the files, ledgers and monthly reports of an intrusive federal organization. Dickering and negotiation have substituted for intra-community relationships developed around performance and its recognition. Perhaps among those who could best perform and be recognized is the choice between going away and staying in such a place not much of a choice at all.

The spectacle of an apparently able people having their affairs administered by outsiders, the prevention of any development of parallel roles by which members of the Indian community could truly identify and participate with their counterparts in the white towns have, to my mind, provided the greatest major source of problems of minority group status. . . . In this situation, a "termination program" which means merely the withdrawal of a necessary subsidy, or the substitution of one set of masters, of outsider initiators of action, for another is not worthy of serious consideration. [Rietz to Sol Jan 28, 1958]

Rietz's invisibility in the historiography of anthropology is not surprising given his decisions to pursue roles such as directing the American Indian Center and work on day-to-day problems of community empowerment, Indigenous rights, and decolonization (although the term was not yet in use). At the same time, his invisibility is also a testament to his humility and success as an action anthropologist or, as Tax anointed him, "the Sainted Bob Rietz." Tragically, Robert Rietz passed away from cancer on May 13, 1971, and the center struggled to overcome the void he left behind before recovering, succeeding, and evolving without him. That is just as Rietz would have wanted it.

NOTES

1. The Meskwaki Nation used to be referred to as the Sac and Fox Indians and by the older spelling *Mesquakie*. I have replaced, even in quotations, old spellings with the contemporary Meskwaki or Meskwaki Nation. Moreover, I refer to what is known in the literature as the Fox Project as the Chicago Project.

2. For the historical and theoretical contexts of anthropology and Indian Policy as they relate to this time period, I have relied on Marc Pinkoski's exceptional work on Julian Steward, which best exemplifies and articulates the context Rietz was working within and against.

3. "HCR 108, passed on Aug 1, declared it to be the new policy of the federal government to abolish federal supervision over the tribes as soon as practical, and to then subject the terminated Indians 'to the same privileges and responsibilities as are applicable to other citizens of the United States, to end their status as wards of the United States, and to grant them all the rights and prerogatives pertaining to American citizenship.' Assimilation was one of the driving forces, although certainly not the lone force, behind this policy. Public Law 280, the second measure, was enacted two weeks later. This act brought Indian lands and their tribal residents in California, Minnesota (except the Red Lake Reservation), Nebraska, Oregon (except the Warm Springs Reservation), and Wisconsin (except the Menominee Reservation) under the criminal and, to a lesser extent, the civil jurisdictional coup. This omnibus act was in principle a unilateral repudiation of treaties between tribes and the United States and severely reduced the tribal governments' inherent powers over civil and criminal issues" (Wilkins 1997, 166–67).

4. To my knowledge, I am the first scholar to analyze, cite, and quote from the Action Anthropology Reader.

5. This portion of my sketch utilizes the exceptional recent work of John J. Laukaitis's dissertation (2009), which is unparalleled in scope and detail. This work is rendered in a more recent book form as well (Laukaitis 2015); I choose to refer to the original dissertation.

6. To name a few: action research; applied research; collaborative research; community-action-research; community-based-participatory-action-research; community-based-research; decolonized research; engaged research; and Indigenous research.

7. I make this observation confidently based on my extensive readings of the Sol Tax papers, voluminous correspondence among action anthropologists, and conversations with both Nancy Lurie and Albert Wahrhaftig.

8. The Robert W. Rietz Papers are in the Regenstein Special Collections Library, University of Chicago. They are part of the larger collection *The Native American Educational Services, Robert Rietz Papers 1876–1982.*

9. On Finding a Place to Stand, see Asch (2001, 2007, 2015).

REFERENCES

Action Anthropology Reader. n.d. Unpublished manuscript. The Sol Tax Papers 126/8.

Arndt, Grant P. 1998. "Relocation's Imagined Landscape and the Rise of Chicago's Native American Community." *Native Chicago* (1998):114–27.

Asch, Michael. 1992. "Errors in Delgamuukw: An Anthropological Perspective." In *Aboriginal Title in British Columbia: Delgamuukw vs. The Queen.* Edited by Frank Cassidy. Vancouver: Oolichan Books, 221–43.

———. 2001. "Indigenous Self-determination and Applied Anthropology in Canada: Finding a Place to Stand." *Anthropologica 43, no. 2: 201–7.*

———. 2007. "Governmentality, state culture and indigenous rights." *Anthropologica 49, no. 2: 281–84.*

———. 2015. "Anthropology, Colonialism and the Reflexive Turn: Finding a Place to Stand." *Anthropologica 57, no. 2: 481–89.*

Barney, Ralph. 1955. "Legal Problems Peculiar to Indian Claims Litigation." *Ethnohistory 2, no. 4: 315–25.*

Bennett, John W. 1996. "Applied and Action Anthropology: Ideological and Conceptual Aspects." In "Anthropology in Public," special issue, *Current Anthropology 37, no. 1: S23–S53.*

———. 1998. "Applied and Action Anthropology: Problems of Ideology and Intervention." In *Classic Anthropology: Critical Essays, 1944–1996.* Edited by John W. Bennet. New Brunswick NJ: Transaction.

Daubenmier, Judith M. 2008. *The Meskwaki and Anthropologists: Action Anthropology Reconsidered*. Lincoln: University of Nebraska Press.

Deloria, Vine Jr. 1969. *Custer Died for Your Sins: An Indian Manifesto*. Norman: University of Oklahoma Press.

————. 1995. "Eulogy for Sol Tax's Memorial Service, January 1995." DVD recording. Sol Tax Papers; Regenstein Special Collections (uncatalogued), University of Chicago.

Laukaitis, John J. 2009. "Community Self-Determination in Uptown Chicago: A Social and Cultural History of American Indian Educational Programs and Experiences, 1952–2002." PhD diss., University of Chicago.

Lawson, Michael L. 1982. *Dammed Indians: The Pick-Sloan Plan and the Missouri River Sioux, 1944–1980*. Norman: University of Oklahoma Press.

Pinkoski, Marc. 2006. "Julian Steward and American Anthropology: The Science of Colonialism." PhD diss., University of Victoria.

Rietz, Robert. 1953. "Leadership, Initiative and Economic Progress on an American Indian Reservation." In *Economic Development and Cultural Change 2*, no. 1 (April): 60–70.

————. 1960. "A Discussion of Contemporary Fox Social Organization, Together with a Proposal for a Combined Program of Social Engineering and Social Science Research." In *Documentary History of the Fox Project*, edited by Fred Gearing, Robert Netting, and Lisa Peattie.

Smith, Joshua. 2010. "The Political Thought of Sol Tax: The Principles of Non-Assimilation and Self-Government in Action Anthropology." In vol. 6 of *Histories of Anthropology Annual*.

————. 2011. "Action Anthropology and the 'Settler Question' in Canada." Paper presented at the Annual Meeting of the American Anthropological Association, Montreal.

————. 2012. "Beyond Collaboration: Action Anthropology as Decolonization." *Journal of Northwest Anthropology*. In *Action Anthropology and Sol Tax in 2012: The Final Word?*, edited by Darcy C. Strapp, 79–95.

————. 2015. "Standing with Sol: The Spirit and Intent of Action Anthropology." *Anthropologica* 57: 445–56.

Tax, Sol. 1988. "Pride and Puzzlement: A Retro-introspective Record of 60 Years of Anthropology." *Annual Review of Anthropology* 17: 1–21.

Trencher, Susan. 2002. "The American Anthropological Association and the Values of Science: 1935–70." *American Anthropologist* 4, no. 2: 450–62.

Wilkins, David E. 1997. *American Indian Sovereignty and the United States Supreme Court*. Austin: University of Texas Press.

IAN PUPPE, NORTH DE PENCIER,
AND GERALD MCKINLEY

4

Sioux Lookout Zone Hospital Archives Project—Barriers in Bringing Medical Anthropology to Medical Practice

*Adrian Tanner, the Sioux Lookout Zone Hospital,
and Cross-Cultural Miscommunication*

In the fall of 2014, medical anthropologist Gerald McKinley came across a set of records in the University of Toronto's Archives & Records related to the operation of the Sioux Lookout Zone Hospital. The hospital operated from 1949 until 1996 to serve the Indigenous communities and reserves of northern Ontario. McKinley sorted through the archive and found one piece in particular that here occupies the majority of our attention, and which helps to flesh out the reception of and resistance to medical anthropology in the health care industry in Ontario by those delivering Indigenous health services. This was a specially commissioned paper written by the British-Canadian anthropologist Adrian Tanner in the summer of 1971 titled "Sickness and Ideology among the Ojibway." The communities of Ojibwe (Anishinaabe), Cree (Nehiyawak) and Oji-Cree people had been underserved and had requested greater assistance from the Canadian nation-state. Officials at the Zone Hospital hoped to provide that assistance, but soon found that encouraging the uptake of services was a struggle, and adequate and appropriate forms of care were not easily provided.

In his report Tanner sought to explain why, for almost fifty years, the hospital and satellite services had failed to adequately address the concerns of community leaders and elders. Tanner's report, though clearly written and founded on intensive fieldwork in the community of New Osnaburg-Mishkeegogamang First Nation, was shelved and remained hidden and unpublished in the archives until McKinley's fortunate rediscovery of the paper. The story of the report's creation and reception (or dismissal) helps to expand our understanding of health care administrators and academics failing to combine their expertise and interests, and offers an intriguing case through which to explore the barriers impeding cooperation between the burgeoning subdiscipline of medical anthropology and health care in practice in the important context of relations between the Canadian nation-state and Indigenous peoples of North America. The vocabularies used by different anthropologists, intended to articulate the importance of culture for the practice of cross-culturally sensitive medicine, often served to impede medical professionals' uptake of these ideas, which allowed representations of cultural, ethnic, and religious or ideological differences to unintentionally subvert the integrity of Indigenous people's ontological orientations and to summon the attention of those who would seek to "improve" Indigenous people through assimilationist means. Often related to a dangerous, though empathetic, paternalism, overgeneralizations pervade the archive. This paper works to correct some of the assumptions that are all too prevalent within the records of the hospital's activity and the practice of health care delivery in the zone.

During his doctoral studies Tanner ethnographically explored experiences of illness and health among community members of New Osnaburg-Mishkeegogamang First Nation through firsthand interviews and participant-observation over the course of three months. The work being undertaken by the Sioux Lookout Zone Hospital Archives Project reassesses the reasons for the report having been undervalued and reconsiders Tanner's report in the wake of the ontological turn in anthropology. Tanner's proposal of a long-term research project to trace culturally situated notions of being-well (Adelson 2009), or *mino-bimadaziwin*, is only now becoming a reality with several projects converging in the area, each working to return stories to the people who have been affected by them.

The zone's Indian Hospital struggled for support after it opened in 1949, and in 1969 was taken over by the University of Toronto Faculty of Medicine, Toronto General Hospital, and the Hospital for Sick Children, who jointly operated the facility until 1996. During that period the organizations amassed a substantial amount of non-personalized health information on the twenty-six First Nations communities serviced by the hospital. The objective of the Sioux Lookout Zone Hospital Archives Project is to use archival research to reconstruct changing health patterns in the region and to document, in ways that will empower communities, the social, cultural, economic, and political factors that contributed to these changes.

Phase one of the project is focused on 1) understanding how formal and informal relationships between First Nations communities, hospital staff, and administrators functioned in the region; 2) exploring the presence and absence of Indigenous voices in the day-to-day running of the hospital; and 3) examining the Scott-McKay-Bain Health Panel report (1989) and the process undertaken to construct it. This important internal report analyzed the operation of the hospital during the transition from the authority of the University of Toronto and Children's Hospital to the First Nations Health Authority, which currently administers health care services in the North. Many of the communities had nursing stations already or had them set up during the expansion of the Zone Hospital into the area, and the report describes the difficulties involved in delivering a less centralized form of health care service.

Phase two examines specific health measures across generations to document changes in population health. Critical issues are related to the relocation of communities; the transition away from foraging, hunting, and gathering as primary modes of acquiring food; sedentary lifestyles introduced by settlement on reserve communities; the impacts of residential schools; and increasingly common health issues such as tuberculosis, diabetes, heart disease, and other illnesses associated with the increasing colonization of Indigenous people's lives and lifeways. This phase will expand on phase one by utilizing a holistic health model to explore factors that contribute to changing health.

Phase three seeks support from individuals and communities (both patients and staff) who were involved with the hospital during its operation so that they can tell their stories. This phase seeks to contribute a mechanism for telling the story of one of Ontario's two Indian Hospitals from the perspectives of people who were there. The final phase of the project is a returning of the story for the benefit of future generations to the communities who were served by the hospital. These phases run concurrently, allowing research to proceed at an appropriate pace in light of the sensitivity of some information contained within the archive, while also allowing us to expedite particular projects given the importance of these stories to those who are dealing with contemporary health care delivery and uptake issues in the northern areas of the province.

THE STORY OF TANNER'S REPORT

Tanner became involved with the Sioux Lookout Zone Hospital when he was contracted for a summer position by Dr. Robin Badgley, the new chairman of the Department of Behavioral Sciences at the University of Toronto. Tanner had no experience in the geographical area, and he had not worked with Ojibwas or Anishinaabe before. Though he had spent time in other northern Canadian Indigenous communities in the Yukon and his doctoral research was focused on Crees of northern Ontario and Quebec, there are some important differences in the ways that these communities apprehend particular issues related to disease and illness. Tanner spent the summer in New Osnaburg (also known as Mishkeegogamang First Nation), located very close to Pickle Lake, a much larger community with similar ideas about health and illness.

Puppe corresponded with Dr. Tanner in 2016 regarding his time in the area working on the project and found Tanner very gracious and forthcoming. He remembered his time there fondly, though he was clearly frustrated by the dismissal of his report and its conclusions. His feeling was that he had naively misunderstood the aims of the project at the time. He had hoped that there would be a push to include the social sciences in medicine where there had previously been much resistance. The project's connection to the newly formed Department of Behavioral Science through Dr. Badgley gave Tanner hope that the developing social science approaches to health being forged in the nascent subdiscipline of medical anthropology might have a much greater impact than it has. Unfortunately, the officials' plans for his work at the time were very different.

Tanner stayed for three months, and, in his words,

> I was a grad student in the Anthropology Department, and one of my professors told me about a summer job with something called the Sioux Lookout project. I met with the director, Robin Badgley. He had recently moved to the University of Toronto to found the Department of Behavioral Science, becoming the department's first chairman. I am a bit vague on this, but at the time I thought the intent of the new department was to bring the social sciences into medicine, because at the time there was resistance to having it inside the U of T medical faculty. He told me the U of T had a history of trying to improve health statistics in the region, with well qualified doctors spending time at the Zone Hospital, but so far this had not made any improvement to the statistics. (Adrian Tanner, pers. comm., 2016)

This estimation is consistent with other documents in the records that stressed the need to find tangible actions that could be taken by professionals in the hospital and dismissed and devalued as superstition issues surrounding different worldviews or philosophies of medical treatment and diagnosis. Physicians held authority over their claimed specialization and defended that privilege on the grounds of positivism and scientific objectivity, in effect becoming the vanguard of settler-colonial hegemony over what constituted health care and well-being, a crucial issue in the funding and delivery of services between the federal government and Indigenous communities in Canada. The defensive posturing of health care providers also meant that issues surrounding the personal affect and bedside manner of physicians and other health care professionals in their interactions with patients were often considered immaterial and therefore superfluous to training, in stark contrast to the centrality of face-to-face interactions for those they were charged with caring for.

The effect of introducing clinics, outpost nurses, and an allopathic medical regime was a destabilization of people's ability to look after themselves in culturally specific ways, or what Illich called "social iatrogenesis," "in which the environment is deprived of those conditions that endow individuals, families, and neighborhoods with control over their own internal states and their milieu" (Illich 1976, 133). Here the effort to control discursive constructions of health care provided a crucial battleground between culturally distinct approaches in a settler-colonial context where Indigenous perspectives became occluded, ignored, and openly derided as superstitious. The empirically grounded assertions of what might be described as Anishinaabe relational etiology was discarded without fair consideration, in part because it required physicians to abdicate some of their authority to define for a patient the cause of an illness.

A CURIOUS INCLUSION

The archive also contains a reprint of a paper by Cliff Bennett titled "Ojibway Consciousness," originally published in the Journal of Ontario Association of Children's Aid Societies. It is impossible to tell when it was reprinted for the files, or who requested it. But the paper offers some interesting clues as to the manner in which the hospital administrators wished to progress, and what they were willing to consider in relation to the obvious differences between how physicians and Indigenous clients perceived health and wellness. It is possible that the Sioux Lookout Zone Hospital reprinted the report prior to the project's takeover by the University of Toronto and the Toronto Children's Hospital. It is also possible that this report became the impetus behind commissioning Tanner's work in the area, furthering the anthropological and sociological knowledge of the area's health care professionals through direct, empirically grounded fieldwork. Bennett's report, like Tanner's, attempts to define the contours of a generalized and broadly shared perspective among Anishinaabe on the workings of the world and how they understand their place in it.

What distinguishes Tanner's report is the care that Tanner takes to outline the limits of his findings in contrast to Bennett's attempts to arrive at a general theory of the "Ojibway" mind by delineating shared patterns of consciousness. Bennett employs the language of the culture and personality school championed by Ruth Benedict, and in doing so supports a vision of the "Indian" as culturally backward and afflicted by ignorance. Bennett describes the "Dionysian" use of alcohol by the "Ojibway" in search of dreams where power and status could be gained, unfairly fitting them into a framework created to describe a people separated from them by leagues and millennia, reductively homogenizing their cultural specificity in the process (Bennett 1966, 2).

Bennett begins by describing ubiquitous racism towards Indigenous people, which positions Indigenous peoples as a group as a "mythical 'underdog'" (1966, 2) in the white imagination. Suggesting that the "white man" has an inferiority complex resulting from the self-conscious historical perspective of British civilization as relatively recently developed compared to the ancient Mediterranean world, Bennett suggests that the imagined Indian plays a role that allows white men to take pride in their civilization by denigrating another as less civilized. But Bennett then describes the "retaliation" of the Indian against whites in the production of an image of "an overfed, over-greedy promise breaker who looks at his watch to see if he is hungry" (1966, 2). This binary view leaves little room for nuance, and fails to capture the importance of such skewed perceptions to the health care professionals who were behind the initiatives to introduce greater access to Canadian health services in the north and the patient community they aimed to serve.

Bennett's discussion moves on to detail the distinctions between the worldview of the Ojibwa and the white man, pointing out specifically that intelligence is not easily understood cross-culturally. Bennett's first interest is children's health and well-being, and he immediately moves from the idea of a mythical authentic Indian trapped in a past state of development toward other concerns, paraphrasing anthropologists as he goes. Bennett describes the inadequacy of measuring children's intelligence in ways that ignore the importance of culture and of relying on evolutionist paradigms to explain cultural differences. Echoing the work done by anthropologist A. I. Hallowell among the northern Ojibwas of the Berens River area in the 1930s and 1940s, Bennett states,

> Labelling Indian children 'slow learners' on the basis of a one-shot IQ test should be questioned, as the test itself is being questioned for its value as an innate intelligence indicator. It cannot measure ethnic learning-ability differences, because although it appears to reveal innate differences between Caucasians and non-whites, when given to large enough groups, the test reveals comparable differences between urban and rural Caucasians. (Bennett 1966, 2)

Here Bennett unintentionally reveals his participation in a regime of racial categorization through the use of the term Caucasian and also, in a more subtle way, his use of the term "ethnic learning." Ostensibly meant to designate the culturally specific pedagogical routines of different societies, he implies innate strengths and weaknesses of ability or interest on the part of different ethnicities stemming from biology in flattened and overly generalized ways. These generalizations conform to a pattern within the archive that infantilizes and derogates Indigenous people, often with the intent to protect, educate, or modernize.

Bennett's is an evolutionist paradigm couched in the rhetoric of a cultural relativism that half-heartedly suggests the need for understanding, insomuch as the failure to recognize the importance of these differences for patients impedes the efforts of health care professionals to teach them "better" ways of living. His unfortunate use of the term Indian, common at the time, flattens culturally distinct differences between people seen from the outside as similar enough to be a single category, but who demonstrated in practice a broad variety of behaviors, practices, worldviews, ontological dispositions, and apprehensions. "Indians" have too often been lumped together through stereotypes that erase cultural differences and deny individuals practicing different traditions their identities and heritages. Bennett's report does nothing to disturb or destabilize the authority of the health care professional, and instead offers a plea that health care professionals take a form of pity on Indigenous patients. In short, Bennett's work perpetuated health care professionals' racist beliefs that Indigenous people may not know what is best for them due to having a perspective on reality affected by stalled evolution—a perspective common among some anthropologists of the time who were interested in the notion of cultural ecology after the work of Julian Steward (Pinkoski 2008).

CONFLICTING PARADIGMS

Tanner detailed the distinctions between "Indian" and "white" illness in a binary pattern of comparison in order to elucidate the power of ontogenetically distinct ways of dealing with illness, and in order to explain how patients and health care providers were likely to differ from one another in a nonjudgmental fashion consistent with the cultural relativism of many anthropologists in the 1970s. The ability to generalize from such materials remains questionable, but, in light of A. I. Hallowell's work in neighboring communities, Tanner's efforts can be seen to bring certain ways of describing Anishinaabe concepts of illness to Western audiences, even while Tanner's and Hallowell's technical language is borrowed from very different sources. While Hallowell primarily used vocabulary borrowed from psychology, social work, and philosophy, Tanner relied on reinvigorated Marxian materialist idioms, likening his analysis to a political economy of belief, to explain and describe his findings. This difference in preference for certain varieties of technical language was met very differently by scholars, medical professionals, and laypeople. Tanner himself said that he was aware of Hallowell's work when he first went to Mishkeegogamang, but that he failed to see its applicability to his own work with closely related communities of Anishinaabe and Crees. Hallowell published widely on the topic of "Ojibwe" (his spelling) notions of illness and provided a fruitful theoretical base from which to pose other empirically grounded ethnological questions about health and healing.

In a Marxian discursive framework "ideology" has a technical meaning that goes beyond its common usage. Tanner's report identifies two distinct ideologies relating to illness and disease in the northern communities that he visited. One follows the Western or biomedical etiological model in which the causes and cures of illness and disease are mainly "material," or objectively determinable through empirically situated experimental science. The alternative constructs a relational etiology of the vectors and appropriate treatments for issues arising from transgressions against "others," broadly understood by Anishinaabe and Nehiyawak to include other-than-human persons, while foregrounding the power of relations to affect daily realities. In the conclusion to his report Tanner refers to "Indian sickness" as "a system of ideas," unintentionally minimizing the critical importance of distinct ontologies in producing perspectives and realities that find friction with one another.

This theoretical approach to Anishinaabe etiological frameworks lends itself to a Marxist understanding of ideology as the false consciousness of the proletariat. Thus Tanner's use of the phrase "false consciousness" might be broadly characterized as accepting the efficacy of "spiritual" cures for illness and disease and aligning with anthropological perspectives that often unintentionally elevated scientific descriptions and approaches above those of the people they meant to describe. In Tanner's work this comes across as the distinction between "white man" and "Indian" illness, and it serves to divide the two distinct etiological approaches by situating them within ideologically inflected worldviews of an unchanging external reality. Tanner understands as environmental the fact that the sicknesses called "Indian" mostly affect Indigenous people, meaning that whites do not experience the same stressors and exposure to these vectors and so do not exhibit such forms of disease and illness. Here Tanner sides with those who would suggest that people's way of life, their economic and material circumstances, determines their experiences of daily reality in a top-down manner. This theoretical position echoes the Marxian notion that an external material reality is the superstructure that determines ideologically premised structures of society and individual psychology.

Closer inspection of the types of illness included by Tanner in the list of Indian sicknesses may shed more light. As mental illness is always considered "Indian sickness" it would seem that, to some degree, a lack of exposure to obviously mentally ill whites could account for some apparent assumptions by Tanner's interlocutors. Conversely, more than one reference in the paper suggests the opposite: that whites are universally mentally ill due to the environmental stressors associated with Euro-American culture, and that only Indian medicines could treat these illnesses inherent in white society. In this way the mental illness described by some Indigenous people may be associated with a breakdown in traditionally secure relations, and, in some other cases, a perspective that taking on the "white man's" ideology demonstrated a form of mental illness, or that in fact all mental illness in Indians was a result of their becoming white. When we consider the construction of illness as social or relational breakdown and alienation we begin to see the value of Bennett's points about the Indian perspective of the white man as perpetually hungry.

Here we must consider the perennial interest of the anthropologist in wendigo tales and the power of this "mythology" (as it is too often denigrated). For Anishinaabe the archetypal monstrous form was the spirit-matter hybrid called a wendigo, a huge, skeletal, insatiable cannibalistic beast striding across frozen landscapes to devour the innocent, or an alluring and persuasive familiar offering to share some meat of dubious provenance that is inevitably revealed to be human flesh. Never too far from the mind during times of stress, conflict, and need, wendigo were often blamed for rash actions and failures to respect the needs of others. Wendigo were understood to sometimes possess individuals, and were eventually categorized by scholars and medical professionals as a culture-bound syndrome called wendigo psychosis (Castillo 1997). In the perspectives outlined by Tanner and Bennett the wendigo plays no discernible role and is not mentioned by name. But it seems the wendigo stalks the margins of some people's notions of mental illness and social disorder, embodying the monstrous potential of antisocial behavior in small communities where social cohesion is highly prized and necessary for harmonious daily life.

If Tanner had been aware of the other-than-human persons many Anishinaabe and Crees recognize as distant kin, he may have chosen to minimize the role they were understood to play in the experience of illness and disease among the people he spoke with in order to avoid suggesting that his subjects were little more than superstitious (Hallowell 2010). But he did find that many thought that there were no accidents. Instead, injuries and illness were understood to follow infractions against other persons who would take revenge. So no experience of illness was understood to be innocent, shifting responsibility for healing toward the person experiencing the issues and away from a healer who could, at best, help people to heal themselves. This a radically different perspective than the one through which health care professionals often authoritatively disempower patients through the use of technical language, which can place patients at a disadvantage as lay people unfamiliar with medical terminology.

A further hint of the opinion held by many Indigenous community members of white men's medicine and its limited efficacy in treating Indian sickness can be discerned in the assertion that only Indians can treat Indian sickness. If Indian sickness is exemplified by behavior likened to that of whites, then healing such illness requires either removing the intractable relationship or removing the person from proximity to the vector, the white man. Tanner reported that people sometimes chose not to report certain illnesses to the nurses at the outpost, and instead sought treatment from other healers with expertise in Indian sickness. But this act of eluding the medical authorities makes apparent that some of the illnesses experienced by people of the community were related to the presence and proximity of whites and the treatment required reintegration into their home society and ontology. The failure of white medicine is simultaneously its inability to accept alternative ontologies of illness and disease and its stubborn refusal to allow Indigenous peoples space to heal on their own. When speaking of a besieged and occupied community afflicted by rampant racism and cultural genocide, it should come as no surprise that some illnesses were associated with the colonizer's presence, and that even the presence of the colonizer could inhibit healing in many cases.

Tucked within Tanner's work is the barely discernible subdiscipline of medical anthropology beginning to distinguish itself from other specializations within social or cultural anthropology. Though it went without a formal name until the early 1990s, medical anthropology as it is most commonly practiced today looks back to predecessors such as Margaret Lock, Nancy Scheper-Hughes, Ronald Frankenberg, and (in the area of transcultural psychiatry) Arthur Kleinman, who all did their most important work in the 1980s and 1990s (Eriksen and Nielsen 2013, 189–90). Tanner came almost two decades before the figures considered to be the founders of medical anthropology, and explored the internal workings of a distinct ontological approach to illness and disease long before others applied theories derived from the social sciences to answer medical questions (Eriksen and Nielsen 2013, 189–90). Tanner participated in a tradition first set forth by Audrey Richards in 1939 in her pioneering effort "Land, Labour and Diet in Northern Rhodesia," which, while subtitled "An Economic Study of the Bemba Tribe," innovated a method of data analysis and refocused subject matter on issues that affected health and well-being rather than simply critiquing economic production through the lens of social inequality.

It seems hardly possible that the health care professionals reviewing Tanner's work did not understand what he was saying, so there are other pressing issues at stake. But the pressures associated with the Zone Hospital's operation, and health care professionals' obvious desire for the hospital to succeed in its mission of improving health in the region, are evident in the language and depth of engagement found in the correspondence and internal reports located in the archive. If health care professionals understood that the Oji-Cree of the area had a different conception of the ways that illness and disease affected people and could be treated, they found ways to disregard these concepts by insinuating themselves into spaces where Indigenous forms of healing and coping with trauma might otherwise flourish. Health care professionals too often denigrated the ontological apprehension of the world common among Oji-Cree, and in doing so exacerbated the tension between themselves and the community they sought to serve. In practice these services often sought to change practices of hygiene and personal comportment, further insinuating Western models of health and healing into Indigenous bodies, exacerbating the alienation of forced assimilation.

The disregard of Indigenous ontologies carried over into other specializations of care, particularly into the care of children, who disproportionately experienced diagnoses of learning disabilities related to language barriers taken for signs of failed intelligence (as noted in a letter from an A. W. Rabhan, MD, to Dr. Harry Bain, director of the Zone Hospital, in 1979). Rabhan even suggested intelligence testing to determine Indigenous children's aptitude for learning other languages. Nowhere in Rabhan's brief report does one find the reflexivity to question the diagnoses' ubiquity in spite of the point made that the Fristoe Woodcock test was too culture-bound to be of use in the zone. This was a test meant to help judge the acuity and clarity of hearing, the presumption being that there may have been some pervasive form of hearing loss behind children's slow progress learning French and English in different provincial contexts. The test was found to be inappropriate for reasons of linguistic habituation. Anishinaabe and Cree languages use many unvoiced vowels that can be voiced in some dialects, so children brought up in environments where the voicing of a vowel may be immaterial to the meaning of a word might very well not discern the distinction between certain voiced and unvoiced vowels out of habit, and not inability, when studying new languages.

The most obvious point of friction is the discursive framework that Tanner applied, which was not borrowed from the health care profession nor any other allied disciplines such as the natural sciences, psychology, or social work. While Bennett (and, incidentally, Hallowell) had a background in social work, and so employed language amenable to interpretation through the lens of health care, great care must be taken when reading Tanner's report not to imbue certain technical terms with their more common vernacular understanding. His use of the word "spiritual," though easily misunderstood, reaches towards a fundamental distinction between European and Indigenous ontologies in their apprehensions of the world, suggesting that each was affected by their own unique spiritualities. For the materialist West, with its objectivist etiology, a thing or object of some variety (a bacteria, virus, etc.), is always at the root of the problem. For the Oji-Cree Tanner interviewed, the source of a problem is always a disturbed relationship, meaning an ostensibly immaterial change is understood to cause a real difference or what Tanner describes as a spiritual disturbance.

Tanner avoided the term *ontology*, instead gesturing toward the different epistemological conditions each culture operated through, structuring their different approaches to etiology and medicine. But in so doing Tanner inadvertently participated in the trend of reducing these differences in approach to behavior and belief rather than making obvious that the differences are not only cognitive or virtual, but also effect material changes to the experience of what is understood to be reality. In the effort to avoid suggesting any ethno-racial or biological differences between white and Indigenous people, Tanner instead represented cultural differences as primarily psychological. Presenting cultural differences as "ideology" allowed health care professionals to operate as though cultural differences were little more than matters of belief.

In the Marxist tradition within which Tanner worked, the term *ideology* is a cover for the notion of false consciousness as it becomes established through bourgeois hegemony, or structures of thought and feeling constructed through the operations of authority (Williams 1977). In this case, it may be that the medical professionals who did have some familiarity with the technical use of the word could have been dissuaded from taking Tanner's findings seriously since they may have understood his description of Oji-Cree "ideology" to mean that patients suffered from a type of false consciousness about sickness and disease from which they needed to be relieved. That is, Tanner's assertions that there were competing notions of what caused and could heal illness may have been a source of further assimilative pressure from health care providers for people to take up Western hygiene practices and ways of thinking about the world, beginning with the need to learn the language of the colonizers in order to assimilate scientific understandings of disease and illness (seen throughout the early period of the Zone Hospital as a laudable goal). The scientism of allopathic medicine and the common positivism of many physicians' training meant that the approach to medicine taken by most health care professionals would dismiss the relational etiology of illness as superstition in need of correction.

Blanket generalizations are rampant within the reports, and often follow a trend of empathizing with the population while continuing to stigmatize and stereotype Indigenous people. In a 1990 report on mental health issues in the zone titled "Cross Cultural Proposal to the Long Term Planning Committee," Harvey Armstrong, director of Child Psychiatry at the University of Toronto, suggested that it is critical that these underserved communities receive more attention than they have, and ascribes the dismal morbidity rate and rampant social issues to the lack of service. In the report Armstrong responds to a memo calling for "Canadian Aboriginal Psychiatric issues" to be made "a separate branch of the cross-cultural psychiatry division" in order to provide more specific care (Armstrong 1990). Armstrong rejects the proposal due to his notion that "Aboriginal" people are the only minority group in Canada not able to "import culture, import new ideas, import professionals" from another country. He continues: "There are very large and active programs in which the University is involved which provide health services to very large numbers of aboriginals [*sic*] in which psychiatry is a very active part. The population served are very large, the psychiatric problems of aboriginal people are very serious" (Armstrong 1990).

The discursive categorization of Aboriginal people as experiencing very serious "psychiatric problems" suggests ubiquitous mental health issues in Indigenous communities, in a reversal of the perspective of the Oji-Crees whom Tanner interviewed. Perhaps Armstrong would have done well to reflect on the assertion that a whole population experienced a specific set of problems due to their ethnic heritage. Certainly the nascent notion that all white men were perceived as potentially mentally ill by many community members would have given him pause. But this is not what happened, and there is no sign that Armstrong or any other administrators or health care professionals at the hospital took time to consider the findings Tanner reported.

CONCLUSION

Tanner's proposed long-term research project tracing culturally situated notions of being-well, or *bimadaziwin*, is only now becoming a reality with several projects converging in the area, each working to return stories to the people affected by them. Projects include Amy Bombay's team's work on the intergenerational effects of residential schools and other forms of trauma (Bombay 2014), Maureen Lux's project concerning the Indian Hospitals of Canada (Lux 2016), and current initiatives to contend with what have been described as crises of mental health, diabetes, stroke, heart disease, and suicide. Gerald McKinley is involved with a project that brings together community members from several reserves in the same zone, the Sioux Lookout First Nations Health Authority, and others to form an early warning system for risk factors that contribute to rises in suicide rates, allowing for more carefully orchestrated responses on the part of the local communities and their partners. The SLZHAP in partnership with the Sioux Lookout First Nations Health Authority will work to further expand on these connections and to trace these relationships in hope that they shed more light on the operation of the hospital and on its shortcomings.

REFERENCES

Adelson, Naomi. 2009. "The Shifting Landscape of Cree Well-Being." In *Pursuits of Happiness: Well-Being in Anthropological Perspective*, edited by Gordon Matthews and Carolina Izquierdo. New York: Berghahn Books.

Armstrong, Harvey, MD. 1990. "Cross Cultural Proposal to the Long Term Planning Committee." Sioux Lookout Zone Hospital Archives.

Bennett, Cliff. 1966. "Ojibway Consciousness." *Journal of Ontario Association of Children's Aid Societies* 9, no. 10 (December): 1–6

Bombay, Amy, Kimberly Matheson, and Hymie Anisman. 2014. "Appraisals of Discriminatory Events among Adult Offspring of Indian Residential School Survivors: The Influences of Identity Centrality and Past Perceptions of Discrimination." *Cultural Diversity and Ethnic Minority Psychology* 20, no. 1: 75–86

Castillo, Richard J. 1997. *Culture & Mental Illness: A Client-Centered Approach*. Toronto ON: Brooks/Cole Publishing Company.

Hallowell, A. I. 2010. *Contributions to Ojibwe Studies: Essays, 1934–1972*. Edited by Jennifer S. H. Brown and Susan E. Gray. Lincoln: University of Nebraska Press.

Eriksen, Thomas Hylland and Finn Sivert Nielsen. 2013. *A History of Anthropology*. 2nd ed. New York: Pluto Books.

Illich, Ivan. 1976. *Limits to Medicine: Medical Nemesis: The Expropriation of Health*. Markham ON: Penguin Books Ltd.

Lux, Maureen. 2016. *Separate Beds: A History of Indian Hospitals in Canada, 1920s–1980s*. Toronto ON: University of Toronto Press.

Pinkoski, Mark. 2008. "Julian Steward, American Anthropology, and Colonialism." *Histories of Anthropology Annual* 4: 172–204.

Tanner, Adrian. 1971. *Sickness and Ideology among the Ojibway: Summer 1971*. Unpublished manuscript. Sioux Lookout Zone Hospital Archives.

Williams, R. 1977. *Marxism & Literature*. Oxford: Oxford University Press.

5

Sickness and Ideology among the Ojibway (Summer 1971)

The following is a report delivered to the Sioux Lookout Zone Hospital administration by Adrian Tanner, a senior Canadian anthropologist of considerable standing, regarding his short time spent in the Oji-Cree community of New Osnaburg-Mishkeegogamang First Nation in northern Ontario, Canada. The Sioux Lookout Zone Hospital was operated by the medical school at the University of Toronto in conjunction with the Hospital for Sick Children from 1949 until becoming incorporated into the Sioux Lookout First Nations Health Authority in 1996. In the summer of 1971 Tanner was sent to the community to help conduct research on the barriers that impeded uptake of governmentally distributed and administered health care services in isolated reserve communities of Indigenous peoples, specifically Crees, Ojibwas, and Oji-Crees.

Tanner explored the perceptions of community members towards different and sometimes competing medical systems and health care approaches, highlighting Oji-Cree notions of illness and disease that complicate the biomedical models employed by the representatives of the Zone Hospital. Written in a direct and uncomplicated style, Tanner's report contains no academic references and was intended for the medical community engaged in delivering health care in Indigenous communities in the Canadian north. It was not directed at an anthropological or theoretically inclined international audience. It is a report intended to be practical. As such, Tanner's language belies the attempt to synthesize Marxist and psychological concerns with theories of culture while eliding the specific influences of various authors on his research. Accordingly, his work intentionally simplifies some of the concepts presented, but in so doing offers a reduced and over-generalized picture of Indigenous people's perceptions, mentalities, ideologies, and beliefs. Further, the use of a single community as representative of an entire ethnic group is questionable, though he remained cautious throughout the paper to frame his understandings in provisional and contingent ways. This Marxist framework unintentionally minimizes the centrality and importance of relationality, and relationships, for these communities and obscures attendant cosmological and ontological considerations and apprehensions in an effort to produce something useful to medical professionals.

For a more detailed discussion of the report and its significance in the genealogy of medical anthropology and the history of Canadian anthropology, see chapter 4 in this volume.

Indian Medicine. When discussing sickness all informants sooner or later made the distinction between Indian sickness and ordinary sickness. Indian sickness can be referred to by the term Inisna-beh Wa:biney. This term refers to a number of sicknesses which have as their special feature that only Indians have the knowledge to cure them. It is also thought that only Indians, by and large, suffer from these sicknesses, but this is related to the causes involved which concern the environment in which Indians tend to live, so that white people are very seldom exposed to them.

One such sickness is called Pa:hta:hsis, which was explained to me as a sickness caused by breaking some spiritual law. Apparently this sickness can be any kind of a persistent pain that does not respond to normal curing techniques. One man told me of a sore that his wife had on her leg. He told me that he tried both medicines obtained from the nurse and medicines made from plants obtained from the bush. His wife also received treatment for the sore in a hospital. Finally, after several years, he had a dream in which he was told that his wife knew about this incident and she admitted that it had indeed happened. After this, I was told of other forms of Indian sickness, one caused by witchcraft practiced by men with magical power and called u:ncineh. Finally, insanity (Ki:wu:skweh) is always considered an Indian sickness, caused by spiritual factors, as is sickness in men caused by pollution from menstruating women.

The other category of sickness, those sicknesses suffered by both whites and Indians, is more difficult to define. According to some informants it only includes accidents (pi:htaha:wtisu:—he hurts himself). Other informants spoke of sickness caused by improper diet, due to the change from bush food to store-bought food. They said that nowadays Indians eat in amounts governed according to taste, and that they do not know the rules for a healthy diet as they did in the past. Some people were of the opinion that diseases like tuberculosis and influenza were unknown to Indians in the past and for this reason Indians did not know how to cure them. However, I was also told that influenza was a disease released by the Europeans in North America specifically to kill off the Indians. When about half of the Indians in North America had died, a powerful shaman discovered the cause in a dream. He also dreamed of the cure, which involved placing certain ingredients in the fire. Another informant who has spent several years in a sanatorium told me that his cure did not come from the white doctors. In the sanatorium he met an Indian medicine man who cured him through the use of dreams, magic, and tobacco.

Apart from accidents, it appears that almost any sickness is potentially "Indian sickness" in the sense that it is believed to have a spiritual cause, and is only amenable to treatment by Indian medical techniques. However, this usually takes a very long time, and when the individual returns from hospital to the community it is thought that the sickness is still inside him, since the real cause has not been dealt with. For this reason, it is felt that such people are liable to become sick again. Heart attacks and other heart troubles are another category of the diseases thought of by the people of the community as having been introduced through contact with white people. In practice, however, it is not always clear at first which sicknesses have a spiritual cause, and which have a material one.

For this reason the nurses are usually the first medical specialists consulted when a person decides he is ill. Whatever the cause of the problem, the treatment given by the nurse or the hospital cannot do any harm. It may relieve the pain even of a sickness which has a spiritual cause. For example, during my visit I interviewed a woman labeled as schizophrenic by the nurses. She was given medication every two weeks, but complained of restlessness, insomnia, and anxiety which built up during the two weeks until she was unable to control herself. She would walk up and down the highway, sometimes eluding her husband, and occasionally getting lost in the bush, or being picked up by passing cars. She had spent a total of five years in Thunder Bay Psychiatric Hospital in three visits. Both she and her husband felt the nurses and the hospital were not doing enough for her, but that they had nowhere else to turn for help. As far as I could discover from interviews they did not believe there was a spiritual cause. However, several others in the community were convinced not only that her sickness was caused by her breaking some religious law, but that she would never become well until she admitted this fact and consulted an appropriate Indian specialist. I was told that drugs merely give this woman temporary relief, and that her hospital visits will become of longer and longer duration.

The element of confession necessary from the start in the Indian curing of sickness is a second reason why patients avoid such cures until some other treatment has been tried. A third reason is that Indian specialists are not as available as government medical services; the community has one each of three kinds of Indian medical specialist, not counting midwives (of which there are several), but these men follow the same working pattern as most of the rest of the community, characterized by frequent changes of residence, and several periods of isolation. Patients may also contact powerful specialists from distant places such as Lansdowne House, Lac Seul, and Long Lac, but this may involve a year or more of waiting. When enough people in the community need such a distant specialist the money is collected for his journey. In addition, payments are made for each cure by the individuals involved.

The question of cost is the final reason nurses are most often the first to be consulted in the event of sickness. Payment for an Indian cure is made up of two parts: a gift for the curer himself, usually consisting of clothes, other store items, or food, and a gift of tobacco for the spirits—those spirits who give to the curer the plant material for his medicines. The patient himself must decide what are appropriate gifts, and place these in front of the curer as an opening gesture of a diagnosis or cure. It is said that the curer needs no other information than these to begin his work. The effectiveness of the cure depends on sufficient gifts having been offered. For instance, to offer the spirits only half the amount of an appropriate gift of tobacco means the resulting cure is only half as effective as a full one. A person consulting a curer for the first time will know in detail what others have paid in the past. I was told by a third person that ethnographic work with a curer would require several pounds of tobacco merely to pay the spirits in charge of the plants.

We have seen how the people of the community attribute spiritual causes to a whole range, in fact the majority, of diseases. While it is true that only Indian medicine is competent to diagnose and cure such disease, other sicknesses can also be cured by non-European techniques. These are the cases of accidents, indigestion, constipation, diarrhea, and many other ailments. The cures for these ailments are known by almost everyone. Today, these cures are mostly used when people are away in the bush, for instance while trapping in winter, or at a fishing camp. In many cases the herbal remedy is seen as the equivalent of some common European medicine, such as aspirin or iodine. Although knowledge of these medicines is not exclusively in the hands of specialists, older people are concerned that the young people who go away to school never get a chance to learn them.

While informants tend to emphasize the two major classes of sickness as being associated with Indians in the case of those involving spiritual causes, and whites in the case of the others, in fact this is not the real distinguishing feature that separates them. For Indians suffer from both kinds of sickness, and there are cases given of whites who have interfered with Indian spiritual matters and have become sick. Both Indians and whites have cures which are effective with non-spiritual sickness. In the case of spiritual sickness European medicine is thought to be out of its depth. However, some Christian missionaries are credited with healing power in these cases. On this point there seems to be a difference of opinion. Some people hold the "Indian sickness" is caused by the devil. I was given the example of biblical Samson's loss of strength; he broke a taboo and therefore became sick. The ultimate cause of this was Satan. Most of my informants held that no amount of prayer to Jesus or God could cure such a sick person. The spirits involved were agents of Satan; it is therefore necessary to deal with these agents by means of activities like dreaming, drumming, dancing, and the shaking tent. This view is in agreement with one commonly expressed by the missionaries, whose purpose was and is to discourage these practices. This did not happen because of a continuing need for cures of this kind. Only recently, with the advent in the region of Protestant sects with spiritual techniques for healing sickness, have some people accepted the view that traditional Indian curing techniques are "wrong." I spoke to only one man about this point of view, although I was told of another who had recently converted and now refused all medical treatment, white and Indian, except for Christian faith healing. In any case, it is accepted that whites are not categorically excluded either from contracting or curing spiritual sickness. Yet, with both whites and Indians, this kind of sickness can be cured only by religious specialists.

To summarize the foregoing and other case material, it appears that several binary contrasts are drawn when speaking of sickness. At the level of ideology—that is, those points which the informants stress in order to indicate why some action was or should be taken—there are two classes of sickness. One is dominated by whites who are responsible for it; the other is similarly the domain of Indians. Upon further examination one learns that the racial contrast is not really crucial, but the real distinction is between accidental damage to the body versus what we would call infections. An examination of actual cases where Indian medicine was used indicates a contrast between sickness that gets better quickly and sickness that lingers. From the point of view of Western medicine, almost every disease can potentially be of the latter category, given unfavorable circumstances. It may, in such a case, be classed as Indian sickness, but is usually diagnosed as such after white medicine is considered to have failed.

Some conflicts do occur between the medical ideas of the nurse and those of the local people. The most common kind of case that I came across concerned the medical treatment of children. I learned of two cases of deformed infants, and one small child with influenza, all of which were not brought to the nurse. One deformed child was hidden from the nurse and other authorities for ten years. In each case this was apparently on the advice of an older person, not the parent. Another case involved an old man who refused to come to the nursing station for any sickness. A son informed the nurse when the old man was sick, without the old man's knowledge. Although circumstances prevented me from doing extensive interviewing in any of these cases, it is probably significant to recall the crucial spiritual role played in the culture by children and old people.

When a child enters the world he is thought to be close to the spirits for two reasons: First, he is all spirit simply due to the absence of other social characteristics which he will later acquire. Secondly, he is unpolluted, particularly from members of the opposite sex; in the case of boys, specifically from menstrual fluid. This state of affairs lasts until puberty. Menstrual fluid is particularly distasteful to the spirits, and in addition it causes sickness in any male who comes near. Children, it is felt, are in communication with the spirits, a process which culminates for boys in the vision quest, held shortly before puberty. This is the last time direct communication with the spirits is possible, except for men who obtain gifts of extraordinary power. For the rest, there are a whole range of techniques by which temporary communication with the spirits may by reestablished. By the time a person is very old he or she has often accumulated expertise in such techniques, and thereby a great deal of spiritual power.

This may in some cases complicate the diagnosis of "Indian sickness" since this sickness is caused by the spirits. Also, parents and others are very reluctant to have such small children away from them in hospital for lengthy periods. In such cases spiritual causes may be immediately diagnosed and for this reason the nurse is not consulted.

White Medicine. The nurse is an established role in the Ojibway social universe in the community. As with most northern trading post settlements, medicine as a specialized white institution has been relatively late in arriving. The job was at first handled by the trading store and the church, and sometimes also the police. Apparently for most of the people, or their ancestors, the first contact with white doctors was at early treaty gatherings to the south. The Albany River, on which the community was then located, was the northern limit of Treaty Number Nine (1905–1906). After the Canadian National Railway was built, communications with the government were oriented in this direction to where the Albany waterway crossed the line. Later mines were opened north of the community. Those Indians who worked in the mine saw company nurses, and a nurse nearby treated other emergencies among the Indian population. In 1958 a road was built from the Canadian North line north to the mines, and the settlement was moved to a site ten miles north, on a small, shallow lake, and just off the new road. Health care continued to be given from the mining community. Apparently at the initial settlement there had been a first aid nurse, at least for one year, but initially there was no white health specialist after the move. From the Indian point of view, this arrangement was bad; patients in most cases had to be taken there from the area and the quality of treatment was not high.

On the other hand, nurses of the time complained of continual battles with the people. When the nurse got a vehicle, a former mining staff nurse told me, the Indians used it as a free taxi, under the pretext of some sickness. One male nurse was taken off into the bush and attacked by several men. There were also several reports of Indians requiring treatment for the aftereffects of home brew and aftershave lotion. Visits were made to the community, particularly after the school was enlarged to about grade seven, and nurses began to regularly treat the children and to give elementary public health education. In 1969 the mines closed and the nursing station was moved to a trailer at the new settlement with a staff of two nurses. Since then relations, it would appear, have improved.

Most interaction between the nurses and adult Indians takes place at the clinic. Former nurses complain that many people used to be very reluctant to come to the clinic, unless they were dangerously ill, when friends would bring them. Today, women are more reluctant than men to come forward for treatment. With children and even babies, it is often a man who accompanies them to the clinic. Comparatively little information seems to be elicited from the patient during examination. This may be partially due to the unfamiliarity of the nurses with the Ojibway introspective description of pain. These descriptions are often highly specific as to the location of internal pain; two common sources given are the heart and the liver. Due to the familiarity with animal butchering, the culture has an elaborate terminology for body parts and organs, which often applies to both animals and humans. In the setting of the clinic the patient is not questioned the way an Indian medical specialist would, nor is the diagnosis or treatment discussed with him.

The nurses also visit people in their homes, particularly in the settlement and particularly for pre- and post-natal examinations. However for much of the year a majority of families lives away from the village, and access to such people depends mainly on proximity to a road. In other cases it is necessary to send somebody in to the community, and a nurse must then decide if the patient is to be treated in the nursing station or at home, or to be sent to the Sioux Lookout hospital.

Views of patients and nurses revolve around (1) the social and cultural significance of health including religious ideas developed recently on the significance of several historically recent epidemics; (2) the social relations between the nurses and the Indian patients, encapsulating as it does the channels of administrator, patron, savior; and (3) following from this the ideologies used by both sides to characterize the total relationships.

First, there is a system of concepts and rules by which significance is attached to sickness. This system is itself timeless but includes a number of historically recent and severe sicknesses. Alongside this system is placed another set of concepts and rules, obtained from the observation of white doctors and nurses. The social relation between the white medical people and the Indian patients fits the familiar social form in which the Indian is socially inferior, and receives small gifts from whites and a dependent status. While this deprived state may seem to place the Indian at the bottom of the heap, socially and medically, Indian thinkers deny this state of affairs by suggesting an alternate model. This model subsumes the two sickness systems, accepting the validity of both. However the relationship made between them is the inverse of the actual power relationship. This overall system of medical ideas places the Indian system of cures in the superior position, but in so doing it emphasizes distinctive features, certain peculiar attributes of the system of causes and cures.

This ideology of sickness particularly emphasizes the importance of religion and spirituality, so that it can be said that the result of contact with whites has been to increase the role of these factors in the curing process. Following from this, it is difficult to see how this medical opposition ideology can be made use of by the hospital and the nurses. For not only do relations between the white medical people and the Indians presume that the patient and his society are dependent, it is also the case that these relations typify the overall pattern of race relations. Medical opposition is political opposition: the evaluation and planning of the community health worker program ought then, it would seem, to be part of a more general community development program.

Medical Opposition. The material obtained on local ideas about health and sickness, incomplete as it is, does raise a number of interesting questions for medical service people. First, why is a distinction drawn between white and Indian sickness? Secondly, do Indian ideas interfere with the work of nurses and doctors, both in treatment and in public health education? Thirdly, are Indian medical ideas becoming acculturated to those of the non-Indian society? And finally, can Indian medical ideas have a role compatible with improved medical services?

As I have indicated earlier, the opposition expressed between white and Indian sickness and medicine is more apparent than real, but informants chose to lay heavy emphasis on it. However, when this information is put alongside other material on Indian worldview a pattern begins to emerge. For instance, in the community, I was constantly having what is assumed to be the white view of the world challenged by informants. That is, not only would people express a viewpoint but they were careful to point out how this differed from that held by white people. For instance, I was told that it was Indians, not Europeans, who invented wheeled vehicles and aircraft. An Indian out in the bush solved the mechanical problems involved by building models using wood and other local materials. One day he showed these to a white man whom he met in the forest. This man copied the ideas and told other white men, and cars, trucks and aircraft were produced in metal. How are such claims to be interpreted?

The obvious message in much of the material gathered takes the form of a challenge to the assumptions with which the white people in the area operate. By and large these assumptions add up to a view that the

Indian culture is powerless and incompetent. It was this point of view which my informants challenged at every opportunity.

Looking back on the material on "Indian sickness" we find that it is constantly being used to challenge white medical views. In reality, they say, it is the Indian who understands the basic causes of most lingering illnesses, and only he has the techniques to deal with the causes, which are spiritual in nature. One old man told me that when he was young, a white doctor told him to wash all over every day in order to be healthy. He told me he did not follow this advice, but has been healthy all the same. Therefore, he concluded, the whites do not really understand sickness. Another man, as I have mentioned earlier, was cured of TB by a medicine man, who told him to continue to use tobacco for the rest of his life. He explained that tobacco was not necessarily "the" cure for TB, but in his case the medicine man obtained special knowledge of the spiritual cause by means of a dream. Tobacco was his medicine, although it could have been another substance in another case of TB. Thus, when he was advised recently to stop smoking by a doctor he was amazed at the fact that the doctor was unaware that tobacco could, in some cases, be beneficial. For the Indians, white medicine emphasizes the importance of cleanliness, and of other material causes, in ascertaining the cause of sickness. It also emphasizes the material aspect of the cure. Informants prepared a model of health in which these factors are inverted. Visible cleanliness is unimportant; invisible pollution is the real danger. In most sickness the cause is spiritual, not material, and cures should also be directed at the spiritual symptoms.

To assess realistically the possibilities of utilizing Indian knowledge of sickness to improve the health of the communities (as was suggested to me by several medicine men) it will be useful to examine the nature of this knowledge. First of all, it is clear that we are not dealing with an aboriginal system of ideas. No doubt most of the current beliefs are part of the established Ojibway cultural repertoire. But in the face of threatening circumstances certain themes have been emphasized and expanded. This was not only as a reaction to the introduction of outside medical services. These ideas serve to reject the whole range of relationships between whites and Indians, of which the nurse-patient relation is merely typical. The emphasis put on "traditional" Indian medicine is typical of a whole range of "revitalization movements" which deny in a symbolic fashion a political reality which is imposed from and controlled by outside forces of another culture.

This phenomenon of the use of "traditional" ideas in the formation of an opposition ideology has relevance to the question of acculturation. Some anthropologists have assumed, because certain ideas make claims of validity based on their intellectual lineage from the precontact past, and because these ideas are expressed only by older people, that they will be replaced by newer ideas picked up by young community members through contacts with the dominant culture. However, here we have the case of a community with recent intensive contacts, such as a mine and a highway. The mine was in operation for over thirty years. The older people are quick to point out that "everything is all mixed up these days—girls are not shy with boys the way they ought to be, children are continually insulting animals because their parents have not taught them properly, nobody seems to care about totem groups when selecting a marriage partner"; however, several middle-aged and younger people gave some of the same information on Indian medicine as the older people. These younger people recognize that their experience is more limited, and that it is not correct for them to make ideological statements at their age.

If I am correct in my assertion that the ideas expressed under the heading of "Indian sickness" are an ideology which opposes itself to another set of ideas, it follows that this second set of ideas is also articulated within the culture. It is clear that the Indians of this community have already learned a great deal about white medical ideas. These new ideas are not always contrasted with Indian ideas in such a way that the white ideas are rejected. Outside the context of political ideology it is possible to compare procedures as they are used in actual cases. However, the cultural meaning and significance of any case of sickness cannot avoid taking account of the political factors, since no matter what treatment is given and what are the results, the case has the potential of a statement about the general situation people find themselves in.

It is important at the present time to view Indian sickness, in the sense of a system of ideas, as having significance at two levels. Examination of cases would reveal the organization of symptoms in a pattern related to a second pattern of spiritual causes, which itself is organized according to the cultural pattern of animal species. This homologous relationship between two sets of ideas is in many cases repeated in the cure, in which the system of floral species is used. It is unclear after a very preliminary research of this question whether it is the case of all sicknesses with animal causes to avoid cures using floral material, or if these two types cover the whole range of Indian sickness. However, as is emphasized elsewhere in this report, the same set of sickness cases are today also fitted into another cognitive structure, one that is part of a very modern political ideology.

6

We Hope That You Will Continue to Teach Us How Best to Learn

Assembling the Pascua Yaqui Tribe at the 89th Wenner-Gren International Symposium

In late November of 1981 an assortment of academics gathered for the 89th Wenner-Gren International Symposium. The majority of previous symposia had been held at the iconic Burg Wartenstein castle nestled high in the Austrian Alps, but the 89th gathering was to be held in arid southern Arizona, split between Pascua Pueblo Yaqui Reservation (also known as New Pascua) and a conference center constructed out of the remnants of an old mining town north of Tucson. Organized around the theme of "Yaqui Ritual and Performance," the event promised a public reenactment and interdisciplinary examination of the Deer Dance, a key component of the Yaqui ceremonial system. An almost forgotten event in a seemingly out-of-the-way place, the Yaqui Conference (as I will refer to it from here on) became an installment in the mutually constructive history of Indigenous recognition and anthropology in Southern Arizona.[1]

My objective in this essay is to show how anthropologists and their institutions became influential participants in the re-articulation of a collective Yaqui identity.[2] I am also concerned with illustrating the subtle ways in which the actions of Yaqui intellectuals left a lasting impression on one of the discipline's most powerful institutions.[3] That is to say, I am concerned with the coproduction of social science and Indigenous politics.

To be sure, numerous principled studies have explored the ways in which anthropology is embedded in systems of recognition and subsequent articulations of Indigenous identity (e.g., Barker 2011; Clifford 1988; Field 2003; McMillen 2007; Simpson 2014). But there have been few event-oriented, interactional accounts of the relationship between anthropology and recognition that are not confined to the courts or official mechanisms of governmental acknowledgment (e.g., the Federal Acknowledgment Process in the United States). By examining a case outside of the legal arena, this essay seeks to cultivate a historically grounded, reflexive, presentist understanding of the less overt and highly contingent ways in which anthropology is implicated in the politics of recognition. Moreover, with attention paid to the margins of both disciplinary and Indigenous histories, this analysis offers insight into the subtle but consequential ways in which Native actors have shaped—not rejected—anthropology on the institutional level.

INDIGENOUS RECOGNITION IN THE MAKING

Studies of recognition typically fall into one of two general camps. In this essay, I pursue an alternative, event-based analysis, which will address what the dominant trends in the literature typically overlook—collective identities in the making. Scholars from across the humanities and social sciences have documented the ways in which collective identity rights have become the dominant means of political mobilization for Indigenous peoples living under liberal institutions (Coulthard 2014; Merlan 1998; 2019; Povinelli 2002; Turner 2006; see also Appiah 1994; Fraser 2000; and Taylor 1994 for broader discussions of recognition and liberalism). However, this literature is by no means uniform. On one end of the continuum, scholars advocate for the wholesale recognition of cultural and linguistic differences with respect to Indigenous communities. While these studies are often critical of the power structures in which groups reside, they focus their attention on the unique and autonomous nature of Indigenous cultures and languages as well as ecological and political traditions (Hinton 2010; Menzies 2006; Powell 2007). More radical, advocacy-oriented versions of this literature deploy biological and ecological metaphors to portray the struggles of Native communities, which are believed to be ever slipping toward the precipice of cultural or linguistic doom (Nettle and Romain 2002; Maffi 2001). Other scholars who are equally committed to the social, economic, and political dilemmas facing Native communities take a more grounded approach. They use the historical and oral historical record to trace the roots of modern Indigenous groups and their associated cultural practices so as to underwrite their historical continuity (Asch 1982; Campisi 1991; McMillen 2007; Ray 2016; Ridington 2014; Shorter 2009). These researchers often emphasize relatively unbroken symbolic articulations of identity over the intricacies of ethnogenesis.

On the other end of the continuum we find critical examinations of the inequitable roots of recognition procedures. This body of literature is primarily and justifiably concerned with rendering recognition a cunning colonialist charade that reproduces longstanding power asymmetries (Barker 2011; Clifford 1988; Coulthard 2014; Povinelli 2002; Simpson 2014). In this mode of analysis, events and individuals are deemphasized as the focus shifts to institutional mechanisms of control, their associated rules of formation, and the ontologies that they produce.

Despite their apparent differences of political commitments (one is supportive of recognition while the other calls for its unmasking), these two orientations share common ground. In particular, both ends of the continuum fail to address recognition through the concrete instances in which "official formulations of Indian identity [emerge] from complex, cross-cultural and intracultural dialogues" (Harmon 1998, 144). To borrow Alexandra Harmon's (1998) terminology, lost are the micro-scale moments of communities "in the making" that enable us to see collective identities as dialogical processes as opposed to primordial essences (Fisher 2010, 9). It then goes without saying that these approaches also prevent us from understanding anthropology's role in practices of acknowledgment. While there have been numerous efforts to critically document anthropology's position in official and unofficial recognition processes (Barker 2011; Clifford 1988; Field 2003; Ray 2016; Simpson 2014), these studies rarely offer an examination of the reversal of roles and the rearticulation of groupness in real-time encounters.[4]

Following recent attempts to view recognition processes and subsequent articulations of Indigenous identity through an explicitly constructionist (Ens and Sawchuk 2016) and event-based prism (Dinwoodie 1998, 2007, 2018), I approach an otherwise marginal occurrence—the

Yaqui Conference—as a nexus wherein anthropology and Yaqui politics met and shaped one another. In doing so, I provide one avenue for unpacking Indigenous engagements with broader political systems and the ways in which anthropology has been caught up in the creative rearticulation of Indigenous subjectivity.

THE TROUBLE WITH RECOGNITION

At the time of the Yaqui Conference, the Yaqui Indians of southern Arizona were in a state of significant political flux, having just achieved federal recognition as an "American Indian Tribe" in 1978. Yaqui recognition was a hard-won and complex campaign, consistent with the rise of Indigenous identity movements and recognition-based politics within and beyond the United States.[5] That being said, recognition of the Yaquis came with its own unique set of complications.

The modern-day Pascua Yaqui Tribe of Arizona is composed of the descendants of individuals who came to the American Southwest in the late nineteenth and early twentieth centuries by way of the push of (Mexican) state violence as well as the pull of railroad and agricultural work. Those who braved the new landscape arrived in multiple waves and never lived in a single area. Migration along agricultural and railroad lines scattered Yaqui individuals and families into ethnically mixed neighborhoods from northern Arizona to Southern California. Arriving from numerous villages in Sonora, a contingent of the displaced and heterogeneous Yaqui steadily aggregated into a small neighborhood in the northwest corner of the developing city of Tucson. In honor of their elaborate Easter ceremonial system, the community was given the name Pascua (Spanish for Easter) by a local U.S. attorney and chair of the Chamber of Commerce who actively supported the cultivation of the Pascua Yaquis as an ethno-tourist attraction (Spicer 1988, x). Despite finding a home in urban Tucson, the community long occupied an uncertain position. Sometimes classified as Mexican refugees, American Indians, and (on at least one occasion) "colonists" (*Tucson Citizen* 1923), Pascua Yaqui identity was surprisingly porous and, at least in the eyes of others, murky and suspect.[6]

In the 1970s Congress became a site for the reimagining of a new American Indian identity for the Pascua Yaquis. While these efforts slightly predate the institutionalization of a U.S. recognition process (Barker 2011; Cramer 2005), Yaquis still found it necessary to perform an essentialized and primordialized version of American Indianness (Miller 2004). Shortly after the bid for recognition, Pascua Yaqui elites suggested they were descendants of the Toltec, the ancient predecessors to the Mexica empire, and that much of what is now the United States (including Arizona) can be considered Toltec and, by association, Yaqui homeland (Castile 2002, 406–7; Pascua Yaqui Tribe 1982). One cannot understate the significance of this narrative shift. Yaquis of Arizona had long understood their position in the region as a product of recent migration (Spicer 1988). Their origin stories marked eight Jesuit towns in Sonora and the incorporation of Christianity as the roots of Yaqui identity (Folsom 2014, 71). Until the 1970s, no part of the present-day American Southwest was included in these narratives. By incorporating Toltec heritage and U.S. territory into their identity, Pascua Yaqui leaders staked their claim to a distinctly American Indian tribal identity. That is to say, they moved along a continuum of imperial incorporation and differentiation, transforming themselves from diasporic Mexican Indians to landed American Indians.

Highlighting the Deer Dance was part of this larger attempt to represent the Pascua Yaquis as an "American Indian Tribe." In September of 1977, Anselmo Valencia, a noted spiritual leader and architect of the Yaqui recognition campaign, went before the Senate Subcommittee on Indian Affairs with this very strategy in mind. Valencia characterized the dance as one of the most significant markers of the Yaquis' "Indianness":

> The Yaquis are Indians in every sense of the word. We have our own language, our own culture, such as the Pascola Dancing, *the deer dancing* and the coyote dancing. These dances are Indian in origin. In the deer dance, we sing to honor the great mountains, the springs, the lakes. We sing of our father the Sun, and of creatures living and dead. We sing of trees and leaves and twigs.... All of the songs sung and played are to the olden times—ancient Yaqui Indian stories. The Catholic faith and the various governments under which the Yaquis have had to suffer have tried for centuries to undermine *our*

'*Yaquiness,*' but after 400 years they have not succeeded. We have retained our language, our culture, and *our Indianness.* (U.S. Congress 1977, 6, emphasis added)

Valencia's conception of "Indianness" displays rhetoric that is typical of recognition proceedings. According to this logic, Yaqui identity can be reduced to select traits (e.g., the Deer Dance, a distinct language, songs, and stories), and these traits are imagined to have emerged in a distant past (i.e., prior to the arrival of "the Catholic faith"). Historians and sociologists of nationalism have argued that the cultivation of essentialized and primordialized symbols such as these are more than mere representations of ethnic communities; they are constitutive elements in the formation of ethnonations (Hobsbawm 1987; Hobsbawm and Ranger 1983; Smith 1999). As described by Anthony D. Smith, the process of "symbolic cultivation" refers to "a wide range of ethnic memories, symbols, values, myths and traditions. Many of these are local in origin, but some of them may be taken up, and adapted, by specialist elites who then communicate these ideas to the world" (2009, 38). Smith goes on to suggest that by operationalizing history and the social sciences, these elites have worked to "place their political projects on firm historical foundations and convince their kinsmen, as well as a hostile world, of the truth of their claims" (2009, 71). In the case of the Yaqui Conference, Valencia followed a similar pattern as he enrolled an anthropological foundation and its cornerstone conference series into his ongoing attempts to frame the Deer Dance as a symbol of the Yaquis' essential and primordial "Indianness."

But the Deer Dance posed a problem for symbolic cultivation under the solidifying essentialized and primordialized logics of recognition. Contrary to Valencia's testimony, the oral historical literature does not paint the dance as an unqualified ancient practice inherently separate from Catholicism and colonial transformations. To see this one must first understand the dance in the context of Yaqui origin narratives. The Yaqui people are believed to be the result of a revelation. In a time before the arrival of Europeans, Yaqui lands were the home of the Surem, an ancient people. One day a tree began to sing to the Surem, foretelling a future of great change that would include the arrival of Europeans and the introduction of Christianity. With the prospect of change on the horizon, many Surem chose to leave and enter the enchanted worlds. Those who remained became the Yaquis. The Surem and Yaquis went on to occupy different realms, but the boundaries between them could be porous. This was especially true of the flower world (*sea ania*), which includes the animals that populate the Sonoran desert. Invoking the figure of the deer, one such animal that exists in both worlds, the deer dancer (*saila maaso*) and its associated singer facilitates a certain degree of communication between the worlds. Thus the Deer Dance occupies an important cosmological position, as it connects Yaquis with their past.[7]

In their influential text *Yaqui Deer Songs, Maso Bwikam: A Native American Poetry* (1987), Larry Evers and Felipe Molina explore numerous oral accounts of the Deer Dance. Rather than reducing the plethora of interpretations to a single perspective, Evers and Molina present a variety of opinions on the origins of the dance. Some elders argue unequivocally that the dance existed before the talking tree's prediction, the birth of the Yaquis, and the coming of Europeans. Some offer a more hybridized narrative that has the ritual developing at the time of Christ's crucifixion, which is said to have occurred in Yaqui lands. Still others are more agnostic on the topic of precolonial ceremonial life. As Molina, a Yoeme educator and cultural practitioner in his own right, notes, "My grandfather and many other Yaqui elders did not really know what kind of dance our ancestors danced during the time just before the arrival of the Spaniards, before the people separated into two groups" (1987, 41).[8]

Although the chronological origins of the Deer Dance may be somewhat unclear, it is apparent that the dance has long been entangled with settler society and Christian practices. In the 1620s, following the aggregation of Yaquis in Jesuit-managed towns in what would become the Mexican state of Sonora, the Deer Dance formed in conjunction with Indigenous interpretations of the Catholic passion play, a dramatization of Christ's crucifixion (Spicer 1980, 70). The introduction of the passion play was a common Spanish colonial practice that symbolically placed newly conquered peoples into an imperial imaginary as subjects of a Catholic crown (Brooks 2002; for a New Mexican case see Rodríguez 2009; for a Nicaraguan case see Field 1999a). Therefore, consistent with Yaqui culture more broadly, the Deer Dance formed as a fusion of Christian and Indigenous practices and beliefs.

In the early twentieth century, the rate at which the dance became increasingly removed from everyday Yaqui life was equal to that of its immersion in local political economies. As Edward Spicer noted at the time of the conference, "Many of the words [in the Deer songs] are not easily translatable into current Yaqui; some words remain wholly untranslatable" (1980, 104). However, the dance was not without a purpose. As Spicer also commented, the striking figure of the costumed dancer with his antlers and rattles became a recognizable symbol in the settler colonial society of twentieth-century Mexico. Northern Mexican states that had once been a locus for Yaqui extermination and exploitation (Folsom 2014; Hu-DeHart 1984) now enshrined the Deer Dancer in public statues and hotel advertisements (Spicer 1980, 274–76). One could say the same of Arizona, where the Deer Dancer became representative of the Pascua Yaquis of Tucson. In the 1920s it was common for Yaquis to perform the ritual out of season at the annual Tucson Rodeo, sometimes under pressure from the Chamber of Commerce to do so in exchange for the city's annual financial support for their Easter ceremonies (Spicer 1980, 275; 1988, 134). Today, it is not uncommon to see representations of the Deer Dancer in restaurants and bars in the Tucson area. While the dance may very well have continued to be significant in Yaqui society (Shorter 2009), it was always enmeshed in local political economies and broader "cycles of conquest" (as Spicer [1962] characterized them).

In distancing the dance from its Catholic and colonial roots, Valencia's congressional testimony attempted to map a layer of ancient Indianness on to the performance. In the end, Valencia successfully persuaded sympathetic politicians such as Arizona Senator Dennis DeConcini to see Yaquis not as "Mexican Indians" but as a "major and unique American Indian tribe" whose "ancestors . . . have lived in what we call the Southwest . . . from time immemorial" (U.S. Congress 1977, 2). In other words, operating under the strictures of partial incorporation and recognition, Valence effectively reassembled Yaquis as an entirely different kind of people.

Even after federal recognition was conferred, however, Yaqui identity remained an open question, especially at the local level, as real estate developers in Tucson began to turn their sights to the newly constructed reservation. When the tribe moved to expand their reservation boundaries in the early 1980s, Joseph Cesare of Broadway Realty and Trust Inc. wrote to Congressman and Pascua Yaqui supporter Morris K. Udall in protest: "There cannot be more than one hundred Yaquis living on that reservation (*who by the way came from Mexico*) and it would be better to integrate them into our society instead of enlarging their reservation" (Cesare to Udall, September 27, 1982, emphasis added).

Mexican refugees, American Indians, colonists, or descendants of the Toltec? As the conference began, the Yaquis of Tucson were a newly recognized tribe still struggling to figure out how best to represent themselves to a hostile world under these newly codified conditions of American Indianness. Echoing the philosopher Ian Hacking, we might say that there was a "two-way interaction" between an emerging category of people (the Pascua Yaquis as an American Indian Tribe) and the kinds of people, such as Valencia, who fit into this category (Hacking 2002, 48). Valencia's congressional testimony was not the end of these interactions, but the beginning. The Yaqui Conference and the continued reframing of the Deer Dance would prove to be another installment in the ongoing effort to re-present and reassemble the Pascua Yaquis under the conditions of recognition.

ASSEMBLING THE CONFERENCE

Far removed from southern Arizona and the political trials and tribulations of the Pascua Yaqui Tribe, the Wenner-Gren Foundation began formulating the Yaqui Conference amid a growing sense of disquiet in institutional anthropology, which caused one of the cornerstone funders of the discipline to open itself to the dynamics of Indigenous recognition. Wenner-Gren's state of uncertainty came at a particular juncture with respect to the foundation's rise to prominence in the field. In 1941 Axel Wenner-Gren established a foundation with the less than noble desire to shield his large financial holdings from a "vexing tax issue regarding the sale of a boat moored in the waters off Florida" (Lindee and Radin 2016, 225). An elite problem if ever there was one! At the suggestion of his lawyers, the Swedish industrialist created the Viking Fund (the name supposedly inspired by his Scandinavian heritage). While the organization asserted what now appear to be vague intellectual pretensions, initial projects in Latin America, such as developing a news clipping service, were motivated largely by Wenner-Gren's hope of extending his business interests into the global south (Lindee and Radin 2016, 225). It was only when Wenner-Gren brought Paul Fejos, a Hungarian aristocrat and avant-garde filmmaker turned nascent social scientist, into the organization as director of research that the foundation, eventually renamed in honor of its founder, took on an explicitly anthropological, not to mention less superficial, focus. Under Fejos's leadership, Wenner-Gren became a leading patron of anthropology in the United States.

In 1957 Fejos persuaded Axel to purchase the twelfth-century Austrian castle Burg Wartenstein, previously owned by the royal family of Liechtenstein, which then became the site of the recently established international symposium series. The palatial estate and the symposia constituted intertwined symbols of the foundation's regal prominence in the field of anthropology. This continued under the guidance of Fejos's widow, Lita (formerly Lita Binns, later Lita Osmundsen), who officially and unofficially led the foundation and the symposium series until the mid-1980s.

Under Osmundsen's stewardship, the already distinguished and exclusive international symposium series took on a highly regimented character. Participants were sequestered and their social and intellectual interactions carefully managed through scheduled discussions, meals, and cocktail hours (Osmundsen 1980).[9] Spouses and children were discouraged from accompanying invited participants. Local scholars who might take an interest in a given event's theme were also barred from sitting in. Such mechanisms of control worked to reconstitute the castle and the symposium series as an authoritative site for the construction of knowledge. By declaring which topics were worthy of discussion, providing the funds and space in which they could be examined, and controlling how conversations (both social and professional) occurred, the foundation was, to an extent, defining the parameters of acceptable anthropological inquiry and discourse. While not exactly constructing facts, Wenner-Gren was certainly (attempting) to frame and guide the future intellectual doings of the field. It appears to have done this with great success. As the foundation approached the bicentennial, Wenner-Gren was popularly understood among U.S. anthropologists to be a leading source of cultural anthropological funding and knowledge production.

In the late 1970s, the foundation's rise to prominence was interrupted. Inflation and a shrinking endowment produced a "crisis mentality" within the organization that compelled the board of directors to sell Burg Wartenstein (Osmundsen 1980; Lindee and Radin 2016, 280).[10] The divestiture of the castle left future conferences—and Wenner-Gren's institutional identity—in a state of "limbo" (Osmundsen 1980, 14). The Yaqui Conference, which was held in November 1981, the year following the sale of the castle, offered the foundation a chance to reconfigure the symposium series for the future. With its relatively novel emphasis on interdisciplinarity and the active pursuit of outside funding from a variety of sources, the Yaqui Conference would serve as a "'mini' symposium," a test case, for future gatherings (Wenner-Gren Foundation 1981).[11] In an attempt to save the series that had lent her great institutional clout, Osmundsen became quite willing to loosen the reins on the Burg Wartenstein model. Participants would no longer be required to pre-circulate papers or even to provide papers at all (Willa Appel to Edward Spicer, July 28, 1981). As planning progressed, the organizers also proved willing to allow participants to forego the requirement of attending all five days of the event. This mini symposium was to be a very different event indeed.

At this point in the planning process, the principal conference organizers had little understanding of Yaquis or contact with Yaqui communities.[12] The initial co-organizers were Victor Turner, the famed interpretative anthropologist of ritual, and Richard Schechner, a well-respected performance studies scholar. Neither man had much familiarity with Yaquis. Similarly, Willa Appel, the appointed project director for the conference, had expertise in other areas. At the time, she was best known as an anthropologist of cults, exploring cult ideologies and leadership practices (Appel 1983). For Turner, Schechner, and Appel,

Yaquis, despite being central to the proposed conference, were something of a mystery.

In September of 1981, a mere two months before the conference was to be held, Appel and Osmundsen attempted to remedy this problem by traveling to Tucson to meet with Edward and Rosamond Spicer, the Pascua Yaqui Tribal Council, and Anselmo Valencia. The Spicers, both of whom were anthropologists, had been fixtures in Pascua Yaqui affairs since the mid-1930s, when they arrived to pursue ethnographic research as graduate students from the University of Chicago. Edward, in particular, made the Pascua Yaquis a primary object of analysis until his death in 1983. Both Edward and Rosamond were also active participants in Yaqui cultural and political affairs throughout this period, starting with small attempts to secure financial support for the Deer Dance and other Yaqui ceremonies from city coffers (Spicer to Tucson Chamber of Commerce January 17, 1938). At the time of the conference, the Spicers had a forty-four-year-old relationship with the Yaquis of Tucson, made stronger by their long-term residence in the city and Edward's position in the Department of Anthropology at the University of Arizona. Oddly, it appears that Turner, Schechner, and Appel had not thought to include the Spicers in their event.

Once the Spicers had finally been suggested to the conference organizers by participant Fred Eggan, Osmundsen and company scrambled to digest Edward's work and the recent history of the Yaquis in Tucson.[13] The conference organizers' behavior suggests not only a lack of familiarity with Yaquis but a naive understanding of the complexities of recognition. Following their September meeting, Osmundsen asked Spicer for a copy of his 1977 testimony before Congress in support of Yaqui recognition. She planned to circulate the statement to the invited participants, the majority of whom had little to no experience with Yaqui issues.[14] Osmundsen stated that she heard that it was the "the most cogent information [they] could obtain as preparation for this conference" (Osmundsen to Spicer, September 28, 1981). What she did not realize was that Spicer's testimony was a carefully crafted and abbreviated attempt to represent the cultural distinctiveness and territorial attachment of the Yaquis to Arizona so as to underwrite their claim to an American Indian tribal identity. The claims made in his testimony were more conjectural and politically pragmatic than they were rooted in empirical research (Barron 2019a, 2019b; Castile 2002, 385). By embracing this testimony, the foundation betrayed a simplified conception of the complexities of recognition in the Yaqui case.

Spicer does not appear to have responded to this request to circulate his testimony.[15] Perhaps this was a subtle recognition of the statement's functional-political (as opposed to scholarly) purpose. However, the couple did agree to attend the conference and provide commentary on the preliminary program, which Osmundsen credited with "Yaqui-izing the issues" (Osmundsen to Spicer, September 28, 1981). Additionally, Edward agreed to be listed as a co-organizer, giving the gathering some semblance of local anthropological approval. Despite the Spicers' aid, the organizers recognized that "Yaqui-izing" the proceedings would, at some point, still require the involvement of actual Yaquis.

A World War II veteran, community organizer, and dynamic political advocate, Anselmo Valencia was far from the unassuming shamanic caricature of Don Juan popularly portrayed in Carlos Castaneda's writings on Yaqui spirituality (2016 [1968]). Valencia was also no stranger to anthropology. During the 1930s and 1940s Valencia's godfather, Lucas Chavez, served as Edward Spicer's primary informant. Chavez, a keen political mind in his own right, was one of the first to recognize how sympathetic anthropologists could be made to serve as advocates for the Yaquis in their dealings with local government (Barron 2019a). Beginning in the late 1940s, Valencia elaborated on this strategy in his own campaigns. The Spicers once again became nodes of advocacy as Valencia relied on Edward to secure support from congressional representatives and federal funding agencies such as the Office of Economic Opportunity (Barron 2019b; Castile 2002; Meeks 2007; Miller 2004). These efforts helped manifest Pascua Yaqui recognition and a tribal reservation, which in turn elevated Valencia's position in the community as a skilled political operator.

However, by the early 1980s, Valencia's positionality had changed. The recognition campaign had put him on confrontational terms with other Yaqui groups who opposed his decision to speak for them as if they were a single homogenous entity (Miller 2004, 110–11). The people of Pascua were but one of several Yaqui communities in the state.

Additionally, leading up to recognition, Valencia faced criticism from more powerful tribes of Arizona who viewed the Yaquis as "Mexican" (not "American") Indians who had made illegitimate claims to already limited federal resources (Miller 2004, 107–8, 112).[16] Faced with opposition on multiple fronts, Valencia entered the conference with a need to represent the Pascua Yaquis to the public as a legitimate and coherent Indigenous entity.

Unaware of this situation, Appel wrote to Valencia following their meeting in Tucson: "We depend upon you, to decide how to present the issues. . . . Our goal is to learn about the Deer Dance and its place in Yaqui culture. *We hope that you will continue to teach us how best to learn*" (Appel to Valencia, September 28, 1981, emphasis added). Fortunately for Valencia, teaching how best to learn would conform quite nicely with his own objectives. Thus organizers had little sense that they would become participants in Valencia's performance of a primordial Indigenous identity.

"WHAT IS THIS WORD SAVAGE?": REASSEMBLING THE DEER DANCE

On the morning of November 19th, 1981, the first official day of the conference, tribal representatives greeted participants at New Pascua and gave their visitors a tour of the facilities before a formal welcome led by Valencia began promptly at 11:30 a.m. The welcoming speech is recounted in participant Edith Turner's reflections:

> Valencia began by introducing the dancers. . . . Then he turned to his listeners and reminded them that they were Anglos, anthropologists, and that he had a lot of trouble from anthropologists. Their incessant questions made it very difficult for the Yaquis. . . . Valencia strode up and down a little, getting indignant. "What is this word, 'savage'?" he asked—a word that Anglos and Mexicans used about the Yaquis. He asked various people in his audience what the word meant. (Turner 1995, 82)

After some unsatisfying responses from Victor Turner and Edward Spicer, "[Valencia] went on to give the definition he had heard from Anglos, that savages were murderous before anything else" (Turner 1995, 82).

It was at this point that Valencia began to reframe his audience's perception of the Deer Dance. Valencia recounted the origins of the ceremonial objects on display before his audience. From flutes to drums, he claimed an Indigenous origin for most of them. Valencia even suggested that the Yaqui use of the cross had precolonial roots (Spicer and Spicer 1981).[17] Later, in his summary of Yaqui history, Valencia emphasized a cunning embrace of colonial society in which Yaquis selectively pruned and incorporated elements of Catholicism while retaining their distinct religion.[18] Echoing his performance before Congress, Valencia framed the Deer Dance as an untouched vestige of a precolonial past. This presentation departed significantly from the ethnographic and ethnohistorical literature, much of which had been produced by Spicer, who was present for this performance. In his notes from the conference, Spicer expressed discomfort regarding Valencia's "idiosyncratic understanding" of the dance, which he felt must have been "much influenced by [Valencia's] recent intensive association (for the purposes of getting federal recognition) with Plains and other American Indians in the National Congress of American Indians and various Pow-wow circuits" (Spicer to Osmundsen January 8, 1982).[19]

When a counter interpretation was offered, Valencia and his extended network of supporters worked to obfuscate such readings of the dance. For instance, at one point, Felipe Molina, Valencia's ceremonial godson and budding cultural representative, suggested that the drum signified the beat of the deer's heart (Turner 1995, 84). Heather Valencia, Anselmo's wife, openly rejected this interpretation. Mrs. Valencia's objection appears to have underwritten her husband's position as an authoritative voice of Yaqui culture.

While the organizers worked to transpose the Burg Wartenstein model to the Arizona location over the next few days, contingencies reigned supreme. The second day of the conference saw a return to the reservation with Valencia once again acting as the master of ceremonies while participants witnessed an abbreviated performance of the Deer Dance organized specifically for the conference.[20] The third day brought Valencia to a conference center located forty miles north of Tucson in the town of Oracle—a more traditional setting reminiscent of the Burg Wartenstein days. Four different sessions were scheduled between 9:30 a.m. and 5:30 p.m., with Valencia serving as the "primary discussant" for the opening session. This session was to be chaired by Keith Basso, an expert on the Western Apaches who reluctantly accepted the invitation admitting his lack of familiarity with the Yaqui case (Basso to Appel, June 2, 1981). But Basso missed the first two days of the conference, rendering him unable to speak specifically about the Deer Dance presentation or Valencia's commentary (Basso to Osmundsen January 9, 1981). The session was also intended to be based on a pre-circulated paper by Alfonso Ortiz, another anthropologist of the Southwest, but Ortiz canceled just prior to the start of the conference due to a family emergency (Osmundsen to Ortiz, November 6, 1981). With an unaware chair and an absent presenter, this left a gaping hole in the day—one that Valencia was more than capable of filling.

Even the strict spatial layout of the symposium fell by the wayside. When conferences took place at Burg Wartenstein, discussions revolved around a round table draped with a green cloth—very reminiscent of King Arthur and his knights (Silverman 2002, 7). After the castle's sale, the green cloth continued to be used, carrying a certain degree of symbolic continuity across symposia. While the tablecloth may have made its way to Arizona, the round table did not. Valencia took a seat at the head of a rectangular table. Subtle though it may have been, this endowed the proceedings with a spatial hierarchy that placed Valencia in an advantageous position from which to critique competing interpretations of "Yaquiness."

From this position Valencia made a lateral move, choosing to discuss and critique Edward Spicer's ethnographic portrayals of Yaquis (Evers to Barron, April 5, 2017). The core of Valencia's comments is not well remembered by participants, nor is it clearly stated in the documentary record. It is very likely that differing conceptions of Yaqui origins and the sacredness of the Deer Dance were in play.[21] As noted above, Valencia increasingly portrayed the community as having a primordial connection to the area that is now southern Arizona. Over the course of his career, Spicer progressively pushed the date of Yaqui arrival in the region further and further back.[22] However, he never endorsed this autochthonous narrative. Relatedly, the year before the conference, Spicer published his epic cumulative monograph *The Yaquis: A*

Cultural History (1980). Part of the book addressed the "absorption" of the Deer Dance into the tourist industries of Arizona and Sonora (275), which did little to support Valencia's depiction of the Deer Dance as a radically Other institution free from colonial or settler influence.

During the early 1990s these anthropological interpretations became the proverbial straw that broke the camel's back, separating Spicer's work and Valencia's imagining of the Pascua Yaquis. In 1993, representatives of the tribe went before Congress again, this time in an effort to reclassify the Pascua Yaquis as a "historic tribe." Though the community had achieved federal recognition in 1978, the Bureau of Indian Affairs (BIA) argued that they had done so as a "created tribe," defined as a recently formulated community of adult Indians. This distinction created roadblocks for the Pascua Yaqui Tribal Council, especially in its effort to ratify a constitution, a right that the BIA did not extended to "created tribes" (U.S. 1977). In their attempt to achieve this reclassification, the Pascua Yaquis had to contend with the fact that the anthropological and ethnohistorical literature stated that they were recent immigrants to the United States. This time, senators noted that the tribe's primary academic advocate, Edward Spicer, had repeatedly made this point in his written work (1940, 1961, 1980). Valencia respectfully argued before the Senate Subcommittee on Native American Affairs that Spicer (now a decade deceased) had erred in his interpretations (U.S. Senate 1993). Thus, in a sense, Valencia's behavior during the conference presaged his future reappraisal of Spicer's work.

We might not know the precise nature of the conflict that emerged between Valencia and Spicer around the green cloth. However, we can see that Valencia used the conference as an opportunity to eclipse dominant anthropological interpretations with his own "idiosyncratic understanding" of the Deer Dance, which better conformed to the essentializing and primodializing demands of federal recognition.

In the aftermath of the conference Valencia continued to cultivate the Deer Dance as a symbol of Yaquiness, and Wenner-Gren continued to be part of this process. With encouragement from Osmundsen, Valencia submitted an application to the foundation for a grant that would help fund a book project about the ritual (Valencia 1982). Because of his participation in the conference, the application was given preferential treatment despite being improperly filled out—Valencia left the majority of his application blank. The section reserved for a one-and-a-half-page description of the aim and scope of the project contained a single sentence. In her response to Valencia, Osmundsen insisted that "the application is short on words, but succinct in intent. It is fine as it is because what you would finally do is what will have a deeper meaning" (Osmundsen to Valencia January 5, 1982).

Despite her expressed enthusiasm and confidence, Osmundsen contacted the Spicers soon after receiving the application asking one or both of them to not only write a letter of support but to "summarize" the project for grant readers. She wrote, "Anselmo finally applied. Given the *cultural problems,* his application is understandable" (Osmundsen to Spicer January 2, 1982, emphasis added). What were these "cultural problems" that would have prevented Valencia from filling out the application? Valencia was new to the Wenner-Gren system, yes. But was this a matter of reaching across vast cultural divides? Hardly. At this point Valencia was no clearly stranger to U.S. bureaucracy. What at first appears to be Osmundsen's limited understanding of the Yaqui is actually evidence of the success of Valencia's performance during the conference. He had presented the tribe in a radically Other light. Osmundsen, not unlike Senator DeConcini before her, appears not to have questioned this depiction. But of course, the impact of the event was not a one-way street. In other words, Valencia's performance shaped more than the public face of Pascua Yaqui identity.

A "CHARISMATIC LEADER"

In indirect, but tangible, ways, Valencia's role in the Yaqui Conference continues to affect the ways in which Wenner-Gren engages academic communities and the general public. As noted above, the foundation conceptualized the Yaqui Conference as a test case at a turning point in the institution's history. The Yaqui Conference became as much a site of experimentation for the foundation as it was for Valencia. As illustrated above, Osmundsen and company relaxed their grip on their strict conferencing model as they worked in an accelerated manner to bring the gathering to fruition. The changes were legion. They chose to have their traditionally elite (if not aristocratic) gathering in what is commonly understood to be a relatively non-elite place—an American Indian reservation. They opened what had previously been a highly exclusive and private affair to the public. They invited non-academic cultural practitioners and intellectuals to not only participate but to take on leadership roles—as Appel phrased it, to *teach how best to learn*. This was all new territory for Wenner-Gren.

Ultimately, the foundation appears to have retained very few of the experimental dimensions of the Yaqui Conference. Some subsequent gatherings have been held in non-elite locales, but the majority of symposia have taken place at more picturesque, attention-grabbing sites that recall the halcyon days of Burg Wartenstein. Events since 1981 have happened at waterfront hotels in Mijas, Spain, and Baja, Mexico, as well as at Tivoli Palácio de Seteais, an eighteenth century estate in Portugal that now functions as a hotel and has hosted twelve Wenner-Gren symposia since 2003. In the few instances in which the Wenner-Gren conference has returned to Arizona, it has steered clear of New Pascua. Even the 102nd symposium, "Daughters of the Desert: Women Anthropologists and Students of the Native American Southwest," which saw a return to Oracle, Arizona, in 1986, was held exclusively at the conference center. The two other events that have been held in southern Arizona were confined to the Hacienda del Sol, a ranch resort that began its life in 1929 as a school for the daughters of wealthy families such as the Vanderbilts, Pilsburys, Maxwells, Westinghouses, and Campbells (Hacienda del Sol n.d.).

Gatherings continue to be highly regimented. Papers are pre-circulated. Participants are required to be present for all scheduled events. Thus social and intellectual activities are once again carefully coordinated.[23] While the symposia are still subject to the contingencies of all conferences (Silverman 2002), the explicitly lax nature of the Yaqui gathering would likely not pass muster today. Furthermore, participants in these invitation-only events continue to be PhDs hailing from research universities. Alice Kehoe suggests that the pool is even more circumscribed now, with many of the universities represented belonging to an elite network of metropolitan east coast schools (Kehoe 2003).

Of course there have been notable changes in the way Wenner-Gren conducts business and presents itself to the world. Through the development of the workshop program the foundation has opened itself to the general public and non-academic intellectuals. However, even this has been quite limited. Unlike the international symposium series, workshops are funded, but not necessarily organized, by the Wenner-Gren Foundation. As a result, there are far more of them each year— roughly fifteen to twenty workshops compared to just two symposia. As with the international symposium series, only those holding doctorates can apply. However, participants do not necessarily need to be traditional academics. For example, in 2016 the foundation funded "Possible Futures: Comparative Perspectives on Collaborative Research in Anthropology in North and Latin America." This event made an explicit effort to join "non-academic scholars from the United States and Canada [with] both academic and non-academic Latin American scholars" in a productive conversation regarding the future of collaborative ethnographic research (Wenner-Gren Foundation, n.d.).[24] That being said, most of these events have been open to formal academics exclusively. The workshops are permitted to have a public component, but the foundation is quite explicit in stating that this must be secondary to the intellectual nature of the event.[25] So, while the workshops illustrate some degree of change, the foundation remains very much within the model Osmundsen tirelessly developed decades ago.

However, and this is crucial for thinking about the co-constructive nature of anthropology and Indigenous politics, might this lack of transformation itself be indirect evidence of Valencia's lasting influence on the foundation?

A consistent feature of the symposium model involved participants submitting detailed notes and reflections after the event. Osmundsen used these comments to gauge the success of the gathering and to facilitate the process of formulating edited volumes. If the Wenner-Gren archives are accurate, most participants did not provide written feedback regarding the Yaqui Conference. Some offered relatively short, vague statements. Consider the comments from J. Richard Haefer, an ethnomusicologist from Arizona State University. Haefer briefly responded, "The entire event, especially the two days at New Pascua were very exciting and I did note several variations in sequence and innovative ideas used in the dance"; however, he lamented, "I do not have any notes from the conference to send to you as I did not take any formal notes" (Haefer to Osmundsen January 28, 1982). The few who did take the time to reflect on the proceedings walked away with a somewhat jaundiced view of the endeavor, which appears to be due in no small part to Valencia. Herbert Blau, the noted performance studies scholar and theater director, made this abundantly clear in his single-spaced six-page response. Reflecting on his brief stay in southern Arizona, Blau noted: "There was, to begin with, Anselmo's presentation of himself as tribal chief, quasi-priest, political leader, pedagogue, real estate speculator, and rationalizing guardian of the enchanted world. . . . It seemed reasonably self-evident that he had this other thing in mind: a ritual occasion for his own gospel of the ceremony, beginning with the chastening enunciation of our hereditary sins" (Blau to Osmundsen, December 4, 1981).

Blau ultimately reduced Valencia's posturing to a mere "critique of anthropological nitpicking" (Blau to Osmundsen, December 4, 1981). There is a rather glib streak in Blau's reminiscences. His characterization of Valencia as a "quasi-priest," "real estate speculator," and "rationalizing guardian of the enchanted world" connotes a flippant view of the well-respected spiritual leader and cultural representative. But in an ironic turn Blau appears to have been attuned to the larger social and political dynamics in which Valencia was operating. Later in his lengthy diatribe he comes to a poignant, albeit somewhat cryptic, point regarding Valencia's *perceived* social hindrances:

> That Anselmo was at a linguistic disadvantage—speaking perhaps in a third language, as [Keith Basso] indicated [. . .]—seemed obvious; [however,] Anselmo was also speaking with a linguistic advantage, since the exchange mechanism was such that in order to be respectful the *other* had to be silent. This is part of the deferential history of the last generation, as well as anthropological practice. Whatever it is for anthropology I felt it as condescending, precisely the behavior I would, in any salutary exchange, want to avoid. When we are dealing with others better adapted than Anselmo . . . we want to

remember that there is a certain kind of deference that gets in the way. (Blau to Osmundsen, November 27, 1981)

While he may have overstated "the deferential history" of anthropological practice (the discipline is littered with tales of scholastic impropriety toward Indigenous peoples), Blau clearly identified the emergent tendency of anthropologists to privilege Indigenous voices as a tool in Valencia's performative kit. The silent "other," in this case, was the academic, not the Indian. While Blau viewed this as a hindrance, something "that gets in the way" of intercultural dialogue and understanding, it was a hindrance that advantaged Valencia.

After reading Blau's critical reflection, Appel wrote to Osmundsen. "Rereading this, I find it very interesting though still opaque. Yet I think it hits some of the core issues . . . shall we talk about it later[?]" (Appel to Osmundsen, September 21, 1982). Appel's note suggests that the foundation flagged Blau's comments. A few months before Blau's ruminations arrived, Osmundsen expressed similar concerns in a letter to Ortiz, bringing him up to date on the events that he missed. While she felt "[the symposium] really came together more at the end," Osmundsen lamented that "we missed the boat in many aspects. Partly, it was the lack of ability to handle *a charismatic spiritual leader* in an academic context. Unavoidable political and historical issues had to enter the scene as they did" (Osmundsen to Ortiz, April 13, 1982, emphasis added). This ambivalent view was echoed in her post-conference communication with Edward Spicer. "The Yaqui conference was a unique experience and probably one of the most difficult ones we have ever been involved in" (Osmundsen to Spicer, February 2, 1982). Osmundsen was clearly intrigued by Valencia on an intellectual level, so much so that she was willing to provide him with additional funding for a book on the Deer Dance. But her comments suggest that she, like Blau, viewed Valencia's behavior as more of a barrier than a bridge to the type of organized intellectual exchanges that the symposium series was designed to achieve.

It may seem too much to assume that Valencia's ability to take command of the proceedings in a manner that irked the institutional guard subtly shaped the symposium series moving forward, except that Osmundsen admitted as much to Spicer. "We held a planning committee meeting recently and based on the Yaqui conference experience completely tore apart our program for the August conference" (Osmundsen to Spicer, February 2, 1982). After the Yaqui Conference the foundation continued to provide limited opportunities for engaging the general public and non-academic intellectuals, but it was just that—*limited*. The foundation had learned firsthand what happens when it curtails its strictures: those operating at the margins of the field with *their own objectives* can step in and voice *their own criticisms* of the discipline.

IMPLICATIONS: NAVIGATING PARADOXES

On the surface, Valencia's performance during the conference recalls aspects of Vine Deloria Jr.'s foundational critique of Native Americanist anthropology (1969). References to the incessant questions that have made things difficult for the Yaqui community echoes Deloria's characterization of "anthros" as "ideological vultures" who "[bury] Indian communities . . . beneath [a] mass of irrelevant information" (1969, 82, 95). However, Valencia neither rendered anthropology "useless" to Native peoples nor did he argue, as Deloria did, that anthropologists stand behind all detrimental federal Indian policies (1969, 81).[26] Rather, he offered his own interpretations of Yaqui culture that aligned with the community's new federal status. In turning the conference into a lecture about the Deer Dance (and Yaqui culture and history more broadly), Valencia continued the work that he had begun before Congress as he placed a premium on the essential and primordial difference of the Pascua Yaquis.

Valencia's use of anthropology brings further clarity to an understanding of anthropology's relationship with Indigenous recognition. When anthropologists participate in Indigenous political projects, they are always already caught between the dynamic vectors of categories imposed from above and the communities labeled by those categories. The limited options available to Indigenous peoples within the norms of collective identity recognition force them into a paradoxical system of representation. They must prove themselves to be authentically Indian without fully acknowledging the colonial and imperial histories that have constituted them as Indian in the first place. Thus they are called upon to identify "with an impossible object of an authentic self-identity" (Povinelli 2002, 6). As a result, recognition proceedings compel Native peoples to articulate ahistorical, essentialized, and primordialized Indigenous identities. As the historian and citizen of the Pawnee Nation Roger Echo-Hawk notes, such identities, insomuch as they reflect outdated racialized conceptions of difference, are "inherently dehumanizing" (2010, 9).

In many cases anthropology has been part of the process of generating typologies that naturalize federal-Indian power relations and popular imaginings of ethnic groups (Barker 2011; Field 2003; Pinkoski 2008; Silverstein 2003; Simpson 2014). However, even when anthropologists work in the service of Native communities, these reductive conceptions have a way of reproducing themselves. Importantly, this is the point that Deloria did not recognize in his assessment of the discipline. Deloria insisted that "anthros" should design their projects to meet the pressing political objects of Indigenous groups (1969, 81). Then and only then can this antiquarian discipline be made to challenge colonial norms and ameliorate the lives of Natives. Deloria did not acknowledge that this kind of work had already been done, with mixed results in such cases as the Indian Claims Commission (ICC). Beginning in the 1950s, anthropologists worked as expert witnesses for tribes to underwrite the legitimacy of claims to land and other resources (McMillen 2007; Ray 2006, 2016). In many instances this meant attempting to reposition Native communities as coherent, homogenous, primordial entities with an essential link to a territory equivalent to Euro-American conceptions of private property. In other words, it meant reproducing the colonial-imperial imaginary that helped render Indigenous groups segregated or landless in the first place. When successful, and they often were, expert witnesses helped secure cash settlements for tribes; the ICC was never designed to directly return land (Kehoe 2014, 109). However, this came at the cost of naturalizing stereotyped notions of Indigeneity.

The case of the Yaqui Conference suggests that the same issue arises outside of the courts or court-like settings whether or not anthropologists are aware of it. The Wenner-Gren Foundation and conference organizers had little sense of the complexity of the political dynamics into which they were stepping. By reconfiguring the event as more of a performance and lecture than a scholastic discussion, Valencia took the helm of the conference. The outcome was clearly not liberatory, nor did it simply replicate relations of domination. Rather, it was consistent with the paradoxes of recognition. Valencia continued to bring cultural and political visibility to a marginalized community, but he did so by reinstituting ideologies with a compromised past. In this case, anthropology was neither an extension of state domination nor a tool of radical Indigenous resistance. It was a means by which an Indigenous intellectual could better navigate the paradoxes of recognition in all kinds of settings, including the mundane and taken-for-granted space of an academic conference.

CONCLUSION

In his final days of a losing battle with cancer, Edward Spicer jotted down his thoughts on the Yaqui Conference and sent them to Osmundsen. Spicer noted a general "lack of a sense of a common understanding as to the purpose of the conference," which left him with "a persistent sense of not communicating that bothered [him] and constituted a disappointment" (Spicer to Osmundsen January 8, 1982). Despite these drawbacks, Spicer identified at least one area in which he felt the conference to be a success.

> The first two days of the conference marked an important new kind of event during which the conference was sponsored by Yaqui singers and dancers on behalf of the Yaqui community of Pascua Pueblo. This inaugurated a constructive kind of relationship between scholars and Indians. The Yaquis involved planned and carried out the presentation of a performance and a spoken introduction for the visitors and made their selections from the Deer ritual without prompting from scholars. . . . Undoubtedly the Wenner-Gren conference established a new model which Yaquis will seek to duplicate in the future in their relationship with all seeking to study Yaqui culture. (Spicer to Osmundsen January 8, 1982)

While the event might have marked a change in Yaqui-anthropological relations insofar as the Yaqui took on a more active role in the conference, the performance carried out over the course of those five days did not emerge *de novo*. As I have illustrated above, Valencia's cultivation of the Deer Dance as a primary symbol of "Yaquiness" and "Indianness" was part of an ongoing attempt to represent Yaquis as a certain *kind of people*—an "American Indian Tribe." The Yaqui Conference and the discipline of anthropology, which had never been too far removed from the Yaquis' political endeavors, arrived as a means of carrying out this performance beyond the halls of Congress.

The conference and Valencia's efforts attest to the importance of the Deer Dance in Yaqui culture and history, an importance for which a constructionist and event-oriented approach is instructive. With his historicization of the Deer Dance and Yaqui culture more broadly, Valencia was not simply displaying "Yaquiness;" he was assembling and reassembling it in relation to the group's new status as an American Indian Tribe. Thus, to borrow Hacking's (2002) phrasing, the category and the kind existed in conversation with one another. Most importantly, such an analysis helps to unpack Indigenous engagements with broader political systems and the ways in which anthropology has been caught up in the creative rearticulation of Indigenous subjectivity. With respect to the case described above, the framework illustrates how Valencia operationalized the conference as a platform upon which to reassemble Yaqui culture and history. More broadly, such an approach to the history of anthropology and indigeneity provides a means to better grasp the discipline's consequential imbrication in the twists and turns of recognition.

NOTES

1. This chapter began as a paper presented in the session "New Directions in the History of Anthropology" organized by Nicholas Barron and David W. Dinwoodie for the annual meeting of the American Anthropological Association in Washington DC, in 2017. Since then I have received critical feedback on drafts from David Dinwoodie, Les Field, Suzanne Oakdale, Susana Sepulveda, and Lindsay Smith. Comments from Richard Handler regarding the conference paper were

wonderfully illuminating. A conversation with Susan Lindee helped me conceptualize the history of the Wenner-Gren Foundation. Emails from Larry Evers and Felipe Molina offered a glimpse into the internal dynamics of the Yaqui Conference. I must also thank Mark Mahoney at the Wenner-Gren Archives and Christina Antipa and Mary Graham at the Arizona State Museum for their guidance during the research phase. Financial support from the UNM-Mellon Dissertation Completion Fellowship, the Center for Regional Studies at the University of New Mexico, and the University of New Mexico Research Grant (General Priority) made this archival research and writing possible. I must also offer a sincere thank you to the Edward H. and Rosamond B. Spicer Foundation for their consistent support of my work.

2. Historically, Yaqui people have referred to themselves as Yoeme among other Yaquis. In the presence of Yoris (white people), the term Yaqui is most commonly used (Spicer 1988, 99). The origins of the term are unclear. One of the first documented accounts of the Yaqui sheds circumstantial light on the origins of this term. According to Andrés Pérez de Ribas, in 1645 Jesuits encountered a group of Indians who said, "Don't you see we are *hiaqui*, 'the ones who make sounds'?" (quoted in Shorter 2009, 7). Because this essay explores intercultural engagements, I follow the recent historical literature and retain the use of Yaqui (Rensink 2018; Schulze 2018). I use the term interchangeably with Pascua Yaqui, which is more specific to the official tribal moniker (the Pascua Yaqui Tribe).

3. Rooted in Gramscian Marxism (Adamson 1980, 143; Gramsci 2000, 301), I understand *Indigenous intellectuals* to be historically produced individuals living among Indigenous groups in contexts where their role is to transmit ideas between the group, civil society, and the settler government. Indigenous intellectuals and Native communities are mutually constitutive. Groups delegate representational authority to select individuals. These individuals help codify a collective identity as they articulate ideas about the group in the public arena (Field 1999b, 2003; Nagata 1987).

4. Even James Clifford's (1988) now canonical account of the Masphee Indians on trial is more of an anecdotal discussion of the broader issues surrounding the case, including epistemological divides between history and anthropology and the paradoxical task of performing authentic indigeneity.

5. These transformations are indexed by the creation of the International Indian Treaty Council (1974) and World Council of Indigenous Peoples (1975) in the United States and Canada, respectively. The 1977 UN NGO conference on Discrimination against Indigenous Populations and the construction of the formal Federal Acknowledgment Process (1978) and the Indian Self-Determination and Education Assistance Act (1975) in the United States are also indications of the turn to Indigenous recognition (Castile 1998; Engle 2010; Merlan 2009).

6. What Edward Spicer, the community's primary ethnographer and ethnohistorian, observed in the 1930s could be said on the eve of federal recognition in the late 1970s. "The political status of the Yaqui [in Tucson] is wrapped up in misconceptions, neither Yaquis nor the majority of Anglo Americans understanding clearly what that status is" (Spicer 1988, 43).

7. This account of the Talking Tree is presented in Evers and Molina (1980).

8. I refer to Molina as Yoeme as this is his preferred designation.

9. While it might appear somewhat draconian in its design, the Burg Wartenstein model and the symposium program was popular among participants (Lindee and Radin 2016).

10. Lindee and Radin also note the implementation of the Tax Reform Act of 1969. Among other things, the act imposed a four percent excise tax on investment income and fines for failure to comply with nonprofit law. See also Wadsworth (1975).

11. I do not mean to say that previous symposia were purely anthropological. It was not unheard of for scholars in related to disciplines to receive an invitation. For example, in 1970, the noted sociologist of interaction Erving Goffman participated in "Ethnic Identity: Cultural Continuity and Change." In fact, several of the Yaqui Conference participants had already been guests at Burg Wartenstein during the 1970s, including performance studies scholars such as Jerome Rothenberg and Richard Schechner. What I am saying is that the Yaqui Conference came during a period when Osmundsen was actively trying to cultivate an explicitly interdisciplinary character for the symposia.

12. Planning did not begin with an eye toward the Yaqui or Arizona. Rather, the idea for the conference began as an epic multi-city tour in which eight distinct cultures and their unique performances would be enacted for participants (Wenner-Gren Foundation, n. d.).

13. Wenner-Gren was nearly done with planning the conference before they ever considered speaking with the Spicers. It was only when Fred Eggan responded to an invitation to participate that Appel and

Osmundsen seemed to even become aware of the anthropological couple. Eggan assumed that Osmundsen had already spoken with the Spicers and that they would be involved in some way. At the time, she had not, and they were not.

14. In his congressional testimony, Spicer went to creative and subtle lengths to emphasize Yaqui discreteness and indigeneity. For example, he led with a characterization of Yaqui distinction based on language. He simultaneously emphasized their connection to the Uto-Aztecan language family and groups like the "Aztec, and the Papagos, Pimas, Hopis, and Paiutes of American Indian language stocks" (U.S. Senate 1977). Notably, Spicer neglected to mention the use of English and Spanish among Yaquis in Arizona. A study from 1979 showed that Spanish was actually the dominant language used by Yaquis in Arizona, with Yaqui spoken only twenty percent of the time and mostly by older family members (Trujillo 1997).

15. I have found no evidence of a circulated copy of Spicer's congressional testimony in the Wenner-Gren papers. Larry Evers does not recall receiving any specific pieces of pre-conference information including a copy of Spicer's testimony (email April 5, 2017).

16. This may help to explain the emergence of the Toltec origin narrative, which the Yaqui tribal council officially adopted in 1981 (Pascua Yaqui Tribe 1981–82, 2).

17. Spicer (1954) wrote about the Yaqui adoption of the cross under Jesuit influence.

18. One of the ways Valencia presented these issues was by suggesting that the Yaquis conflated the Judeo-Christian God with the Sun, which he identified as a sacred element in Yaqui cosmology. According to Larry Evers, "Anselmo was talking about the Yaqui's Father the Sun long before this meeting" (Evers to Barron, April 5, 2017).

19. This is Spicer's full note on the matter: "The senior Deersinger's emphasis on Sun symbolism and the concept of Sun the Father rather than on God the Father and the Trinity constitutes a re-reading of Yaqui religious tradition. His exalting of the Sun symbolism is much influenced by his recent intensive association (for the purpose of getting federal recognition) with Plains and other American Indians in the National Congress of American Indians and various Pow-wow circuits. The Sun-Father concept among Arizona Yaquis had fallen into an almost lost state until these recent efforts at resurrection and revitalization. He ties it to the Deer Song content and few features of Deer-

Pascola ritual which had become unimportant, almost non-existent, for Yaquis generally. It is true nevertheless that among Sonora Yaquis the concept is somewhat more alive as a result of the vigor there of the Military Society, in the ritual of which the Sun plays still an important part. In Arizona, on the other hand, the Military Society ritual has been entirely dead for at least sixty years" (Spicer to Osmundsen January 8, 1982).

20. The dance is typically an all-night affair.

21. Another issue would be Spicer's changing view of the Deer Dance. During this period and prior, Spicer had reached a somewhat instrumental interpretation of the Deer Dance as practiced in Arizona, seeing it more as an avenue for Yaqui representation in the tourist market than a sacred ritual (Spicer 1974, 312).

22. In his letter to Congress Spicer settled on 1796 as the earliest date. There is evidence to suggest that missionaries brought a group of converted Yaquis to Tumacacori to model behavior. He also notes the use of Yaqui labor in gold and silver mines during and after this period. In *The Yaquis: A Culture History* (1980) Spicer states that, despite the abandonment of the mission in 1828 and intrusion of Apache raids, the settlement was "still inhabited by descendants of the earlier group" (1980, 237). Castile notes, however, that Spicer provides no evidence to support this belief (2002, 385).

23. The conference format is now explicitly stated for all applicants on the foundation's website: http://www.wennergren.org/programs /international-symposia/format-international-symposia.

24. Details for this particular workshop can be found here: http://www .wennergren.org/grantees/lassiter-luke-eric.

25. According to the foundation's website, "workshops may be coupled with public symposia to present the debates to a broader audience. However, the workshop must be the primary focus of the proposal." http://www.wennergren.org/programs/conference-and-workshop -grants/eligibility

26. The somewhat reductive nature of Deloria's depiction of anthropology must always be understood within the context of the 1960s, a period in which the discipline's mainstream was only beginning to voice overt critiques of the discipline's entanglement with American empire and the treatment of colonized peoples. One might understandably credit Deloria (and others) with pushing self-reflexive anthropologists to make their own critiques explicit. Relatedly, Deloria's longstanding

and close engagements with such sympathetic anthropologists (e.g., Nancy Lurie) suggest that Deloria held a more nuanced and forgiving view of the discipline (Arndt 2019). Additionally, one should not ignore Deloria's own family's contributions to the anthropology of Native North America (Cotera 2008; King 2019).

REFERENCES

Archival sources

Wenner-Gren Foundation Archives. Symposium Main Files series, boxes SMF-074 to SMF-076.

Edward H. and Rosamond B. Spicer Papers, 1911–2000. Arizona State Museum. University of Arizona.

Fred Eggan Papers. Special Collections Research Center. University of Chicago Library.

Published sources

Adamson, Walter L. 1980. *Hegemony and Revolution: A Study of Antonio Gramsci's Political and Cultural Theory*. Berkeley: University of California Press.

Appel, Willa. 1983. *Cults in America: Programmed for Paradise*. New York: Holt, Rinehart, and Winston.

Appiah, Anthony K. 1994. "Identity, Authenticity, Survival: Multicultural Societies and Social Reproduction." In *Multiculturalism*, edited by Amy Gutmann, 149–63. Princeton NJ: Princeton University Press.

Arndt, Grant. 2019. "Rediscovering Nancy Oestreich Lurie's Activist Anthropology." *American Anthropologist* 121, no. 3: 725–28.

Asch, Michael. 1982. "Dene Self-Determination and the Study of Hunter-Gathers in the Modern World." In *Politics and History in Band Societies*, edited by Eleanor Burker Leacock and Richard B. Lee. Cambridge: Cambridge University Press.

Barker, Joanne. 2011. *Native Acts: Law, Recognition, and Cultural Authenticity*. Durham NC: Duke University Press.

Barron, Nicholas. 2019a. "Applying Anthropology, Assembling Indigenous Community: Anthropology and the Pascua Yaqui Indian Tribe in Southern Arizona." PhD diss., University of New Mexico.

———. 2019b. "Assembling 'Enduring Peoples,' Mediating Recognition: Anthropology, the Pascua Yaqui Indians, and the Co-Construction of Ideas and Politics." *History and Anthropology*. https://doi.org/10.1080/02757206.2019.1695203.

Brooks, James. 2002. *Captives & Cousins: Slavery, Kinship, and Community in the Southwest Borderlands.* Chapel Hill: University of North Carolina Press.

Campisi, Jack. 1991. *The Mashpee Indians: Tribe on Trial.* Syracuse: Syracuse University Press.

Castaneda, Carlos. (1968) 2016. *Teachings of Don Juan: A Yaqui Way of Knowledge.* Berkeley: University of California Press.

Castile, George Pierre. 1998. *To Show Heart: Native American Self-Determination and Federal Indian Policy, 1960–1975.* Tucson: University of Arizona Press.

———. 2002. "Yaquis, Edward H. Spicer, and Federal Indian Policy: From Immigrants to Native Americans." *Journal of the Southwest* 44: 383–435.

Cesare, Joseph. 1982. "Joseph Cesare to Morris K. Udall," September 27, 1982. Morris K. Udall Papers Box 621, Folder 13. University of Arizona Special Collections.

Clifford, James. 1988. *The Predicament of Culture: Twentieth-Century Ethnography, Literature, and Art.* Cambridge: Harvard University Press.

Cotera, Maria Eugenia. 2008. "Telling the Story of Her People." In *Their Own Frontier: Women Intellectuals Re-Visioning the American West,* edited by Shirley Anne Leckie and Nancy J. Parezo, 245–68. Lincoln: University of Nebraska Press.

Coulthard, Glen Sean. 2014. *Red Skin, White Masks: Rejecting the Colonial Politics of Recognition.* Minneapolis: University of Minnesota Press.

Cramer, Renée Ann. 2005. *Cash, Color, and Colonialism: The Politics of Tribal Acknowledgment.* Norman: University of Oklahoma Press.

Darnell, Regna. 2001. *Invisible Genealogies: A History of Americanist Anthropology.* Lincoln: University of Nebraska Press.

Deloria Jr., Vine. 1969. *Custer Died for Your Sins: An Indian Manifesto.* New York: Macmillan.

Dinwoodie, David W. 1998. "Authorizing Voices: Going Public in an Indigenous Language." *Cultural Anthropology* 13, no. 2: 193–223.

———. 2007. "'He Expects We Would Be Off from His Lands': Reported Speech-Events in Tsilhqut'in Contact History." *Anthropological Linguistics* 49, no. 1: 1–26.

———. 2018. "Recognizing Aboriginal Perspectives in Land Claims Litigation." Paper presented at the American Anthropological Association, San Jose, California, November 15, 2018.

Echo-Hawk, Roger C. 2010. *The Magic Children: Racial Identity at the End of the Age of Race.* Walnut Creek CA: Left Coast Press.

Engle, Karen. 2010. *The Elusive Promise of Indigenous Development: Rights, Culture, Strategy*. Durham.

Ens, Gerhard J., and Joe Sawchuk. 2016. *From New Peoples to New Nations: Aspects of Métis History and Identity from the Eighteenth to the Twenty-First Centuries*. Toronto ON: University of Toronto Press.

Evers, Larry. 2017. "Larry Evers to Nicholas Barron," April 5, 2017.

Evers, Larry, and Felipe S. Molina. 1987. *Yaqui Deer Songs, Maso Bwikam: A Native American Poetry*. Tucson: University of Arizona Press.

Field, Les W. 1999a. *The Grimace of Macho Ratón: Artisans, Identity, and Nation in Late-Twentieth-Century Western Nicaragua*. Durham NC: Duke University Press.

————. 1999b. "Complicities and Collaborations: Anthropologists and the 'Unacknowledged Tribes' of California." *Current Anthropology* 40, no. 2: 193–210.

————. 2003. "Unacknowledged Tribes, Dangerous Knowledge." *Wicazo Sa Review* 18, no. 2: 79–94.

Fisher, Andrew H. 2010. *Shadow Tribe: The Making of Columbia River Indian Identity*. Seattle: University of Washington Press.

Folsom, Raphael Brewster. 2014. *The Yaquis and the Empire: Violence, Spanish Imperial Power, and Native Resilience in Colonial Mexico*. New Haven CT: Yale University Press.

Fraser, Nancy. 2000. "Rethinking Recognition." *New Left Review* 3: 107–21.

Gramsci, Antonio. 2000. *The Gramsci Reader: Selected Writings 1916–1935*. Edited by David A. Forgacs. New York: New York University Press.

Hacienda del Sol. n.d. "Our History." Accessed May 1, 2019. https://www.haciendadelsol.com/about-us/history/.

Hacking, Ian. 2002. *Historical Ontology*. Cambridge: Harvard University Press.

Harmon, Alexandra. 1998. *Indians in the Making: Ethnic Relations and Indian Identities around Puget Sound*. Berkeley: University of California Press.

Hinton, Leanne. 2010. "Language Revitalization in North American and the New Direction of Linguistics." *Transforming Anthropology* 18, no. 1: 35–41.

Hobsbawm, Eric J. 1987. *The Age of Empire, 1875–1914*. New York: Pantheon Books.

Hobsbawm, Eric J., and Terence. Ranger. 1983. *The Invention of Tradition*. Cambridge: Cambridge University Press.

Hu-DeHart, Evelyn. 1984. *Yaqui Resistance and Survival: The Struggle for Land and Autonomy, 1821–1910*. Madison: University of Wisconsin Press.

Kehoe, Alice B. 2003. "Review of The Beast on the Table: Conferencing with Anthropologists, by Sydel Silverman." *Bulletin of the History of Archaeology* 13, no. 1: 12–14.

———. 2014. *A Passion for the True and Just: Felix and Lucy Kramer Cohen and the Indian New Deal.* Tucson: University of Arizona Press.

King, Charles. 2019. *Gods of the Upper Air: How a Circle of Renegade Anthropologists Reinvented Race, Sex, and Gender in the Twentieth Century.* New York: Penguin Random House.

Lindee, Susan, and Joanna Radin. 2016. "Patrons of the Human Experience: A History of the Wenner-Gren Foundation for Anthropology Research, 1941–2016." *Current Anthropology* 57 (Supplement): s218-s301.

Maffi, Luisa. 2001. *On Biocultural Diversity: Linking Language, Knowledge, and the Environment.* Washington DC: Smithsonian Institution Press.

McMillen, Christian W. 2007. *Making Indian Law: The Hualapai Land Case and the Birth of Ethnohistory.* New Haven CT: Yale University Press. http://www.loc.gov/catdir/toc/ecip0620/2006029347.html.

Meeks, Eric V. 2007. *Border Citizens: The Making of Indians, Mexicans, and Anglos in Arizona.* Austin: University of Texas Press.

Menzies, Charles R. 2006. *Traditional Ecological Knowledge and Natural Resource Management.* Lincoln: University of Nebraska Press.

Merlan, Francesca. 2009. "Indigeneity: Global and Local." *Current Anthropology* 50, no. 3: 303–33.

Miller, Mark Edwin. 2004. *Forgotten Tribes: Unrecognized Indians and the Federal Acknowledgment Process.* Lincoln: University of Nebraska Press.

Nagata, Shuichi. 1987. "From Ethnic Bourgeoisie to Organized Intellectuals Speculations on North American Native Leadership." *Anthropologica* 29, no. 1: 61–75.

Nettle, Daniel, and Suzanne Romaine. 2002. *Vanishing Voice: The Extinction of the World's Languages.* New York: Oxford University Press.

Osmundsen, Lita. 1980. "Wenner-Gren Foundation for Anthropology Research 1980: Turning Point in Perspective." Fred Eggan Papers, Box 30, Folder 1. Special Collections Research Center, University of Chicago Library.

Pascua Yaqui Tribe. 1982. "The Emerging Pascua Yaqui Tribe, 1981–1982." Edward H. and Rosamond B. Spicer Papers, Box 89, Folder 317. Arizona State Museum.

Pinkoski, Marc. 2008. "Julian Steward, American Anthropology, and Colonialism." *Histories of Anthropology Annual* 4: 172–204.

Povinelli, Elizabeth. 2002. *The Cunning of Recognition: Indigenous Alterities and the Making of Australian Multiculturalism*. Durham NC: Duke University Press.

Powell, Timothy B. 2007. "A Drum Speaks: Partnership to Create a Digital Archive Based on Traditional Ojibwe Systems of Knowledge." *RBM: A Journal of Rare Books, Manuscripts and Cultural Heritage* 8 (2): 170–71.

Ray, Arthur. 2006. "Kroeber and the California Claims: Historical Particularism and Cultural Ecology in Court." In *Central Sites, Peripheral Visions: Cultural and Institutional Crossings in the History of Anthropology*, edited by Richard Handler, 248–74. Madison: University of Wisconsin Press.

———. 2016. *Aboriginal Rights Claims and the Making and Remaking of History*. Montreal: McGill-Queen's University Press.

Rensink, Brenden. 2018. *Native but Foreign: Indigenous Immigrants and Refugees in the North American Borderlands*. College Station: Texas A&M University Press.

Ridington, Robin. 2014. "Dane-Zaa Oral History: Why It's Not Hearsay." *BC Studies* 183 (Autumn 2014).

Rodríguez, Sylvia. 2009. *The Matachines Dance: A Ritual Dance of the Indian Pueblos and Mexicano/Hispano Communities*. Santa Fe NM: Sunstone Press.

Schulze, Jeffrey M. 2018. *Are We Not Foreigners Here?: Indigenous Nationalism in the U.S.-Mexico Borderlands*. Chapel Hill: University of North Carolina Press.

Shorter, David Delgado. 2009. *We Will Dance Our Truth: Yaqui History in Yoeme Performances*. Lincoln: University of Nebraska Press.

Silverman, Sydel. 2002. *The Beast on the Table: Conferencing with Anthropologists*. Walnut Creek CA: AltaMira Press.

Silverstein, Michael. 2003. "The Whens and Wheres—As Well as Hows—of Ethnolinguistics." *Public Culture* 23, no. 1: 531–57.

Simpson, Audra. 2014. *Mohawk Interruptus: Political Life across the Borders of Settler States*. Durham NC: Duke University Press.

Smith, Anthony D. 1999. *Myths and Memories of the Nation*. Oxford: Oxford University Press.

———. 2009. *Ethno-Symbolism and Nationalism: A Cultural Approach*. New York: Routledge.

Spicer, Edward H. 1940. *Pascua, a Yaqui Village in Arizona*. Chicago IL: University of Chicago Press.

———. 1954. "Spanish-Indian Acculturation in the Southwest." *American Anthropologist* 56, no. 4: 663–78.

———, ed. 1961. *Perspectives in American Indian Culture Change.* Chicago IL: University of Chicago Press.

———. 1962. *Cycles of Conquest: The Impact of Spain, Mexico, and the United States on the Indians of the Southwest, 1533–1960.* Tucson: University of Arizona Press.

———. 1974. "Context of the Yaqui Easter Ceremony." In *New Dimensions in Dance Research: Anthropology and Dance—The American Indian: The Proceedings of the Third Conference on Research in Dance, March 26th—April 2nd, 1972, the University of Arizona and the Yaqui Villages of Tucson.* Vol. 6. 309–46. New York: Committee on Research in Dance.

———. 1980. *The Yaquis: A Cultural History.* Tucson: University of Arizona Press.

———. 1988. *People of Pascua.* Edited by Kathleen M. Sands and Rosamond B. Spicer. Tucson: University of Arizona Press.

Spicer, Edward H., and Rosamond B. Spicer. 1981. "Notes from the 89th Wenner-Gren International Symposium." Edward H. and Rosamond B. Spicer Papers, Box 86, Folder 70. Arizona State Museum.

Taylor, Charles. 1994. "The Politics of Recognition." In *Multiculturalism,* edited by Amy Gutmann, 25–74. Princeton NJ: Princeton University Press.

Trujillo, Octaviana V. 1997. "A Tribal Approach to Language and Literacy Development in A Trilingual Setting." In *Teaching Indigenous Languages,* edited by Jon Reyhner, 10–21. Flagstaff: Northern Arizona University.

Tucson Citizen. 1923. "Entire Easter Ceremony Dance of Yaquis Record on Film to Advertise," April 2, 1923.

Turner, Dale A. 2006. *This Is Not a Peace Pipe: Towards Critical Indigenous Philosophy.* Toronto ON: University of Toronto Press.

Turner, Edith. 1995. "The Yaqui Deer Dance at Pascua Pueblo, Arizona." In *By Means of Performance Intercultural Studies of Theatre and Ritual,* edited by Richard Schechner and Willa Appel. Cambridge: Cambridge University Press.

U.S. Senate. 1993. *Pascua Yaqui Status Clarification Act: Hearing Before the Subcommittee on Native American Affairs of the Committee on Natural Resources on H.R. 734, to amend the act entitled "An Act to Provide for the Extension of Certain Federal Benefits, Services, and Assistance to the Pascua Yaqui Indians of Arizona, and for Other Purposes."* 103rd Congress, First Session.

U.S. Senate. 1977. *Trust Status for the Pascua Yaqui Indians of Arizona*. Washington DC.

Valencia, Anselmo. 1982. "Deer Dance Ritual: Application for a Grant-in-Aid from the Wenner-Gren Foundation for Anthropological Research, Inc." 89th Wenner-Gren International Symposium. Wenner-Gren Foundation.

Wadsworth, Homer C. 1975. "Private Foundations and the Tax Reform Act of 1969." *Law and Contemporary Problems* 39: 255–62.

Wenner-Gren Foundation. 1981. "Wenner-Gren Foundation Application for National Endowment for the Humanities Grant." 89th Wenner-Gren International Symposium. Wenner-Gren Foundation.

GEOFFREY GRAY

7

His Past Rose Up to Defeat Him

F. G. G. Rose and Academic and Political Freedom

From the late 1940s through the 1970s, during the height of the Cold War, Western democracies underwent a period of anti-communist hysteria that resulted in the intellectual suppression and often public humiliation of social scientists and scientists (Buckley-Moran 1986; Deery 2010). While the extremism of McCarthyism in the United States did not occur in Australia, some scientists and social scientists were publicly accused of being communists and their careers were curtailed and hindered. Academic suppression entailed the blocking of funds, denial of promotion or publication, outright harassment, subtle undermining of reputation, or, in extreme cases, dismissal. Each case involved a government instrumentality acting in concert with the often sympathetic collaboration of a timid or politicized academic establishment. The treatment of anthropologist F. G. G. Rose was one of several blatant denials of academic and political (civil) freedom (Gray 1993, 1998).

Rose's career as a public servant and anthropologist was impeded by Australian security agencies, especially the Australian Security Intelligence Organisation (ASIO). Indeed, the surveillance and harassment were key factors in his resettlement (he referred to it as "exile") in the German Democratic Republic (GDR) in 1956. Three years before his death he wrote that Australia "has at the very least a moral obligation to make recompense (or as it is frequently expressed in the German word *Wiederhutmachung*) for what I was subjected to in 1954 and during the following years."[1] He overlooks his own actions and overstates and exaggerates his victimization.

Frederick George Godfrey Rose (1915–1991), public servant, anthropologist, and Communist, was born at Croydon, London, on 22 March

1915, the second of three children of George William Rose, a municipal clerk, and his wife, Frances Isabel, née Godfrey. He attended Whitgift Grammar School, founded in 1596, a school "suited to the needs" of the lower middle class.[2] Awarded a scholarship to St. Catharine's College, Cambridge, in 1933, he enrolled in the Science and Mathematics Tripos but changed to Anthropology and Archaeology in his final year.[3]

To understand and assess Rose's victimization, this paper discusses two periods of his life, concentrating on his attempts to conduct anthropological research in northern Australia. The first covers the period from his arrival in Australia in late 1937 to his departure for the GDR in 1956. It focuses on Rose's initial attempts to make a career in anthropology, in which he was hindered in part by his political allegiances and activities as well as his theoretical position. The second period begins in 1962 and covers his attempts to return to Groote Eylandt, the site of his first fieldwork trip from 1939 to 1941, which highlights Australian security services indirectly blocking his field research. To enter Groote Eylandt, an island off the Arnhem Land coast in northern Australia, designated an Aboriginal reserve, Rose needed a permit issued by the director of Native Welfare, who was advised by ASIO as to Rose's character and suitability.[4] His first hurdle, however, was obtaining sufficient research funds, which meant applying for Australian research funds. Rose was a graduate of Cambridge University. David Mills, in his history of modern British social anthropology, states that, during the 1930s, in contrast to the London School of Economics (LSE) and Oxford University, "Cambridge remained relatively marginal, dominated as it was by biological anthropologists and administrative ethnographers" (Mills 2008, 6). George Stocking is harsh in his assessment: "After the election of TC Hodson to the readership in 1926, Cambridge anthropology had entered a long period of decline" (Stocking 1995, 430). In his view Cambridge languished until the election of Meyer Fortes to the William Wyse chair in 1951 (Stocking 1995, 431).

Rose's interest in Australia he attributed to Cambridge anthropologist Alfred Cort Haddon (1855–1940), who told him there was still much work to be done in Australia (Munt 2011, 112).[5] Haddon's experience in Australia comprised the Cambridge Expedition to the Torres Strait in 1898 and advising on government appointments such as that of a government anthropologist in New Guinea (Stocking 1995, 407; Gray 2003). He had little firsthand knowledge of the state of research in Australia. This is reflected in Rose believing that "if Haddon was right in what he told me, I could do the same as Malinowski for some groups of the Australian Aborigines."[6] It was an ambitious yet fanciful aspiration and reveals an ignorance of what went before. In his enthusiasm Rose overlooked the scope of the research undertaken by the Sydney department and Australian museums, especially the Museum of South Australia (Elkin 1938a, 1938b; Jones 1987).

In 1926, with the establishment of a Chair of Anthropology at the University of Sydney, there was put in place a systematic research plan to cover the Aboriginal tribal groups least impacted by European settlement. This resulted in anthropologists working at sites of Aboriginal displacement and non-indigenous settlement in an attempt to record and witness Aboriginal lifeways (concentrating on kinship) before it was too late (Gray 2007a). These field sites were tricky spaces, as anthropologists were often "identified closely with the people they studied . . . [and] thought to be subversives (in thought, if not necessarily in deed)" (Kuklick 2011, 15; see also Turner 1979; Gray 1994a, 2019). It is not surprising that imperial and national security services viewed anthropologists with suspicion founded on a belief that anthropology "naturally attracts an inherently subversive element" (Kuklick 2011, 15). As if to prove this point an unnamed ASIO officer made the aside that the work of social anthropologists provided "the most perfect cover possible for subversive activities among undeveloped peoples."[7] Membership in the Communist Party, or any groups deemed fellow travelers, was sufficient to bring a scholar under suspicion and thus to the attention of the security services (Price 2004; Cain 1983; Deery 2000; Zogbaum 2004; Gray 2006, 2014, 2019, 2020).

Before World War II Australian security agencies depended upon the British MI5 to keep them informed of possible security threats arriving from Britain. This continued after the war, including, for example, notifying ASIO about Peter Worsley (1924–2103). In fact there is a long history of cooperation between Australian security services (housed in the attorney general's department) and MI5, which protected the empire and dominion nations from subversive threats (Andrew 1989;

Gray 2009; 2014; Goody 1995, 44–57; Zogbaum 2004; Forsyth 2015). When Rose left for Australia at the end of 1937 he was not on the radar of MI5. During the war Australian Military Intelligence did check out Rose's wife, Edith Linde, a German national, but showed little interest in Rose. He did, however, come to the attention of Australian security services after the war, due to his membership in the Communist Party of Australia (CPA), which he joined in 1942. Rose expected that with his Cambridge degree he would find some form of employment or financial assistance to study Aboriginal people. He arrived in hope. He had no institutional support, no academic supervisor or mentor, no supporting or introductory letters from his teachers at Cambridge, so he sought, successfully, an interview with A. P. Elkin (1871–1979), professor of anthropology at the University of Sydney. Elkin was recognized as the leading scholar of Aboriginal anthropology.

The Sydney department, consisting of the professor, a lecturer in Melanesian anthropology, and a linguistics lecturer assisted by temporary lecturers, was the only anthropology department in any of Australia's six state universities. Funding for research was limited to those projects previously funded by the Rockefeller Foundation funds from 1926 to 1935. This was supported by internal university funding. A further source of funding was the New South Wales Aboriginal Welfare Board, of which Elkin was vice-chairman, for investigation into adjustment and assimilation policies. Funding restrictions meant that Elkin focused on matters associated with assimilation in urban and rural New South Wales (Gray 2000). Elkin suggested Rose have a look at the situation of Aboriginal people at La Perouse on Botany Bay, a fifteen-minute tram ride from the city.[8] Rose found the Aboriginal people he encountered a very depressed group, far from what he envisaged.[9] Without realizing it he had missed a funding opportunity. Rose's interest, however, was firmly fixed on finding supposedly pristine, untouched Aboriginal people. He decided to train as a meteorologist, which he thought would enable him to work in northern Australia and in his spare time investigate Aboriginal life and help establish his credentials as an anthropologist.

Rose travelled to Melbourne to do his training. While there he contacted Donald Ferguson Thomson (1905–1970), considered one of Australia's leading anthropologists outside the Sydney networks (Rigsby and Peterson 2005; Gray 2005a). Thomson had no department, no students, and no funding for visiting researchers, only a personal chair. Thomson advised Rose to gain experience by working among Aboriginal people living along the railway line from Darwin to Birdum in the Northern Territory.[10] It seems Thomson, like Elkin, saw Rose as ill-equipped to conduct fieldwork away from the centers of settlement.

On completion of his training Rose was sent by the Commonwealth Meteorological Bureau to establish a weather station at Groote Eylandt, a staging post for flying boat flights to and from London.[11] The Church Missionary Society (CMS) established Groote Eylandt Mission in 1921 at Emerald River. Museum of South Australia curator and ethnographer Norman Tindale (1900–1993) visited at that time (McCaul and Roberts 2015). By 1924 the mission operated a school and dormitories for Aboriginal children from the mainland. After 1933 most local children were sent to Roper River Mission at Mirlinbarrwarr on the mainland.[12] Rose sought permission to make contact with "the Native inhabitants for the purpose of anthropological study."[13] This was granted. Rose was largely confined to working with people on the Groote Eylandt Native Settlement (a private reserve) at Umbakumba, the east side of the island and the site of the flying boat base. It was supervised by the reserve's "protector" Fred Gray, and his wife Marjorie (Rose 1968, 133). Groote Eylandt was by no means a site of untouched culture, which Rose acknowledged in *Australia Revisited* (Rose 1968, 130–42). Nevertheless, he investigated and recorded Aboriginal life, concentrating on kinship. This work was interrupted when he was sent to establish a weather station at Broome in northwest Western Australia.

Rose applied to A. O. Neville (1875–1954), the West Australian chief commissioner of Native Affairs, for a permit to visit Aboriginal reserves in the Broome area. Initially he wanted to make a "representative collection of the material culture" (Rose to Neville, 26 June 1939) of the area for the University Museum of Archaeology and Ethnology at Cambridge University. After enquiries were made by the resident magistrate and the local police Neville denied him permission.[14] Rose persisted. He sought permission to photograph Aboriginal people at Beagle Bay Mission. It was denied. Neville asked the Inspector of Natives at

Broome to make further inquiries regarding Rose's actions, as he had been in the area for several months. Neville wanted further information on Rose's behavior and intent.[15] There was always the suspicion that, without institutional support and oversight, such activities could be a front for gaining access to Aboriginal women.[16] Were his studies of a private nature or was he working in association with some scientific institution?[17] Rose explained that he had "lived in the Northern Territory and Tropical Western Australia (the Kimberley) for the past three years making wide contacts with aboriginals here in Broome, Darwin and in the Groote Eylandt reserve."[18] He provided details of his qualifications as proof that he was a bona fide anthropologist. This satisfied Neville, who guarded his domain assiduously, wary of outside criticism and scrutiny, especially from anthropologists (see Gray 1994a).

Neville received correspondence from Kimberley residents, as well as reports from the local police and protectors, informing him of the behavior of people, especially those who were not regular visitors. In this way he heard that Rose and his "German wife," Edith, had supposedly accompanied A. T. H. Jolly, the district medical officer, on his monthly visit to Beagle Bay.[19] It was reported that Rose had taken photographs. Neville reminded Rose that he did not have permission to take photographs.[20] Rose wrote that he had not taken photographs or visited Beagle Bay with Jolly. It was, however, an opportunity to further underline his scholarly legitimacy, and to that end he informed Neville that he and Jolly were working on "a thesis dealing with the Evolution of Primitive Society and primitive forms of marriage relations" (Rose to Neville, 6 October 1940). He had written to J. H. Hutton (William Wyse Professor of Anthropology, Cambridge), outlining a PhD topic, "The place of the Australian Aborigine in the evolution of society. A vindication of Lewis Morgan."[21] The photographs—head and shoulders, full face and profile—were to "serve as a permanent record of information in an appendix to the thesis."[22] There is no evidence that Hutton accepted Rose's thesis topic. Certainly Rose never went ahead with it.

What he and Jolly wanted to show was that, over the course of evolution, humankind had learned to avoid incest. In short, their argument was that, if patrilineal societies were a later stage of development, why, in "primitive" communities like those in Australia, had patrilineage, in some instances at least, already established itself? Jolly had introduced or reintroduced Rose to Lewis H. Morgan's *Ancient Society* (1877), which argued that the earliest human domestic institution was the matrilineal clan, not the patriarchal family, and to Friedrich Engels's *Origin of the Family* (1884), which used Morgan to posit an argument that the shift from matrilineage to patrilineage was "evidence of the historic defeat of the female sex which heralded the arrival of class society" (Munt 2011, 117–21). Marriage rules, his initial analysis stressed, were based on incest (consanguinity), but later it was economics that underpinned them.[23]

Neville was uninterested in such musings. He reiterated that permission was needed for inducing "any native to take part in the representation of any scene or incident which is being photographed for the purpose of being published or which when photographed is capable of being reproduced in moving pictures or in still pictures of a dramatic character."[24] He had not forgotten S. D. Porteus and Paul Withington's film *The Blonde Captive*, which used photographs and films taken at Beagle Bay (Gray 2006). Neville imposed himself on all matters to do with Aboriginal people in Western Australia, including those of visiting scholars and others interested in Aboriginal cultural and social life. He was a gatekeeper par excellence to the field (Jacobs 1990). Elkin, on the other hand, was gatekeeper to the academic networks; he was keen to control knowledge and was a compiler of people's ethnographic lives, a clerk of their ethnographic records. Moreover, he controlled what funding was available and how it was dispensed.

Rose, still thinking Elkin was supportive of his endeavors, asked him for information on kinship terminology and a copy of a paper on kinship by Ursula McConnel (1936), who had worked in northern Queensland.[25] In return, as was his wont, Elkin sought information from Rose on "an aboriginal from Beagle Bay," a Nyul Nyul man who had been one of Elkin's informants when he had passed through Beagle Bay in 1927–1928.[26] Cassima, as Elkin had named him, was a fully initiated man, a valuable source of ethnographic knowledge, a man familiar with the queries of anthropologists. Rose probably met Cassima (Rose called him Cassimir) when he stayed at the Continental Hotel in Broome, where Cassima/Cassimir was employed doing menial work. Rose inveigled him from the hotel and employed him as a cleaner. Rose supplied Elkin with the information he sought.

Elkin and Rose maintained a regular correspondence. Rose sent Elkin cultural material, some from Nyul Nyul, which included "five [barks] made by Groote Eylandt aboriginals."[27] Rose was attentive to detail. He attached "short descriptions of the artefacts."[28] He described how the barks were prepared, named the painters, and provided an explanation of the meaning of the barks.[29] Elkin considered them "very good samples indeed and your diagrams and descriptions make them all the more valuable."[30] He placed them in the department's ethnographic collection.[31] He offered to assist Rose to make his description of the barks acceptable for publication in the journal *Oceania*, as he frequently did with material sent for publication or for his perusal. Rose took up Elkin's offer and the paper was subsequently published (Rose 1942, 170–76). In spite of Elkin's seeming encouragement there was developing a wide divide over their understandings of Aboriginal life and social organization; material culture was a neutral area.

Possibly emboldened by Elkin's apparent support, Rose sent him an article for publication in *Oceania*, "Mother-in-law Taboo and Moiety societies," which he and Alec Jolly cowrote. In their view the Cambridge anthropologist W. H. R. Rivers (1864–1922) had "missed entirely the dialectic interpretation of fusion viz. progressive avoidance of incest." He surmised that Elkin would "no doubt . . . agree that the article's content is of first importance and you are at liberty to publish it in *Oceania*. You may disagree with some points . . . but I trust you will find space for it."[32] Not only was he confident, he was perhaps arrogant in his assertion that it was suitable for publication. Elkin was recognized as the leading scholar on Australian Aboriginal anthropology. The content and theoretical positioning of Rose's article did not fit *Oceania*. It was a turning point in their professional relationship.

Despite once being attached to "old theories"—Elkin's doctoral thesis was supervised by the diffusionists W. J. Perry (1887–1954) and Grafton Elliot Smith (1871–1937)—Elkin proclaimed Rose engaged in an arcane discussion over the mother-in-law taboo, noting that it was "unfortunate that people read historical meanings into them."[33] Elkin made some observations: Rose was "expecting a highly intellectual attitude to be taken by primitives with regard to exogamy and incest"; he doubted whether all anthropologists accepted the idea of the evolution of patrilineal to matrilineal societies. He queried Rose's idea "that originally there were matrilineal moieties," although he conceded "it may be that in some regions there were matrilineal moieties before patrilineal. . . . It used to be the fashion to do so but, of course, fashions change." Nevertheless, it "would be quite possible to have a patrilineal locally organized society preceding a matrilineal organized one. I am thinking of my experience amongst the Aluridja" in Central Australia (see Elkin 1938c, 419–52; 1939, 41–78).

Elkin had written to the missionary superintendent on Groote Eylandt, L. J. Harris of the Church Missionary Society of Australia. It appears he was checking on Rose's evidence, as Harris informed Elkin that he had "checked two separate families who possess the relationships mentioned by you and the results are the same" (Harris to Elkin 28 May 1943). Harris sent a "few actual genealogies" and was attempting to "get more genealogies etc. in my spare time" which further questioned Rose's data.[34]

Despite this rebuff from Elkin, Rose considered his findings so important that he sent a "major" paper—"Relationship System of the Groote Island Aborigines"—to the minister of the Department of the Interior, seeking to have it published as a government report. It was over four hundred foolscap pages long with over four hundred photographs. He described "the research work and method of approach as entirely original . . . among Aborigines about whom little is known." Moreover, work such as his, he informed the minister, addressed the rapid detribalization (the beginnings of which he witnessed) of Aboriginal people, so that it would be "doubly valuable in the years to come."[35] The old trope "before it's too late" was in play once more.

Naturally, Elkin was asked for an opinion on the quality of the paper.[36] Elkin told the secretary of the Department of the Interior that he was familiar with Rose's previous publications, which he described as "very poor in quality." Elkin made the point that in making this assessment he had "examined the kinship system of Groote Eylandt with the help of my former students," a small exaggeration. In his usual patronizing manner he told him that he hoped "some day [to] have the chance of helping Mr. Rose see the weakness of his arguments and methods, the insufficiency of his observations and the natural and true interpretation of the facts." He assured Carrodus that Rose "does not understand the kinship system, nor indeed Australian kinship"; secondly, Rose's "photographic method" has "some value as an adjunct to the well-tried genealogical method"; and, finally, attempting to vindicate Morgan was "old-hat." He concluded that there was no purpose in printing Rose's manuscript: "It would be a waste of money and would bring adverse criticism from those who understand better."[37] Such publications as Rose's proposal depended on the Department of the Treasury agreeing to fund the printing. Paper was in short supply.

In spite of his poor opinion of the text, Elkin offered to help Rose bring his photographic and statistical method into shape for publication in *Oceania*, an offer Rose declined.[38] Rose remained confident in the worth of his work, and submitted it to *American Anthropology*, where it was similarly rejected. The reviewer wrote that it was his "considered opinion that Mr. Rose's manuscript . . . is not suitable for publication in a reputable American journal such as *American Anthropology*."[39] Rose, not giving up, submitted it to the Royal Society of Victoria, arguing that, while he recognised that a request to publish an ethnographic paper of such size was unusual, the society had previously published a number of large ethnographic papers.[40] It "had undertaken to publish the description of the method employed while at the same time the National Museum in Melbourne has undertaken to meet the cost of limited number of reproductions of the data and photographs."[41] The paper was not published by the society.

After 1942 Rose had one further opportunity to continue his anthropological investigations. In 1948 he was seconded to the American Australian Arnhem Land Expedition (Thomas and Neale 2011). The expeditioners spent about three months investigating cultural and social life on Groote Eylandt. Rose had written to Charles Mountford (1890–1976), leader of the expedition, as early as 1945 with a request to join the expedition; he shared Mountford's distrust of Elkin. He gave Mountford his own notes on Groote Eylandt "social organisation and totems, and negotiated with key elders for the performance of the ceremonial cycle" (Jones 2011, 50–51; Gray 2007a, 192–94).[42]

Although employed as a public servant, he had not given up on finding an academic position. There were, however, few academic positions available in Australia or even the British empire. Indeed, in the United Kingdom there were fewer than a dozen permanent university posts. Fortes reckoned in 1953 that there were "perhaps only twenty British trained anthropologists in the Empire" (cited in Owusu 1975, 19).[43] Having failed to win the chair of geography and anthropology at the University of Aberystwyth, Wales, he turned his attention to the Australian National University (ANU), which had advertised two research fellowships.

Established in 1946, the ANU was a research university consisting of four schools, of which one, the Research School of Pacific Studies, offered research fellowships and doctoral scholarships in anthropology (Foster and Varghese 1996). Rose applied for a research fellowship. There were four applicants: Rose, Cyril Belshaw, Kenneth E. Read, and Lesley Ella Cunningham, a graduate of Sydney university. Belshaw and Read had recently completed doctoral studies at LSE.[44] The university registrar, Ross Hohnen, wrote to the LSE anthropologist Raymond Firth (1901–2002), academic advisor on Pacific Studies to the ANU, that "we used our judgment in excluding Mr. Rose and Miss Cunningham." Hohnen explained the university's view was that Rose's *vita* was not that of a first-class scholar. Cunningham had a BA.[45]

Hohnen informed Rose that "the question of quality was the major factor in determining appointments," implying that he was not considered suitable for the position. Rose responded stating that he had "experience which might be useful" to Firth, so Hohnen asked "him to go away and write a note" which he would pass on. It is a rambling three-page explanation of his anthropological interests, achievements, and differences with the functionalists. He was, he wrote, a functionalist when he left Cambridge "and many were the hours that I have been entranced by Malinowski's facile pen." But Malinowski, he now realized, was solely responsible for "leading anthropology into the backwater in which it now finds itself." It took Rose three years among the Australian Aborigines "to be in a position to reject functionalism," his "metamorphosis as a result of field experience." He had a "new method of approach, particularly with regard to kinship"; he considered "normal anthropological work as 'metaphysical slush.'"[46] He acknowledged that his criticism of functionalism—that it was "anti-evolutionism"—might be "considered presumptuous because of the great eminence of the school's principal exponents. However, such field experience as I have had leads me away from the views held by the accepted contemporary schools of thought and I feel bound to voice my criticism even though it may prevent me, as it apparently has done in the past, from securing academic recognition."[47]

Firth handed it over to S. F. Nadel (1903–1956), foundation professor of anthropology at the ANU, who was in London at the time. Was Rose of any interest? Nadel replied with typical directness:

> Frederick Rose . . . is probably a crank . . . certainly a poor anthropologist, inadequately trained (in spite of his Cambridge degree) and intellectually arrested. . . . In fact I should go beyond pointing out the obsolence [sic] of Rose's anthropological opinions. I would say that a person having his interests and approaching anthropology from his point of view is unlikely to contribute anything of value to the kind of research you and I have in mind.[48]

After this rebuff Rose considered applying for a position of staff anthropologist (sometimes described as government anthropologist) in the Department of District Services and Native Affairs in the Australian Territory of Papua and New Guinea.

The newly appointed administrator of Papua and New Guinea, J. K. Murray (1889–1979), invited Elkin to visit. It was his first trip to Papua and New Guinea. Asked to advise on a number of matters, Elkin argued for the importance of appointing a government anthropologist, preferably a husband and wife team who could put in twenty years and thus "become familiar with the native background and thought in some large part of the region."[49] He had in mind his protégés Ronald and Catherine Berndt (Gray 2005b, 77–106).[50]

Elkin's suggestion was picked up by the anthropologically trained educationalist William C. Groves (1898–1967), the director of education, who, with the support of the newly appointed director of health, John T. Gunther (1910–1984), "put up a proposition for a specified term appointment of a male and female Anthropologist to work almost exclusively on problems of depopulation, which, of course, have particular reference to health factors" (Murray to Elkin, 10 July 1951). General approval was given by the Papua and New Guinea administration but refused by the minister for territories, Paul Hasluck (1905–1993) (Gray 1994a, 195–213). Murray explained the difficulties in getting the idea for anthropologists off the ground.

> I was rather hoping that the ways in which the advertisement for [an] anthropologist in this Territory would be advertised and worded might allow of their [Ronald and Catherine Berndt] joining the Administration but there have been a great deal of cross purposes and, I think, misunderstandings involved in consideration of anthropological work which it is desirable should be undertaken in this Territory. The views of Dr. Gunther and Mr. Groves for instance are far from coinciding with those of Messrs. Jones and Ivan Champion [director and assistant director, District Services respectively], and, in addition there are the requirements of the ASOPA [Australian School of Pacific Administration].[51]

The upshot was it became a staff position in the Department of District Services and Native Affairs and limited to the requirements of that department and "not available . . . for the purposes of other departments such as Health and Education."[52]

Rose considered himself an ideal candidate. He was sure his lack of experience and knowledge about Papua and New Guinea would not be a problem.[53] As with all applications for Papua and New Guinea, ASIO was alerted. In a handwritten memo it was stated that Rose was "a security risk and his appointment as anthropologist to the Department of District Services and Native Affairs . . . is not recommended." The grounds for this recommendation were his association with Alec Jolly, his membership and his appointment as "official anthropologist" of the CPA.[54]

It is likely his application would have been given only cursory consideration as Charles Julius, a 1937 Sydney graduate (he had a research MA from Sydney) was the preferred candidate.[55] Groves had informed Elkin that "I have reason to know that Julius will be selected."[56] Julius had experience in Papua before the war as an education officer, and during the war he was with the Australian New Guinea Administrative Unit (ANGAU), the military government of Papua and New Guinea. After the war he was senior research officer in the Department of Education, where he planned the "special training in principles of Native Education [which] every incoming Education Officer" was required to take. He was part of a research section in the education department that Groves envisaged including not only Julius (anthropology), but Stephan Wurm (linguistics), and a "third person specialized in Applied or Educational Psychology." He was confident it would be a "pretty strong research team able to do the work which I have always been convinced was essential to the development of a fully-satisfactory educational organization for this Territory."[57] Julius's appointment to district services signaled the collapse of Groves's grand scheme. Having failed to ban the Communist Party, Australian Prime Minister Robert Menzies (1894–1978) established the Royal Commission into Espionage; it smeared left-wing politicians and intellectuals, although its proclaimed purpose was to uncover a Soviet spy ring in Australia.[58] Rose's reputation was destroyed after he reluctantly appeared as a witness.[59] Deemed a security risk, he was downgraded and forced to leave the public service.[60] Rose sailed for the German Democratic Republic in 1956. His wife and their three children had preceded him in 1953.[61] A new life beckoned, one where he was able to realize his lifelong ambition of being appointed to an academic institution.

Before he left Australia, his father-in-law, Richard Linde, a patents lawyer in the GDR, arranged for Rose to be offered a teaching position at Humboldt University in East Berlin. After some difficult negotiations, Rose was awarded his Habilitation for his previously unpublished manuscript, "Classification of Kin, Age Structure and Marriage Amongst the Groote Eylandt Aborigines: A Study in Method and a Theory of Australian Kinship." It was published in 1960 with the same title.[62] He was forty-five years old. He was appointed professor and head of anthropology soon after.[63]

The establishment of the Australian Institute of Aboriginal Studies (AIAS) in 1961 was an unexpected opportunity for scholars in Aboriginal Studies. It was not formally established until 1964 but it was in receipt of funds for research several years earlier.[64] University funding for Aboriginal research was limited, so the AIAS in effect increased funding for academic anthropologists under the rubric of Aboriginal Studies. As anthropologist Jeremy Beckett commented, "there was money like Aboriginal research had never seen before" (Beckett 2001, 96).[65]

William C. Wentworth (1907–2003), a strident anti-communist parliamentarian, and the politically conservative W. E. H. Stanner (1905–1981), reader in anthropology at the ANU, founded the AIAS (Lambert 2011; Clohesy 2010).[66] It was unsympathetic to unorthodox research projects (Lambert 2011, 63–84). It took no interest in urban or rural Aboriginal people, seeing such research as the domain of state Aboriginal welfare departments or sociology. Broadly speaking, its brief was to record and collect the remaining cultural knowledge of Aboriginal people "before it was too late."[67] Its founders expected to have their work complete within a decade, when all available knowledge of traditional Aboriginal life would be safely deposited (and captured) in the institute's archives.

Of course Rose wanted to continue his work on Aboriginal kinship. To this end he planned a secret trip to Australia so that he would not be stopped at his point of entry.[68] He was worried that he could be refused entry or even lose his passport.[69] He also wanted to make a personal presentation for research funds. He attempted to enlist the support of Elkin, who was lukewarm. He had retired in 1955, although he remained editor of the journal *Oceania*. He was no longer the sole authority on Aboriginal ethnography and his influence had waned. Rose sought advice from the director of the Research School of Pacific Studies at the ANU, who promptly informed ASIO. He also wrote to Minister for Territories Paul Hasluck to seek funds for a research project comparing Walbiri and Pintupi in Central Australia with his findings on Groote. Hasluck, like the others, was unable to provide any funding and advised Rose to apply to the AIAS, which he did.[70]

The Interim Council of AIAS, chaired by Arthur Dale Trendall (professor of Greek and deputy vice-chancellor of the ANU) consisted of sixteen members drawn from government, academia, and business. The AIAS anthropology committee, which made recommendations on research proposals to the Interim Council, advised against Rose's application.[71] The reasons were scientific, academic, and political. First, the

University of Melbourne anthropologist Donald Thomson "had firm plans" to work in Eastern Arnhem Land and it was "thought he should have ... priority" (Interim Council Minutes, AIATSIS, File 65/85 Part 1). Thomson, a member of the committee known for his concern over the disruption to Aboriginal people caused by contact, added that, in order to avoid unduly disrupting the Aboriginal way of life, it would not be wise to sponsor fieldwork in this area by others (see Thomson 1936, 1937a, 1937b). Secondly, Rose's field—kinship studies—was "highly specialized" and not a priority for the AIAS. Thirdly, there was concern he would "adjust the facts to his (Morganite-Marxist) theories."[72] It was the decision hoped for by ASIO. The director-general of ASIO, Brigadier Charles Spry, firmly believed that communists—individually and collectively—were "disloyal to Australia, if not actively subversive on behalf of the Soviet Union" (Maher 1998, 343). Rose was, in his view, a representative of a hostile foreign government. Indeed Spry believed there were at least sixty thousand potential subversives in Australia.[73]

The government was well aware of Rose's propensity to seek publicity and the subsequent likelihood of questions in Parliament. The prime minister's representative on the Interim Council, E. J. B. Foxcroft, advised that the prime minister should deny any knowledge if questioned. He should, however, inform the Parliament that he would endeavor to ascertain the reasons from the AIAS. His minister for territories, Paul Hasluck, would provide an explanation if needed.

Rose was sure his unsuccessful application was due to his past, his membership in the CPA, and his residence in the GDR. He made an appeal for support from his fellow anthropologists to bring pressure to bear on the government. No local academic support for Rose was forthcoming. There was no need to get offside with the government by publicly supporting Rose; after all, the decision was made by an eminent and senior group of scholars.[74] It is not surprising, nonetheless, that those making decisions at AIAS had vested interests in supporting their colleagues, their students, and each other. Moreover, Rose's kinship studies, it needs be stressed, were at this time considered anachronistic, and his published work, *Classification of Kin*, had not found support from the Australian anthropological establishment. Peter Worsley, for example, described it as "the work of one initially trained in an older school of anthropology who, however, used his own wits, sharpened by natural-scientific training, to construct a rigidly methodical analytical procedure" (Worsley 1963, 77). To sum up: Rose's reputation internationally as anthropologist was limited to the GDR, and to a few scholars in the West who were interested in Marxist kinship studies (Kauffman 1978; Munt 2011).

Lacking funds and a permit to enter a government Aboriginal reserve, he ended up at Angas Downs, a cattle station owned by Arthur Liddle, whom Rose described as a half-caste. Rose worked for his keep. He was free to pursue his research unhindered by ASIO or government authorities. From this research he produced *The Wind of Change in Central Australia*, far removed from his aim to continue researching traditional Aboriginal life, especially kinship. He wrote to Aboriginal historian and Arrente man Gordon Briscoe that "personally I have never regarded this [research] as important ... although I appreciate—as you do—its historical implications as a piece of ethnography describing a group in the process of change i.e. as a slab of local history."[75]

He returned to Australia in 1965. He did not seek funding from AIAS. Taking advantage of his notoriety, he held a press conference at CPA headquarters in Sydney, where he explained that his intention was to investigate the living conditions of Aboriginal people, noting that "Australia does not stand very high in the east or the west because of its unjust treatment of Aborigines."[76] He explained he had no intention on this visit to enter reserves. He traveled around Australia without hindrance but surveillance remained.[77] He visited Groote Eylandt as part of a union delegation but he was not able to conduct research other than taking photographs and generally engaging in superficial observation. By this time there was a manganese mine on the island. He remained on the island for two days. There is little doubt that the visit to Australia was to highlight the shortcomings of Australian treatment of its Aboriginal inhabitants, matters on which Rose had commented previously. He produced two books for a German audience.[78] For English speakers he wrote *Australia Revisited: The Aborigine Story from Stone Age to Space Age* (Rose 1968).

Not deterred by his previous failure, he applied to the AIAS for research funding in 1968. W. C. Wentworth, who led the attack on

Communists and fellow travelers in the Australian Parliament (Clohesy 2010), was present at the council meeting but conveniently missed most of the first day, when the discussion on Rose's application took place. There is no written evidence that he tried to influence the council's decision, which doesn't preclude discussions he may have had before or after the meeting. In the same year Wentworth noted Rose's role in the Royal Commission on Espionage, saying that "it is not just that Professor Rose is a Communist . . . he has had a particularly bad record of treachery and he has prostituted his position as an anthropologist to further the aims of the Communist Party."[79] His attempts to block Rose even extended to a plan he canvassed with then Attorney General Billy Snedden to deny Rose entry to Australia. They did not proceed with it as it would have given Rose undue prominence. Overall, whether Rose was awarded a grant mattered little as far as Wentworth was concerned, as he could be confident that Harry Giese, the director of welfare in the Northern Territory, would not grant Rose a permit to enter Groote Eylandt.[80] The AIAS could therefore appear as though "political matters were not its concern" (Barnes 1969, 27; Turner 1979, 18).[81]

It was an ambitious project: "Proposal for Social Anthropological Research among Four Tribes of Australian Aborigines." After the council rejected Rose's initial proposal, he modified it on the advice of University of Sydney anthropologist L. R. Hiatt (1931–2008); again it was rejected.[82] His third attempt, focusing on Groote Eylandt, was successful. A condition of the grant was that if he was denied a permit to enter Groote Eylandt, it would be rescinded. In spite of the problems already encountered, and the uncertainty of obtaining a permit, Rose arrived in Australia at the end of May 1968. Keen to establish that he was a bona fide researcher, and to counter the idea that he was a threat to the good governance of Aboriginal people, Rose announced that all he wanted "to do was study their kinship, marriage and age structure."[83] He described himself in the article as an "objective scientist," and a "friend of the Native." Rose stressed that he was a "scientist," not an agitator, a pointed response to Wentworth's charge that he had prostituted his position as an anthropologist.

Despite newspaper stories highlighting Rose's position, the end result was that the Northern Territory government did not alter its stance.

So Rose travelled to Darwin where he made another unsuccessful attempt to get a permit.[84] Again he traveled as part of a union delegation to Groote Eylandt but was forcibly removed. He then travelled from Darwin to Wave Hill to support Gurindji pastoral workers who were on strike over land, labor conditions, and treatment of women by white stockmen. He stayed there for two days (Hardy 1968; Attwood 2003, 257–82; Hokari 2011; Ward 2016).

Rose left Australia soon after, but not before attempting to create trouble for the government. With little firsthand knowledge, but no doubt informed by his North Australian Workers Union comrades, he handed out a press release that stated there was the "possibility of violence on Groote Eylandt because of the increasing resentment among the local population. B H P [Broken Hill Proprietary Co.], with the help of the government, was riding roughshod over the cultural heritage of the Aborigines."[85] The government brushed aside such allegations. Yet it was not without substance, as alluded to by anthropologist David H. Turner (who had his own problems obtaining a permit to enter Groote Eylandt) the following year (Turner 1979; Brian 2001, 273).[86]

Turner, a University of Western Australia doctoral student, was denied entry to Groote Eylandt the year after Rose, despite having "secured written permission to stay from the local Aborigines at the local mission and government settlement and even from the Administration's own representative on the island" (Turner 1979, 17). After patiently sorting out the Northern Territory's decision, it was reversed. Turner had no political affiliation and he had not published any damning articles or made critical statements. A S I O had asked the Royal Canadian Mounted Police for information on Turner, as it had done with other anthropologists. The government had to show, Turner argued, that it was not against research per se, only "against subversive researchers, like Rose" (Turner 1979, 17). Two years later, in 1971, he was once more refused a permit. This time he thought it was due to the closeness anthropologists have with the people they study, which resonates with the idea that researchers are inherently subversive. This creates problems for administrators—colonial officials—as well as for the local Aboriginal population. There was a need to be patient and work with officials, missions, and Aboriginal people despite the obstacles and contradictions, a luxury Rose did not have (Turner 1979, 22). Indeed, it would not have mattered what approach Rose took.

In December 1972 a Labor government replaced the conservative Liberal Country Party Coalition government that had been in power for twenty-three years. The new government established a separate Department of Aboriginal Affairs. The minister, Gordon Bryant (1914–1991), was a longtime advocate for a change in the status of, and civic rights for, Aboriginal people. He set up the National Aboriginal Consultative Council, the first official body to represent Indigenous interests.[87] There had also been changes at a local level that gave Aboriginal Councils the ability to recommend (if not decide) who could come onto their land, although it did not necessarily alleviate the influence of government and mission authorities (Turner 1972, 1979). Former ANU anthropologist J. A. Barnes (1918–2010) had argued, several years earlier, that researchers should ascertain whether Aboriginal people were interested in their research and be enabled to review and comment on the proposed research. Barnes, as an AIAS council member, had proposed that the council adopt a system "whereby aboriginals decide on their visitors and on the extent to which they will co-operate in scientific inquiries" (Barnes 1969, 27–30). This was a radical view that was taken up some years later and is now standard practice in the AIATSIS ethical guidelines.[88] This shifted the way in which researchers and Aboriginal people negotiated over research proposals.

Coincidentally, with the change of government there had been a change at AIAS. Peter Ucko (1938–2007), a young archaeologist from Southampton University in the United Kingdom, had been appointed principal. He brought a fresh perspective, an energetic disposition, and an enthusiasm for change, and broadened the research agenda. His appointment also coincided with an increase in the budget, which led to more internal appointments and increased funding for external research grants. The change of government, a new minister who had supported Rose in the past, and a new principal must have given Rose hope.

In March 1973 Rose was awarded a grant to undertake research to examine the changes, especially in kinship and marriage rules, that had occurred on Groote Eylandt since his last fieldwork in 1941 (and his short stay in 1948).[89] He was in receipt of data from Peter Worsley and David Turner, so he had a base from which he could work. Like Rose, they were interested in the structure and function of traditional marriage relationships. Turner, as indicated earlier, had recently completed fieldwork on Groote Eylandt (Turner 1974).[90]

Rose applied for permission to enter Groote Eylandt, which was now administered by an Aboriginal Council. He may not have been aware of the difficulties Turner had experienced in 1971, or he simply disregarded them as there was a new government and a supportive minister. An Aboriginal Council had assumed legal responsibility for Angurugu and Umbakumba, and former superintendents were renamed community advisors. BHP had built Alyangula, a town north of Angurugu, where most of the Europeans who worked on manganese mining lived.[91] Turner had noted that the "island was a sensitive area. . . . A manganese mine had been established in 1966 and a prawning factory was getting underway in 1969. At that time, the Aboriginal population was 800 and the White was 200 and rising" (Turner 1979, 18).

This time Rose was not denied entry by the minister or the Northern Territory administration acting on ASIO advice. Rather, he was informed that the Commonwealth Department of Aboriginal Affairs had been unable to obtain "any firm expression of opinion from the islanders" on Rose's proposed research. In fact, the chairman of the combined Groote Eylandt Aboriginal Council had informed Aboriginal Affairs in Darwin that they did not want to see Rose on this visit. Turner was also refused because the Aboriginal Council did not want him. Perhaps they had had enough visitors—foreign mine workers, managers, anthropologists, and missionaries. This is certainly a point made by Kauffman (1978, 9–11).

After representations from Rose, the minister decided that, as there was no evidence that the joint council had discussed Rose's proposed visit and fieldwork, the department would arrange for a "suitable Aborigine" to negotiate on Rose's behalf. The representative sent to negotiate returned empty handed.

With funds authorized by Bryant, Rose travelled to Darwin in the hope that he could personally resolve what he portrayed as an impasse. In anticipation of being granted a permit he had begun field work with

Groote Eylandt Aborigines at Bagot Reserve, Darwin. According to Rose they encouraged him to persist with seeking a permit. Rose suggested to Aboriginal Affairs that "Kulpejer (77), Albert (118), India (121) and Nengbinarra (159)" should be invited to meet with him. (The numbers and names corresponded with those in his *Classification of Kinship*.)

His plans were dealt a blow, however, when he received a telegram (transcribed in a letter to Peter Ucko) dated 14 September 1973, via Aboriginal Affairs, from India Mamarika (121), chairman of the joint council: "We do not know why professor rose wants to come stop if he wants to talk about old ways tell him to see fred gray who knows about Groote Eylandt stop people still say definitely no but please send us a message to tell us why he wanted to come." It is difficult to ascertain why Rose received such an impersonal response from people he confidently believed would remember him warmly and facilitate his research. Fred Gray stated that if he were superintendent of Umbakumba he "would welcome him back as a helper" and he was confident that "so would the Andilyaugaugwa people."[92] Rose ignored the dismissive tone of the telegram, and set out what he wanted to do on the island. He also sent a copy of *Classification of Kin*, a massive 572 pages. It is unlikely his book would have clarified his research proposal, other than to affirm the belief of council members that he was interested in the past. It was most likely the first time people on Groote had seen any of his publications or realized what he was doing.[93] The council did not bother to reply.

So, how was Rose remembered? Did his past brief and uninvited visit with union officials have an impact on their decision? Were the local people tired of anthropologists? It is difficult to ascertain what factors were in play. Rose seemed unfamiliar with the changes that had occurred since his 1948 visit. Medical anthropologist D. C. Biernoff, who was in Eastern Arnhem Land in 1972, reported a change of context for anthropologists: "The old men . . . are anxious that Europeans, particularly those in positions of authority and those in close contact with the tribal groups, *learn about those things which are of importance to tribal people.* . . . Many of the ceremonial leaders in Eastern Arnhem Land believe that if the 'law' can once more become strong, at least in their countries, their people will regain their lost strength, security and tranquillity."[94] Rose's research project on kinship, marriage rules, and change was not, it appears, of much interest to Groote Eylandters. Rose's visit also occurred at the beginning of the outstation movement—the movement of local groups away from established settlements to recreate their own communities on land to which they have traditional claims (Peterson and Myers 2016; cf. Turner 1979). These factors most likely weighed on the minds of council leaders.

It is not surprising, nor unreasonable, that he inferred outside sources influenced the council's decision. Rose, an egotistical man, feeling persecuted and paranoid, wrote to Ucko: "The official departmental view . . . is that mine was a specific case of a general apathy of the Aborigines towards anthropologists . . . exacerbated in my case by visiting illegally [in 1968]. The official view would also be that the Aborigines on Groote Eylandt . . . had not been subjected to outside manipulation or influence. . . . For my part, [I] do not accept this simplistic view."[95] He was unable to entertain the possibility that local people were able to make decisions independently (even if in line with administrators and missionaries), or that they could be uninterested in his research.[96] Turner certainly offers a more nuanced explanation that retains the integrity of Aboriginal decision making. Moreover, in a later article he points to the divisions within particular groupings and individuals (Turner 1979), which may have been factors in Rose's case.

Not one to give up, Rose manufactured an interest in photographing the ruins of the old flying boat base in an attempt to circumvent the council's decision, apparently for a book he was writing. The minister could not go against the decision of the council so it was suggested, by someone in the minister's office, that Rose should take his own initiative and the minister would turn a blind eye. As he had on a previous occasion, he made a quick visit to Groote Eylandt as an organizer of the Federated Miscellaneous Workers Union of Australia, North Australian Workers Union branch. What did Rose expect to achieve? Was it simply a gesture that he could visit the island in spite of the decision of the joint council?[97] Did he wonder what his reception would be among Groote Eylandters? Did he talk with any of the council members? We don't know, as records of these events are silent. It can be assumed that the council was unmoved, and probably irritated.

In one sense Rose treated people on Groote Eylandt as colonized subjects, dependent people unable to act independently. Rose, himself "hardly a colonialist or imperialist, was nevertheless a . . . privileged *white* person, invariably identified with the colonial system of *white* domination by the people he studied" (Owusu 1975, 18). And this is a position he adopted when he arrived unannounced and against the wishes of the council. Rose, as alluded to above, appeared unaware of the changes that decolonization had had on anthropological research and the ability of colonized people to determine, through consultation, research fitted to their needs (Iamo 1992, 75–99; Uddin 2011, 455–67; Berreman 1968; Gjeesing 1968; Gough 1968). By his actions, Rose seemed ignorant of such changes, or disregarded them, sure in the knowledge that such problems could not exist for Marxist anthropologists who were by inference and practice anti-colonial. This attitude led him to misread the people and the situation on Groote Eylandt and Eastern Arnhem Land.

Rose made no further applications for funding, although he remained in contact with AIAS. He continued to visit Australia. On those occasions he was provided with support from AIAS in the form of a room and library access. He also sought to have his *Classification* (1960) and *Winds of Change* (1965) republished by Aboriginal Studies Press.[98] The managing editor of the press responded, grumpily, that there was "no way I would want to reprint books published in 1960 and 1965 by anybody."[99] He was also unenthusiastic over a proposal for a festschrift for Rose.[100] Rose died in Berlin on 14 January 1991.

It was not only his political beliefs that impeded his work as an anthropologist. From the time he arrived in Australia Rose struggled to gain acceptance as an anthropologist, let alone make a career as an academic anthropologist. He faced several obstacles: He was not part of any anthropological network in Britain or Australia; he had no patron who could mentor and promote him; he was poorly qualified to win an academic position in Australia, especially after World War II; and he had no independent funding. To blame Elkin alone for hindering his anthropological career in Australia is to simplify the relationship he had with Elkin, which was at times supportive in spite of opposing theoretical positioning. Elkin could be capricious in his support for fellow anthropologists; Rose was by no means the exception, and in fact Elkin's actions against Piddington far exceeded any against Rose (Gray 1994a; Gray and Munro 2011; see Gray 2005a).[101] His failure to win an academic appointment was due primarily to his theoretical stance and his dismissal of functionalism, as Nadel pointed out. Furthermore, he had not followed the usual sequence of a supervised research degree and thus a proper initiation into the world of professional anthropologists.

Initially the security services took little interest in Rose. War time security did not impede his anthropological research nor his career choices. He was further impeded by other factors, such as his employment in the Australian public service, where he held senior positions. His membership of the CPA and the belief that Rose was a spy led to his (forced) resignation in 1954 from the Australian public service. His membership of the CPA, as well as living in the GDR, were critical factors. On each visit Rose made to Australia his past rose up to defeat him. His research was hindered by the refusal of government authorities to grant him permission to enter government- and mission-run Aboriginal reserves in the Northern Territory, particularly on Groote Eylandt.

His relations with AIAS were problematic. AIAS files scrupulously avoid politics mainly by silence; the minutes of meetings are minimal. The members of the council protected their integrity by pretending to remain at arm's length in the process. AIAS was able to hide behind the knowledge that any problems arising from a research grant, such as the need to obtain permits, were not at its door. The institute deftly avoided any concern for Rose's academic and political freedom. Once the grant had been awarded it was up to the recipient to make arrangements to undertake the research. It was the recipient's responsibility to obtain a permit. Such a demand militated against Rose as ASIO would always file an adverse report.

Rose's treatment by government security services highlights the difficulty progressive left-wing anthropologists had in the Cold War period. Rose's activism was conducted in print, such as writing pamphlets in support of Aboriginal rights groups. He was, for example, critical of the position of Aboriginal people and supported demands for land rights, as did his most strident critic, W. C. Wentworth.[102] To be sure Rose was opposed to the oppression of colonized peoples, but he was able to separate his political activism from his work as an anthropologist, despite his declaration in 1969 that anthropologists should work to liberate oppressed peoples.[103] Peter Worsley, himself subject to ASIO and British MI5 surveillance, states that administrators and settlers were often "'hysterically intolerant' even of those anthropologists whose credentials were impeccably orthodox, or even reactionary" (Worsley 1992, 37). He commented that

> it is hard to see what even the most dedicated Reds like Rose or myself could have hoped to achieve had we set out to agitate among the Aborigines. But we didn't. What both the colonialist and some Marxist accounts fail to grasp is that those of us who did not choose to live "professionally at peace" with colonialism, were nevertheless, qua anthropologists, primarily concerned with intellectual issues, not with agitation. The irony is that Rose, Turner and I produced studies mainly concerned with the intricacies of Aboriginal kinship.[104]

Rose, a man who liked to be the center of attention, made himself a victim, the aggrieved party.[105] This was set out when he was seeking a pension from the Australian government. Rose described himself as "a recognized international, albeit controversial, authority in my discipline of social anthropology." He maintained he was unable to work in Australia because the Royal Commission into Espionage "effectively precluded me from following in Australia my chosen profession for which I had been trained." He had left "my country for my country's good, [and] . . . sought asylum in the GDR."[106] This is an exaggeration. He certainly did not seek asylum; it was a self-imposed exile. He retained his British citizenship and was able to come and go from the GDR without serious restrictions on his movement. The main restriction on his movement in Australia was his lack of access to government reserves.

The conservative Australian government and its security service were linked in denying Rose any semblance of academic or political freedom. He was, however, not the only anthropologist to have his career disrupted or to have been forced to leave Australia to continue their career.[107] No matter how we view Rose's treatment, it is overstating it to claim, as did Worsley (1991, 35), that Rose held the record for "sheer duration of victimization."

Over the course of my work on academic freedom and political perse-
cution of academics by Australian security services, Christine Winter
has been invaluable in so many ways, and I want to acknowledge her
contribution. I would like to thank Doug Munro, Woodrow Denham,
and Phillip Deery for the comments on earlier drafts. Valerie Munt
answered my queries about Rose. Finally, this paper is part of a project
that examines, through selected case studies, academic and political
freedom during the interwar and postwar period in Australia.

1. Rose to Department of Social Services, 21 March 1988, copy in AIAT-
   SIS, 65/85 Part 2. Wiederhutmachung refers to the reparations the
   German government paid directly to the survivors of the Shoah,
   forced laborers, and other victims of the Nazis.
2. https://wellesleyroad.github.io/whitgift.html accessed 10 October 2019.
3. Edmund Leach is scathing in his assessment of Cambridge anthropology
   before World War II. In his view, despite the history propagated at Cambridge that it started in 1901 with the appointment of Haddon and Rivers, "the most remarkable feature of Cambridge anthropology during this
   period was that Haddon and Rivers failed to establish anything at all." His
   successors were former Indian public servants. Anthropology was revived
   by the appointment of Meyer Fortes to the William Wyse Chair.
4. For detailed discussion regarding the foundation of ASIO see Maher
   (1993, 103–18), Horner (2014, 33–121), and Andrew (1989, 226–30). See
   also Ball and Horner (1998) and Manne (2004).
5. Rose studied anthropology under Thomas Callan Hodson, who held
   the first William Wyse Chair of Anthropology from 1932 to 1937. He
   was a retired member of the Indian Civil Service and a writer on
   Indian anthropology although he was not a trained anthropologist (cf.
   Munt 2011, 114).
6. "An Unapologetic Anthropologist." Rose Papers.
7. ASIO officer (unknown), NAA, A6119,1231, vols. 1 and 2.
8. La Perouse is known as Gooriwal to the Muruora-dial people of the
   area (Nixon 1947).
9. http://www.sbs.com.au/news/article/2012/11/29/la-perouses
   -unknown-historical-significance
10. The railway line was completed in 1929 with plans to extend it to Alice
    Springs. It was never completed. http://www.southaustralianhistory
    .com.au/adrail.htm

11. "Lonely Groote Eylandt. Perfect Site for Airport. The Cooee's Progress," newspaper report from a "special representative aboard the "Cooee" on her inaugural flight in the Empire Flying Boat Service," unnamed newspaper, 8 July, 1938. Copy in Rose, box 34.

12. For a brief history of settlement and re-settlement of people on Groote Eylandt see Worsley (1992, 36–43).

13. Cook to Rose, 5 July 1938; Rose to Chinnery, 11 May 1940, Rose Papers, box 39. Elkin to Carrodus, 4 June 1940. NAA, A659, 44/1/4313. Chinnery checked Rose's qualifications with Elkin.

14. Rose to Neville, 26 June 1939, Neville to Resident Magistrate, 7 July 1939; Resident Magistrate to Neville, 13 July 1939; Neville to Rose, 3 August 1939. SROWA, ACC993, 608/39.

15. Neville to Inspector of Natives, Broome, 30 September 1940; Inspector of Natives to Neville, 10 October 1940. WASA: ACC993, 608/39.

16. Rose had a reputation in Canberra as a womaniser.

17. Neville to Rose, 26 October 1940, SROWA, ACC993, 608/39.

18. Rose to Neville, 6 October 1940, SROWA, ACC993, 608/39.

19. Inspector of Natives to Neville, 8 November 1940. SROWA, ACC993, 608/39. Cf. Elkin to Neville, 15 December 1927, SROWA, ACC993, 365/27.

20. Neville to Jolly, 9 December 1940; Neville to Inspector of Natives, 9 December 1940; Jolly to Neville, 13 December 1940; Inspector of Natives to Neville, 24 December 1940. SROWA, ACC993, 608/39.

21. Rose to J. H. Hutton, 3 January 1940. Rose, box 34.

22. Rose to Neville, 16 December 1940, SROWA, ACC993, 608/39. Rose and Jolly, 1942, 15–16; 1943, 44–87; 1942.

23. See F. G. G. Rose, *The Traditional Mode of Production of the Australian Aborigines* (1987).

24. Neville to Rose, 2 January 1941, SROWA, ACC993, 608/39. See Gray (2006, 69–90).

25. Rose to Elkin, 8 November 1940, EP, 40/1/5/52.

26. He spent nearly six months between La Grange, eighty five miles south of Broome and Sunday Island, one hundred and sixty miles north of Broome.

27. Elkin to Rose, 20 December 1940; Rose to Elkin, 21 October 1941; Rose to Elkin, 23 October 1941; also Rose to Elkin, 13 November 1941, EP, 40/1/5/52.

28. The list is three pages. He describes the item and the maker and names the various parts of the object: spear head, bark, etc. The list includes twenty-seven items: spear heads, shafts, traded spears from Roper R.

and Caledon Bay, child's spear, bamboo spear (a fighting spear made only in the southwest as this is the only place bamboo grows), hair string, dilly bag, armbands, necklace, hair girdle, coolaman, and types of paint. Rose to Elkin, 29 January 1942, EP: 40/1/5/52. These were added to the department's collection.

29. Rose to Elkin, 25 August 1941, EP, 40/1/5/52.

30. Elkin to Rose, 9 September 1941, EP, 40/1/5/52.

31. The barks Rose collected are now in the Australian Museum, Sydney. Rose to Jane Forge (AIAS), 11 September 1978. AIATSIS, file 65/85 (Rose) Part 2.

32. Rose to Elkin, 17 September 1941, EP, 40/5/52.

33. Elkin to Rose, 15 October 1941; Rose to Elkin, 21 October 1941; Rose to Elkin, 23 October 1941, EP, 40/1/5/52. "The Place of the Australian Aboriginal in the Evolution of Society: A Vindication of Lewis Morgan." (n. d.) unattributed but most likely sent by Rose to Elkin. Elkin's thesis "was a vast historical survey of burial rites, initiation rites, the making of medicine men and mythology . . . studded with maps on the distribution of circumcision rites, subincision rites, the use of shell and ending with a token bow to Elliot Smith's pet hobbyhorse: the diffusion of mummification rites out of the Egyptian XXI Dynasty" (Wise 1985, 49).

34. Harris to Elkin, 28 May 1943, EP, 40/1/5/51. He attached three pages on "marriage rules," which Elkin used to question Rose's interpretation.

35. Rose to Minister, 15 November 1944. NAA 659, 1944/1/4313. His ignorance of the work by W. Lloyd Warner (1898–1976) in Eastern Arnhem Land is reasonable, because *A Black Civilization: A Social Study of An Australian Tribes* was published in 1937 and Rose had limited access to academic publications.

36. Elkin was considered the unofficial advisor on Aboriginal affairs and "good friend to this department" of the Interior. Carrodus to AL Driver, Administrator (NT), 15 July 1946, NAA, F1, 1946/767.

37. Elkin to Carrodus, 14 March 1945, NAA: A659, 44/1/4313. For a comprehensive discussion on the various anthropologists who worked on kinship problems on Groote see Worsley (1992); Kauffman (1977). See also J. A. Barnes's book *Three Styles of Kinship* ([1971] 2004).

38. Elkin did this for many young anthropologists and his students. It was not an unconditional act of generosity.

39. William Ewart Lawrence to Leslie A. White, 23 December 1949, ROSE, box 34. Lawrence was described as an expert on Aboriginal kinship (see Lawrence and Murdock 1949, 58–65).

40. Rose to Secretary of Royal Society of Victoria, 19 January 1949; Rose to Tindale, 1 August 1949; Tindale to Rose, 5 August 1949. Royal Society to Rose, 19 October 1949. Rose, box 34.

41. Rose to Hohnen, 2 February 1950. FIRTH 7/5/9.

42. Rose was seconded to assist the research of Margaret McArthur, who investigated the quality and quantity of food consumed by the people of Arnhem Land and compiled a groundbreaking report that changed the generally accepted views on women's contribution to Aboriginal diet and social economy.

43. There were few positions available, and until the early 1960s anthropology departments were small. See Gray, Munro and Winter, *Chicanery: Foundation Chairs of Anthropology in Australasia*. Forthcoming.

44. K. E. Read, "The Relationship between Food Production and Social Structure in Simple Societies" (1948); C. S. Belshaw, "Economic Aspects of Culture Contact in Eastern Melanesia, with Special Reference to the Influence of a Monetary Economy" (1949).

45. Hohnen to Firth, 28 February 1950, FIRTH 7/5/9.

46. Elkin to Nadel, 4 September 1952. Nadel to Elkin, 8 September 1952; Elkin to Nadel, 10 September 1952. EP, 41/4/2/414.

47. Rose to Hohnen, 6 February 1950, FIRTH 7/5/9.

48. Nadel to Firth, 24 February 1950, FIRTH 7/5/9. See also Monteath and Munt 2015, 81, 317n2.

49. Before the war there were three government anthropologists: E. W. P. Chinnery in the League of Nations "C" Mandate Territory of New Guinea (1924–1938), and F. E. Williams in the Australian Territory of Papua (1922–1943). William Strong was the chief medical officer and held the position of government anthropologist and he was initially supported by W. E. Armstrong (see Urry 1985); Williams was assistant government anthropologist until 1928, when he replaced Strong on his retirement.

50. Elkin to Murray, 15 September 1949, EP, 172/4/2/217.

51. Murray to Elkin, 10 July 1951, EP, 183/4/2/338

52. Groves to Elkin, 28 August 1951, EP, 182/4/2/325.

53. Historian Peter Elder (2001) argues that, had Rose succeeded in becoming a government anthropologist, an enlightened administration less subservient to the civilizing colonial mission and the colonizer's economic interests may have been possible. Elder misreads the nature and limitations of the position. Elder worked off the position

and influence exerted by the pre-war government anthropologists (see Gray 2003 and Griffiths 1977, for example).

54. Rose to Secretary, Department of Territories, Canberra, n. d. See also Memo, Regional Director, ASIO, ACT, 27 April 1953; Memo, unsigned to "Director" C, 17 October 1951. NAA, A6119/1007, Frederick George Godfrey Rose (vol. 1).

55. Elkin was of the view that a Sydney MA dissertation was the equivalent of an ANU doctoral dissertation. See Gray (2015, 38).

56. Groves to Elkin, 28 August 1951, EP, 182/4/2/325.

57. Groves to Elkin, 28 August 1951, EP, 182/4/2/325. It signaled the collapse of a "New Deal" for Papua and New Guinea and created a hiatus in colonial policy.

58. For a discussion on the Royal Commission and its outcomes see Manne (1987).

59. The official transcript of the proceedings of the royal commission on espionage (1954–1955) contains an account of his travails attending the royal commission. NAA, A6119/1007.

60. See http://guides.naa.gov.au/land-of-opportunity/chapter17/ for an outline of Rose's work for the Australian government.

61. Edith (née Linde) had not seen her family since 1938 when she sailed for Australia and married Rose.

62. Akademie-Verlag, Berlin, c.1960. It is 572 pages and essentially his Habilitationschfrift, Humboldt Universität Berlin. Worsley: "it contains 244 pages of text, another 221 pages of tables showing the kinship terms used by each of 221 Aborigines to refer to other Aborigines (approximately 25,000 'identifications' of between 50 and 60 per cent. of the tribe), 221 photographs of the subjects, plus 20 other photographs and various diagrams" (Man, 193, 77).

63. It was, he declared, "a measure of the magnanimity of the GDR that I [a non-citizen] was given the possibility of rising in my profession to become head of a university department." Rose to Department of Social Services, 21 March 1988, copy in AIATSIS, 65/85 Part 2.

64. It was an independent statutory body funded by the commonwealth government.

65. In the act establishing AIAS, the definition of "aboriginal studies" as "anthropological research and study in relation to the aboriginal people of Australia (including research and study in respect of culture and languages)" enshrined the dominance of anthropology.

66. In May 1961 Stanner convened a conference on the state of knowledge of Aboriginal Studies and to lay out future problems to be investigated (Sheils 1963).

67. Political scientist Colin Tatz, a founding member of the AIAS, characterized it as "near extinction rescue scholarship" (Colin Tatz, pers. comm., 12 February 2014).

68. He was able to travel freely to Australia, which at the time did not recognize the GDR. Other Australians, such as Salomea Genin, who moved from Australia to the GDR, had to relinquish their Australian citizenship and their travel was restricted. https://storymaps.arcgis .com/stories/f668709350ea47e38b07df0541ab8fc0

69. Rose travelled on a British passport. British nationals were able to obtain Australian citizenship and had easy entry into Australia. The Australian government could revoke a passport, as happened with the journalist Wilfred Burchett (based in Vietnam), who like Rose was British born. "In 1955 Burchett lost the British passport on which he had always travelled. He applied for an Australian one and requested that his two children be registered as Australian citizens. At (Sir) Robert Menzies's direction, the government rejected both applications and asked the British Foreign Office not to grant him a new passport" (Heenan 2007). Rose avoided such a situation.

70. AIAS was in the prime minister's department.

71. The anthropology committee convened by Elkin reflected the range of disciplines encompassed by the discipline at that time and included representatives from psychology (Don McElwain) and ethnomusicology (Trevor Jones) as well as anthropologists J. A. Barnes (ANU), W. E. H. Stanner (ANU), J. H. Bell (Sydney), Marie Reay (ANU), D. F. Thomson (Melbourne), Ronald and Catherine Berndt (UWA), and William Geddes (Sydney).

72. Memo, E. J. B. Foxcroft to Prime Minister, 30 April 1962. NAA, A6119/1012 vol. 6, 75.

73. The Australian population in 1960 was 10.3 million.

74. See Gray (2007a) for consequences of questioning the status quo.

75. Rose to Gordon Briscoe, 1 April 1988, AIATSIS, file 65/85 Part 2 (F. G. G. Rose). See Briscoe (2010).

76. "Aborigines Treatment 'Slur on Reputation'" *The Australian* 14 April, 1965.

77. See various folios in NAA, A6119/5025, vol. 7.

78. Both German books were translated from English. Presumably the books met GDR Socialist Unity Party guidelines for propaganda value.

Anthropologist Andre Gingrich, Vienna Academy of Science, University of Vienna, explained to me that Rose's books were well produced, with higher production standards than usual, which was an indication of the status Rose held in the GDR (Andre Gingrich, pers. comm., 19 August 2009). Indeed Worsley commented that "no expense has been spared by his original East German publishers, and it is indeed difficult to conceive of 'Western' publishers producing such a work" (Worsley 1963, 77).

79. Commonwealth Parliamentary Debates, House of Representatives, 4 June 1968, 1887; ASIO Minute Paper on CPA Interest in Aboriginal Affairs, 16 May 1968, NAA, A6119, 4070. See also Spry to Bowen, 17 May 1968, NAA, A6119, 4070.

80. The director general of ASIO provided information on Rose (and other communists) to Wentworth, usually via the attorney general, as the protocol required. ASIO minute on meeting with Wentworth, 28 March 1968; ASIO Minute on Communist influence in Aboriginal Affairs, NAA, A6119, 4070. See also Spry to Billy Snedden, 16 September 1965, NAA, A6119, 4068.

81. The ANU similarly appeared neutral over the appointment of scholars who were declared by ASIO to be communists or suspected to be members of the Communist Party (Gray 2014, 2020).

82. Hiatt was a member of several AIAS committees and later chairman of the council. He was a noted libertarian.

83. *The Age*, "Open Entry Sought to Aboriginal Reserves," 1 June 1968.

84. This situation was creating problems for the AIAS. The following year in response to the institute's "draft application for grant form and code for fieldworkers (the combined fieldwork document)" several members strenuously objected with Les Hiatt, who would later be chair of the AIAS Council, setting out his objections including his objection to the permit system. He referred to the opposition to the permit system articulated by the social anthropology section at the biennial general meeting of the AIAS in May of the previous year. There was "resentment at a situation in which the Institute's scientific task maybe hindered by the stroke of an administrator's pen" (L. R. Hiatt to AIAS Secretary, J. S. Boydell, 21 February 1969, file 64/129, Fieldworkers' conditions and regulations, part 1, AIATSIS). In 1966 the social anthropology group raised the matter of the "growing resistance among Aborigines in some areas to the conduct of fieldwork.... It would appear that this may be due in part ... to thoughtless pressures exerted by scientists intent only on their own concerns" (AIAS

General Meeting Minutes, 18–21 May 1966, Recommendations by the Social Anthropology Group, 5).

85. "Trouble forecast on N.T. Island," *Sydney Morning Herald*, 3 September 1968. See also Rose to the editor, *The Australian*, 7 June 1968.

86. The greatest problem faced by the mining company and the government was industrial action by the white Australian workers.

87. Peter Gifford, "Bryant, Gordon Munro (1914–1991)," Australian Dictionary of Biography, National Centre of Biography, Australian National University, http://adb.anu.edu.au/biography/bryant-gordon -munro-18365/text30004, published online 2015, accessed online 12 March 2020.

88. See Australian Institute of Aboriginal and Torres Strait Islander Studies. Research of Interest to Aboriginal and Torres Strait Islander peoples, 1995–7. Commonwealth of Australia, Canberra. 1999. See also https://aiatsis.gov.au/research/ethical-research/aiatsis-code-ethics.

89. The structure and function of traditional marriage relationships were of major interest to Rose, Worsley, and Turner. Warner's data collected from Groote Eylandt informants between 1927 and 1929 (Warner 1933, 1937) was overlooked. Worsley and Turner were specifically concerned with social and cultural change. Other anthropologists who worked on Groote Eylandt included Tindale (1923, six months), Mountford (1948, three months), van der Leeden (1964–1965; 1972–1973), and Biernoff, (1971–1972). See also Kauffman (1978) and Jefferies (2018).

90. He had little firsthand field experience after 1948. Kauffman (1978, 97), who reviewed the literature on Groote Eylandt and made a two-month field visit in 1977, believes that Rose's data "fairly accurately reflect a pre-settlement distribution of classificatory kin" at the time and was useful in 1978. The fact that Rose was unable to conduct fieldwork after 1948 resulted in an ethnography bounded by ideology, grounded in time: a frozen segment of Aboriginal kinship, which served as the foundation for all his future writing on Groote Eylandt.

91. Groote Eylandt Mining Company (Gemco).

92. "Banned Expert Is Friend of Natives," *The Australian*, 1 June 1968

93. Cf. Monteath and Munt 2015, 251–58.

94. Quoted in Kauffman 1978, 19. My emphasis.

95. Rose to Peter Ucko, 14 September 1973, AIAS file, 65/85 Part 2.

96. Too often in the literature the hand of the white person is always highlighted. It is premised on the idea that colonized people are unable act in their own interests.

97. Aboriginal people would see this as disrespecting their wishes and decisions.

98. Rose to Warwick Dix, 30 March 1988, AIATSIS, 65/85 Part 2.

99. David Horton to Warwick Dix, 21 April 1988, AIATSIS, 65/85 Part 2.

100. David Horton, pers. comm., 5 March 2010.

101. Monteath and Munt (2015) single out Elkin for Rose's failure to establish himself in Australia; he is described as Rose's "nemesis." One of the authors, Valerie Munt, goes so far as to claim Rose's fieldwork findings were suppressed by Elkin (Munt 2011, 124). Elkin retired in 1955 but Monteath and Munt maintain that Elkin continued to pull the strings. More importantly, by the time Rose returned to Australia, there was an expansion of anthropology departments resulting from the growth of the university sector.

102. Wentworth and Rose supported Aboriginal land rights, as historian Bob Boughton documents. So, too, does Lachlan Clohesy, in his 2010 PhD diss, "W. C. Wentworth, Australian Cold Warrior: The Anti-Communism of W.C. Wentworth."

103. "On the New Road for Ethnography in the GDR," n.d. (probably January 1969). Rose papers, box 15.

104. Letters, Peter Worsley, RAIN, no. 53 (December 1982), 12–14.

105. Rose arranged for all his personal papers to be deposited in the Mitchell Library, State Library of New South Wales, Sydney, Australia. This was before the fall of the Berlin Wall and suggests a lack of faith in a united Germany.

106. Rose to Department of Social Services, 21 March 1988, copy in AIATSIS, 65/85 Part 2.

107. This list is not comprehensive: Ralph Piddington never returned to Australia after falling afoul of government authorities and the Australian National Research Council in the early 1930s. Elkin did his best to destroy his career (Gray 1994; Gray and Munro 2011, 70–71). The German communist anthropologist Paul Kirchhoff, denied entry to Australia in 1931, was unable to undertake fieldwork in British colonial Africa, but found a safe refuge in Mexico (Gray 2009). Phyllis Kaberry moved her research site from the Mt. Margaret mission station to the Kimberley after being denied entry to the mission station (Gray 2002). Olive Pink was marginalized for her views (Marcus 1987; Cheater 1989). Peter Worsley made a shift from anthropology to sociology (Worsley 1992; Gray 2014). Jeremy Beckett was refused entry to Papua New Guinea, as were Jack Golson, Max Gluckman, and Bill Epstein (Gray 1993, 1998,

2020; Beckett 2001). Ronald and Catherine Berndt were denied permits to visit Aboriginal reserves in the 1940s (Gray 2019). David H. Turner was initially denied entry to Groote Eylandt (Turner 1972, 1979).

REFERENCES

Archival sources

AIAS/AIATSIS. Australian Institute of Aboriginal Studies/ Australian Institute of and Torres Strait Islander Studies, Canberra.

EP. Elkin Papers, University of Sydney Archives.

FIRTH. Archive of Sir Raymond Firth, British Archive of Political and Economic Science, London School of Economics (FIRTH, followed by series, box and file numbers).

NAA. National Archives of Australia.

ROSE. FGG Rose Papers, uncatalogued and unsorted mss, Mitchell Library, State Library of New South Wales.

SROWA. State Records Office of Western Australia, Perth.

Published sources

Andrew, Christopher. 1989. "The Growth of the Australian Intelligence Community and the Anglo-American Connection." *Intelligence and National Security* 4, no. 2: 226–30.

Ball, Desmond and David Horner. 1998. *Breaking the Codes: Australia's KGB Spy Network, 1944–1950.* Sydney: Allen & Unwin.

Barnes, J. A. 1969. "Politics, Permits and Professional Interests: The Rose Case." *Australian Quarterly* 41, no. 1: 17–31.

Beckett, Jeremy. 2001. "Against the Grain: Fragmentary Memories of Anthropology in Australia." In *Before It's Too Late*, edited by Geoffrey Gray 82–100. Sydney: Oceania Monograph 51.

Berreman, Gerald D. 1968. "Is Anthropology Alive? Social Responsibility in Social Anthropology." *Current Anthropology* 9, no. 5: 391–435.

Boughton, Bob. 2001. "The Communist Party of Australia's Involvement in the Struggle for Aboriginal and Torres Strait Islander Peoples' Rights 1920–1970." In *Labour and Community: Historical Essays*, edited by Raymond Markey, 82–100. Wollongong: University of Wollongong Press.

Buckley-Moran, Jean. 1986. "Australian Scientists and the Cold War." In *Intellectual Suppression: Australian Case Histories, Analysis and Responses*, edited by Brian Martin, Ann Baker, Clyde Manwell, and Cedric Pugh, 11–23. Sydney: Angus and Robertson.

Brian, Bernie. 2001. "The Northern Territory's One Big Union: The Rise and Fall of the North Australian Worker." PhD diss, Northern Territory University (Charles Darwin University).

Briscoe, Gordon. 2010. *Racial Folly: A Twentieth Century Aboriginal Family.* Canberra: ANU Press.

Cain, F. M. 1983. *The Origins of Political Surveillance in Australia.* Sydney: Angus and Robertson.

Cheater, Christine. 1989. "Olive Pink and the 'Native Problem.'" *Olive Pink Bulletin* 1, no. 1: 14–16.

Clohesy, Lachlan. 2010. "Australian Cold Warrior: The Anti-Communism of WC Wentworth," PhD diss. Melbourne: Victoria University.

Deery, Phillip. 2000. "Scientific Freedom and Postwar Politics: Australia, 1945–55." *Historical Records of Australian Science* 13, no. 1: 1–18.

Elder, Peter. 2001. "The Winds of Change: E.W.P. Chinnery (1887–1972) and F.G.G. Rose (1915–1991) in the Australian Territories." *South Pacific Journal of Philosophy and Culture* 5: 50–93.

Elkin, A. P. 1938a. *The Australian Aborigines; How to understand them.* Sydney: Angus and Robertson.

———. 1938b. "Anthropological Research in Australia and the Western Pacific, 1927–1937," *Oceania* 8, no. 3: 306–27.

———. 1938c. "Kinship in South Australia." Part 1. *Oceania* 8, no. 4: 419–52.

———. 1939. "Kinship in South Australia." Part 2. *Oceania* 9, no. 1: 41–78.

Forsyth, Hannah. 2015. "The Russell Ward Case: Academic freedom in Australia during the Cold War." *History Australia* 11, no. 3: 31–52.

Foster, Stephen and Margaret Varghese. 1996. *The Australian National University, 1946–1996.* Sydney: Allen & Unwin.

Gjeesing, Gutorm. 1968. "The Social Responsibility of the Social Scientist." *Current Anthropology* 9, no. 5: 391–435.

Goody, Jack. 1969. *Comparative Studies in Kinship.* Stanford CA: Stanford University Press.

———. 1995. *The Expansive Moment: Anthropology in Britain and Africa 1918–1970.* London: Cambridge University Press.

Gough, Kathleen. 1968. "New Proposals for Anthropologists." *Current Anthropology* 9, no. 5: 391–435.

Gray, Geoffrey. 1993. "Sympathetic Collaboration: Anthropologists, the Australian National Research Council and Government." *Olive Pink Society Bulletin* 5, no. 1: 23–26.

———. 1994a. "'Piddington's Indiscretion': Ralph Piddington, the Australian National Research Council and Academic Freedom." *Oceania* 64, no. 3: 217–45.

———. 1994b. "'I was not consulted in any way about matters in New Guinea': A. P. Elkin, Papua New Guinea and the Politics of Anthropology, 1942 to 1950." *Australian Journal of Politics and History* 40, no. 2: 195–213.

———. 1998. "(This Often) Sympathetic Collaboration: Anthropologists, Academic Freedom and Government." *Humanities Research* 2(1998): 37–61.

———. 2000. "[The Sydney school] seem[s] to view the Aborigines as forever unchanging: Southeastern Australia and Australian Anthropology." *Aboriginal History* 24: 176–200.

———. 2003. "There Are Many Difficult Problems: Ernest William Pearson Chinnery—Government Anthropologist." *Journal of Pacific History* 38, no. 3: 313–30.

———. 2005a. "A Deep-seated Aversion or a Prudish Disapproval: Donald Thomson and AP Elkin." In *Donald Thomson: The Man and Scholar*, edited by Bruce Rigsby and Nicolas Peterson. Canberra: Academy of the Social Sciences in Australia.

———. 2005b. "'You Are . . . My Anthropological Children': AP Elkin, Ronald Berndt and Catherine Berndt, 1940–1956." *Aboriginal History* 29: 77–106.

———. 2006. "Looking for Neanderthal Man, Finding a Captive White Woman: The Story of a Documentary Film." *Journal of the Australian and New Zealand Society for the History of Medicine Health and Society* 8, no. 2: 69–90.

———. 2007a. *A Cautious Silence: A Political History of Australian Anthropology*. Canberra: Aboriginal Studies Press.

———. 2007b. "'Cluttering up the department': Ronald Berndt and the Distribution of the University of Sydney Ethnographic Collection." *reCollections: Journal of the National Museum of Australia* 2, no. 2: 153–79. http://recollections.nma.gov.au/issues/vol_2_no2/papers/cluttering_up_the_department/

———. 2009. "Not Allowed to Stay and Unable to Leave: Paul Kirchhoff's Quest for a Safe Haven, 1931–1941." *Histories of Anthropology Annual* 5. Lincoln: University of Nebraska Press.

———. 2014. "'A Great Deal of Mischief Can be Done': Peter Worsley, the Australian National University, the Cold War and Academic Freedom, 1952–1954." *Journal of the Royal Historical Society of Australia* 101, Part 1: 25–44.

———. 2019. "Anthropology and Sociology Were of 'No Value . . . in War Time': Ronald and Catherine Berndt and War-time Security, 1939–1945." *Anthropological Forum* 29, no. 2: 116–33.

———. 2020. "'In my file, I am two different people': A. L. Epstein, Max Gluckman, the Australian National University and the Australian Security Intelligence Organisation, 1958–1960." *Cold War History* 20, no. 1: 59–67. DOI: 10.1080/14682745.2019.1575367.

Gray, Geoffrey and Doug Munro. 2011. "Australian Aboriginal Anthropology at the Crossroads: Finding a Successor to A. P. Elkin, 1955." *Australian Journal of Anthropology* 22, no. 3: 351–69.

Griffiths, Deidre Jean Fyfe. 1977. "The Career of F. E. Williams, Government Anthropologist of Papua, 1922–1943." MA thesis, ANU.

Hardy, Frank. 1968. *The Unlucky Australians*. Melbourne: Nelson.

Heenan, Tom. 2007. "Burchett, Wilfred Graham (1911–1983)." *Australian Dictionary of Biography*. National Centre of Biography, Australian National University, http://adb.anu.edu.au/biography/burchett-wilfred -graham-12265/text22015.

Hokari, Minoru. 2011. *Gurindji Journey. A Japanese Historian in the Outback*. Kensington: University of New South Wales Press.

Horner, David. 2014. *The Spy Catchers. The Official History of ASIO 1949– 1963*. Sydney: Allen & Unwin.

Iamo, Warilea. 1992. "The Stigma of New Guinea: Reflections on Anthropology and Anthropologists." In *Confronting the Margaret Mead Legacy: Scholarship, Empire, and the South Pacific*, edited by Lenora Foerstel and Angela Gilliam, 75–79. Philadelphia PA: Temple University Press.

Jacobs, Pat. 1990. *Mister Neville, a Biography*. Fremantle: Fremantle Arts Centre Press.

Jefferies, Tony. 2018. "Close—Distant: An Essential Dichotomy." In *Skin, Kin and Clan: The Dynamics of Social Categories in Indigenous Australia* edited by Patrick McConvell, Piers Kelly, and Sébastien Lacrampe, 363– 400. Canberra: ANU Press.

Jones, Philip 1987. "South Australian Anthropological History: The Board for Anthropological Research and Its Early Expeditions." *Records of the South Australian Museum* 20: 71–92.

———. 2011. "Inside Mountford's Tent: Paint, Politics and Paperwork." In *Exploring the Legacy of the 1948 Arnhem Land Expedition*, edited by Martin Thoma and Margo Neale, 33–54. Canberra: ANU Press.

Kauffman, Paul. 1978. *The New Aborigines: The Politics of Tradition in the Groote Eylandt Area of Arnhem Land*. MA thesis, ANU.

Kuklick, Henrika. 2011. "Personal Equations: Reflections on the History of Field-work, with Special Reference to Sociocultural Anthropology." *Isis* 102: 1–33.

Lambert, J. A. 2011. "A History of the Australian Institute of Aboriginal Studies 1959–1989: An Analysis of How Aboriginal and Torres Strait Islander People Achieved Control of a National Research Institute." PhD diss., ANU.

Lawrence, William Ewart and George Peter Murdock. 1949. "Murngin Social Organization." *American Anthropologist* 51, no. 1: 58–65.

McCaul, Kim and Amy Roberts. 2015. "Editorial." *Journal of the Anthropological Society of South Australia* 39: 147–75.

McConnel, Ursula H. 1936. "Totemic Hero-Cults in Cape York Peninsula, North Queensland," parts 1 and 2. *Oceania*, vol. 6, no. 4: 452–77; vol. 7, no. 1: 69–105.

McConvell, Patrick, Piers Kelly, and Sébastien Lacrampe, eds. 2018. *Skin, Kin and Clan: The Dynamics of Social Categories in Indigenous Australia*. Canberra: ANU Press.

Maher, Laurence W. 1993. "The Lapstone Experiment and the Beginnings of ASIO." *Labour History* 64: 103–18.

———. 1998. "Downunder McCarthyism: The Struggle Against Australian Communism 1945–1960: Part One." *Anglo-American Law Review* 27: 341–89.

Manne, Robert. 2004. *The Petrov Affair*. Melbourne: Text.

Marcus, Julie. 1987. "Olive Pink and the Encounter with the Academy." *Mankind* 17, no. 3: 185–97.

Mills, David. 2008. *Difficult Folk? A Political History of Social Anthropology*. New York: Berghahn Books.

Munt, Valerie. 2011. "Ideology and Political Repression: The Cold War Experience of FGG Rose." *Anthropological Forum* 21, no. 2: 109–29.

Nixon, Pamela. 1947. "The Integration of a Half-caste Community at La Perouse, NSW." MA thesis, University of Sydney.

Owusu, Maxwell, ed. 1975. *Colonialism and Change: Essays Presented to Lucy Mair*. The Hague: Mouton & Co.

Peterson, Nicholas, and Fred Myers, eds. 2016. *Experiments in Self-determination: Histories of the Outstation Movement in Australia*. Canberra: ANU Press.

Price, David. 2004. *Threatening Anthropology: The FBI's Surveillance and Repression of Activist Anthropologists*. Durham NC: Duke University Press.

Rigsby, Bruce, and Nicolas Peterson, eds. 2005. *Donald Thomson: The Man and Scholar*. Academy of the Social Sciences in Australia.

Rose, Frederick 1942. "Paintings of the Groote Eylandt Aborigines." *Oceania* 13, no. 2: 170–76.

Rose, F. G. G., and A. T. H. Jolly. 1942. "An Interpretation of Taboo between Mother-in-Law and Son-in-Law." *Man* 42: 15–16.

———.1943. "The Place of the Australian Aboriginal in the Evolution of Society," *Annals of Eugenics* 12, no. 1: 44–87.

———. 1960. *Classification of Kin, Age Structure and Marriage Amongst the Groote Eylandt Aborigines: A Study in Method and a Theory of Australian Kinship*. Berlin: Akademie-Verlag.

———. 1965. *The Wind of Change in Central Australia: The Aborigines at Angas Downs, 1962*. Berlin: Akademie-Verlag.

———. 1965a. *The Australian*, 14 April 1965.

———. 1968. *Australia Revisited: The Aborigine Story from Stone Age to Space Age*. Berlin: Seven Seas.

———. 1987. *The Traditional Mode of Production of the Australian Aborigines*. London: Angus and Robertson.

Sheils, Helen, ed. 1963. *Australian Aboriginal Studies: A Symposium of Papers Presented at the 1961 Research Conference*. Melbourne: Oxford University Press.

Stocking, George W. Jr. 1995. *After Tylor: British Social Anthropology, 1888–1951*. Madison: University of Wisconsin Press.

Thomas, Martin, and Margo Neale, eds. 2011. *Exploring the Legacy of the 1948 Arnhem Land Expedition*. Canberra: ANU Press.

Thomson, Donald. 1936. *Interim General Report of Preliminary Expedition to Arnhem Land, Northern Territory of Australia. 1935–1936*, Report to the Commonwealth. Canberra: Government Printer.

———. 1937. *Report on Expedition to Arnhem Land, 1936–1937*. Canberra: Government Printer.

———. 1937a. *Recommendations of Policy in Native Affairs in the Northern Territory of Australia*. Report to the Commonwealth Parliament. Canberra: Government Printer.

Turner, David H. 1972. "Nimda Rites of Passage: A Comparative View." *Anthropological Forum* 3, no. 2: 112–35.

———. 1974. "Tradition and Transformation. A Study of the Groote Eylandt Area Aborigines of Northern Australia." Canberra: AIAS.

———. 1979. "An Aboriginal Outstation Movement in Arnhem Land and the Perils of Advocacy Anthropology." *Nomadic Peoples* 3, no. 1: 8–21.

Uddin, Nasir. 2011. "Decolonising Ethnography in the Field: An Anthropological Account." *International Journal of Social Research Methodology* 14, no. 6: 455–67.

Urry, James. 1985. "W. E. Armstrong and Social Anthropology at Cambridge 1922–1926." *Man* NS 20, no. 3: 412–33.

Ward, Charlie. 2016. *A Handful of Sand: The Gurindji Struggle, After the Walk-off*. Clayton: Monash University Publishing.

Warner, Lloyd W. 1933. "Kinship Morphology of Forty-One Australian Tribes." *American Anthropologist* 35, no. 1: 63–86.

———. 1937. *A Black Civilization: A Social Study of an Australian Tribe.* New York: Harper & Row.

Wise, Tigger. 1985. *The Self-Made Anthropologist: A life of A. P. Elkin*. Sydney: Allen & Unwin.

Worsley, Peter. 1963 "(Review of) Rose F.G.G. *Classification of Kin, Age Structure and Marriage Amongst the Groote Eylandt Aborigines*, Berlin: Akademie-Verlag." *Man*, no. 75–77: 63–64.

———. 1991. "Iconoclast of the Outback: Obituary for Professor Rose." *Guardian*, 18 February 1991.

———. 1992a. "The Practice of Politics and the Study of Australian Kinship." In *Dialectical Anthropology: Essays in Honour of Stanley Diamond*, vol. 2, edited by Christine Ward Gailey, 36–43. Gainsville: University of Florida Press.

———. 1992b. "Foreword." In *Confronting the Margaret Mead Legacy: Scholarship, Empire and the South Pacific*, edited by Lenora Foerstal and Angela Gilliam. Philadelphia PA: Temple University Press.

Zogbaum, Heidi. 2004. *Kisch in Australia: The Untold Story*. Melbourne: Scribe Publications.

CHARLES D. LAUGHLIN

8

Extraterrestrial Anthropology and Science Fiction

A Review and Reflection

What we think, imagine or dream about cultures beyond the earth not only reflects our own hidden fears and wishes, but alters them.

—Alvin Toffler

One day we might receive a signal from a planet like Gliese 832c, but we should be wary of answering back.

—Stephen Hawking

My father studied real cultures and I make them up—in a way, it's the same thing.

—Ursula K. Le Guin

It was on a warm, clear summer night in Dallas back in 1954 when I and a fellow bag-boy at the local A & P grocery store sat on lawn chairs staring up at the sky and chatting about the universe. Suddenly I had an epiphany. I realized, in a moment of extreme clarity, that we were not alone in the universe; that we nearly hairless apes were not the apogee of consciousness, sentience, and civilization in the cosmos; and that there were millions of worlds orbiting stars with all kinds of beings evolving upon them. This realization came with such certainty that it marked me for the rest of my life, although it occurred before astronomers had found a single exoplanet. It also occurred a couple of decades before several young anthropologists, including myself, conceived of a new marginal subdiscipline of anthropology sometimes called extraterrestrial anthropology (Maruyama and Harkins 1975;

Backe 2015; Funaro 1994; Laughlin 1997; Wescott 1975; Sisson 1977; Baird 1987; Dick 2006; Battaglia, Valentine, and Olson 2015). The running joke at the time was that it was the only branch of anthropology that had no subjects to study.

Extraterrestrial anthropology (EA) gradually became an umbrella term for a number of associated research interests, such as developing first contact scenarios (Finney 1990), creating compelling aliens and sociocultural simulations in science fiction (Funaro 1994; Slusser and Rabkin 1987; Bohannan 1990), ethnological engagement with the search for extraterrestrial intelligence (SETI) projects (Denning 2018; Finney 1992; Hough 1991), the ethnography of UFO cults as quasi religions (Balch and Taylor 1977; Cook 1999), anticipating the cultural reaction of humans to first contact (Harrison 2002; Vakoch 2011), using communication with other earth animals as models for problems faced in communication with alien beings (Herzing 2010), evaluating xenoarchaeological theories and research (McGee 2010), helping NASA develop realistic sociocultural lifestyles for space colonies and long-term space voyages (Aiken 2015; Almon 2018; Finney 1987; Finney and Jones 1986; Connors, Harrison, and Akins 1999; Harris 1986; Smith and Davies 2012), studying government and other organizations related to space exploration (Davis-Floyd, Cox, and White, 2002; Olson 2018), studying scientists working and living in extreme environments (Helmreich 2009; Olson 2010), evaluating the role of tourism and other motives for space exploration (Smith 2000), and addressing social issues (gender, race, sex, etc.) within the practical limits of living in outer space (Oman-Reagan 2017).

Core issues in EA revolve around the quest for, the impact upon humans of, and the possibility of contact with *extraterrestrial intelligences* (ETIs; see Dick 2015). Human interest in the heavens is ancient, dating from Upper Paleolithic times (Wescott 1975), and the debate over whether there exist sentient beings on other worlds is centuries old (Crowe 1997). Those who consider such life forms as being likely in our universe should be called "sentientologists," "ETI-ologists," "astropologists," or even "extraterrestrial multispecies ethnographers" (Kirksey and Helmreich 2010). By definition, of course, anthropology is the study of humans by humans, and, in American anthropology, the focus is on human *culture*—what we humans learn and share with each other living in groups. The presumption, however, is that any extraterrestrial beings technologically advanced enough to communicate with or visit us will also be both highly intelligent and *culture bearers*—that is, their psyches, their consciousness, as well as their social values and collective knowledge will be obtained from their social group. I suspect ETIs sufficiently advanced enough to visit us will be in many senses post-cultural (Laughlin and Richardson 1986), but for the moment let us suppose ETIs are conditioned by culture. If so, anthropologists' vast experience in (1) mapping the evolution of humanity and the human mind, (2) communicating between radically different human cultures, and (3) studying the patterns of enculturation (also known as socialization) of immature group members contributes valuable skills that will be necessary for optimal communication with and understanding of ETIs (Dick 1996, 2006; Harris 1986, 1989, 211–14). Thus extraterrestrial matters certainly lie within the purview of the discipline, augmenting the research of other scientific disciplines such as astrobiology (Sullivan and Baross, 2007), exoplanetology (Charbonneau 2008), astrosociology (Pass 2009, 2011) and extraterrestrial psychology (Harrison and Elms 1990; Todd and Miller 2017).

In this article I wish to trace the history of anthropological involvement in the space program and briefly introduce a rather curious cluster of research projects nestled within the greater discipline of anthropology that in one way or another touch upon the future of humankind in outer space. I wish to parse out some of the common elements that run through the thinking of EA researchers. I will focus on several of the areas mentioned above, including anthropological involvement with NASA and SETI, problems of communicating with ETIs, studies of the relationship between culture and ETI, and the kinds of cultures that may optimize permanent space colonies and multigenerational space voyages. A major emphasis of this piece, however, will be the intimate interaction between anthropology and science fiction.

ANTHROPOLOGY AND SCIENCE FICTION

In the early 1970s I met a young anthropologist named Jim Funaro who was teaching at Cabrillo College, a community college in Aptos,

California. We carried on a correspondence for a few years, discussing our mutual interest in science fiction (SF) and the possibilities of contact with ETIs. It was from Funaro that I got the idea of teaching anthropology through the medium of science fiction. He had been using science fiction in his anthropology courses since 1966 (Funaro 1994). There also were textbooks published in the early 1970s for this type of course (Mason 1974; Stover and Harrison 1972), and discussions appeared in journals about anthropology and SF (Stover 1973). My first course, Anthropology through Science Fiction, was offered at the State University of New York at Oswego in 1972, and I continued to teach this course after I moved to Carleton University in Ottawa, Ontario, until my retirement in 2001. This was always my favorite course. I assigned ten novels per semester as texts, including such novels as Alexei Panshin's *Rite of Passage*, Ursula K. Le Guin's *Left Hand of Darkness* (Ursula was the daughter of the famous anthropologist Alfred Kroeber), Orson Scott Card's *Speaker for the Dead*, Larry Niven's *Ringworld*, Greg Bear's *Blood Music*, Chad Oliver's *Unearthly Neighbors*, and William Gibson's *Neuromancer*. Each novel illustrated some issue in contemporary anthropology that was discussed in class. The term paper was a science fiction short story, and I recall that several were of publishable quality. I should note perhaps that I am from a generation that draws a fuzzy line between the genres of science fiction and fantasy. John W. Campbell, perhaps the most influential editor of science fiction stories in the twentieth century, insisted that true science fiction be grounded in solid, plausible science. Many authors write in both genres, of course, but there is an effort to make their science, when it enters into the story, grounded upon plausible "hard" science, as well as psychological and social science. My bias here is toward science fiction in Campbell's sense, as is evidenced by the selection of stories I use to illustrate this essay.

Funaro went on to found both the popular EA simulation game called *Cultures of the Imagination* (COTI; Funaro 1994) and CONTACT, a series of annual conferences that "bring together some of the nation's foremost scientists, science fiction writers and artists to exchange ideas, explore possibilities and stimulate new perspectives about humanity's future. Our goal: To encourage serious and creative interdisciplinary speculation about what lies ahead as we enter the space age" (Funaro 1994, 10). One of the most difficult challenges SF writers face is creating realistic and compelling ETIs. Most ETIs in SF stories are in one way or another anthropomorphized Earth dwellers (Traphagan 2015)—either they remind us of humans (human-like lizards, tigers, vegetables, etc.), or they are antithetical to humans (alien enemies routinely look like bugs; e.g., the nasty, drooling xenomorphs in the *Alien* franchise, Heinlein's aliens in *Starship Troopers*, sandworms in Frank Herbert's *Doom*). The CONTACT conferences have brought together anthropologists and SF writers, and each has benefitted from the other with respect to producing realistic scenarios involving ETI cultures and the problems of engaging with alien societies. Incidentally, Paul Bohannan (1990), one of anthropology's distinguished ethnographers, attended one of the CONTACT conferences and wrote about the experience. In addition, some SF writers have had backgrounds in anthropology. Kurt Vonnegut took some graduate courses in anthropology at the University of Chicago; Chad Oliver earned his PhD in anthropology at UCLA, and had this to say about combining the anthropological perspective with creative writing:

> When I was first exposed to anthropology, as an undergraduate, I experienced an immediate sense of familiarity; I felt that I was in the same universe of discourse [as SF]. The problems of culture contact and culture conflict, the discussions of cultural relativism, the idea of cultural evolution, the whole emphasis on looking at things from different perspectives, the questions about what it meant to be human—all of these were as characteristic of science fiction as they were of anthropology. (quoted in Collins 2004, 243)

I never used the COTI game in my courses, but it is a brilliant tool for inviting serious, creative, and out-of-the-box thinking about ETIs and possible first contact scenarios. Funaro describes the game this way:

> One team, the Aliens, constructs a solar system, a world and its ecology, an intelligent native life form and its culture, basing each step on the previous one and utilizing the principles of science as a guide to imagination. The other team, the Humans, designs a future

human colony, planetary or space faring, "creating and evolving" its culture as an exercise in cultural structure, dynamics and adaptation. Finally, through a structured system of progressive, real-time revelation, the teams simulate—and experience through unrehearsed roleplaying—contact between the two cultures, in order to explore the problems and possibilities involved in inter-cultural encounters.

Perhaps one of the most important results of the interplay between sf and anthropology has to do with the orientation of the latter toward time. As Samuel Collins (2003) demonstrates, anthropology was conceived in the nineteenth and early twentieth centuries as an exercise in the study of our evolutionary past. Living traditional peoples were treated as primitive case studies illustrating what our civilized (Western) societies were like in the distant past. It took a long time before ethnologists began to treat living non-technocratic societies as alternative social arrangements in the present—a present they share with us, albeit with different cultures and types of subsistence. Even so, the tendency of anthropologists in the latter part of the twentieth century and into the new millennium has been to focus on the past (through historical anthropology, archaeology, and historical linguistics), the ethnographic present (i.e., treating all ethnographies of living peoples in a timeless fashion as though fieldwork for each was carried out contemporaneously), and the real present (societies living today). Margaret Mead (1978) noted this temporal-historical bias and wrote that "anthropology has to date made very meager contributions to man's developing concern with the future" (1978, 3).

Robert Textor, Asian ethnographer and founder of the American Anthropological Association's Robert B. Textor and Family Prize for Excellence in Anticipatory Anthropology, called this pervasive attitude *tempocentrism*, and argued for a future orientation he called *anticipatory anthropology* (Textor 1999). Textor had this to say about his own transformation:

One way to characterize my lack of the necessary skills in 1958 is to say that I was "tempocentric," or centered in my own temporal context—which was natural enough for me, but inappropriate for the problem at hand. Like most anthropologists, I was concerned primarily with the past, the ethnographic present, and the actual present. I should have been more explicitly concerned about *just how, through future time, a given set of technological, economic, social or political inputs could, would, or should bring about the type of change I visualized—in the form of one or more comprehensive, connected, consistent, and contextualized scenarios.* (1999, 2, emphasis added)

This temporal reorientation is implied in EA and has led to many future-oriented studies (Hakken 2000; Dobbert 2000; Textor 2009; Nutall 2012). An important application of anticipatory anthropology is to analyze the relations between social relations and technologies and, based upon the changes in these relations in the past, to anticipate future scenarios that may arise because of new technologies. For instance, given what we know about changes in labor opportunities due to advances in AI, what are the likely implications of self-driving vehicles, smart warehouses, or medical diagnostic devices? In 1985, Textor and his associates demonstrated the efficacy of this method in analyzing the impact upon human well-being of what he called the telemicroelectronic revolution. His motivation was this:

By "anticipatory anthropology" we mean the use of anthropological knowledge and ethnographic methods, appropriately modified and focused, to anticipate change. We take the position that the time has come for cultural anthropology to add an anticipatory dimension to its long-existing and successful historical, descriptive, interpretive, comparative, and social-science-generalizing dimensions. *The results of an anticipatory anthropology project ought, in most cases, to facilitate the development of public policy that will be proactive rather than reactive.* (Textor 1985, 4, emphasis added)

This describes nicely the motivation of many anthropologists interested in both SF and the space program.

CYBORG ANTHROPOLOGY

Engagement with SF has aided the reorientation of many anthropologists to future studies. SF and anticipatory anthropology certainly influenced my own thinking about the future of cyborg technologies and their impact upon human consciousness and culture (Laughlin 1997, 2000). What I have called cyborg anthropology has nothing to do with the use of that term by anthropologists who were influenced by Donna Haraway's (1991 [1985]) left-wing sociopolitical essay "A Cyborg Manifesto," in which she uses the concept of the cyborg metaphorically, referring to the relationship between humanity and technology. I use the term in a more literal sense, as did Manfred Clynes and Nathan S. Kline (1960), who first coined the term *cyborg*, attempting to anticipate the probable evolution of cyborg technologies—the physical merger of the human body (skeleton, muscles, organs, nerves, and brain) with AI technologies—and the implications of this merger for the future of human consciousness.

The use of the cyborg in fiction provides us some indication of the extent to which people generally have understood the implications of the organism-machine merger (see Porush [1985, 2–3] on cybernauts and soft machines; see also Zebrowski and Warrick [1978] and the essays by Andrew Gordon, Anne Hudson Jones, and Gary K. Wolfe in Dunn and Erlich [1982]). Although the term *cyborg* had yet to be coined, in his 1923 novel *The Clockwork Man* E. V. Odle depicted a person with a device in his head that allowed him to flip into alternate realities. Most treatments of the cyborg idea, however, have followed the brain-in-metal-body motif (e.g., L. A. Eshbach's "The Time Conqueror" in 1932, Curt Siodmak's *Donovan's Brain* in 1943, and Damon Knight's horrifying short story "Masks" in 1968). A more developed theme began to emerge when Cordwainer Smith wrote about cyborgs designed for space travel in "Scanners Live in Vain" in 1950. Frederik Pohl's *Man Plus* in 1976 and Barrington J. Bayley's *The Garments of Caean* in 1976 continued this theme, as did Anne McCaffrey's *The Ship Who Sang* from 1961, in which a human brain is incorporated into the command structure of a spaceship. Martin Caiden's novel *Cyborg*, published in 1972, led to the popular "Six Million Dollar Man" TV series, which brought the cyborg or "bionic man" concept to the awareness of the public. The novel and series followed a more modern trend in cyborgian thinking: the awareness that parts of the human body can be replaced and even augmented by machines. William Gibson's 1980s cyberpunk novels (*Neuromancer, Burning Chrome,* and others) portray a near future dystopian era in which street people have microchips implanted in their brains and can access the World Wide Web by an act of will. Gibson's vision of street culture and advanced technology led to a subgenre that continues today in such novels as Ernest Cline's *Ready Player One*, in which a teenager jacks into a virtual reality world known as the OASIS and stumbles upon information that can get him killed. Social science, however, was slow to realize the importance of cyborg technologies for the future of human society and consciousness. Thus early SF writers may be considered truly prescient in this respect.

In one of my papers I defined four stages in the evolution of cyborg technologies:

> Stage I Cyborg: Replacement or augmentation of the human skeleton. Examples: wooden leg, hook for lost hand, armor, false teeth.
> Stage II Cyborg: Replacement or augmentation of muscle. Examples: mechanical hand for lost hand, other prosthetic devices, mechanical heart valve, replacement of lens in eye.
> Stage III Cyborg: Replacement or augmentation of parts of the peripheral nervous system, autonomic nervous system, and endocrine system. Examples: bionic arms and legs, pacemakers, automatic biochemical pumps.
> Stage IV Cyborg: Replacement or augmentation of parts of the central nervous system. Examples: video "eyes," Air Force cyborg fighter plane control, cochlear implants. (Laughlin 1997, 152)

Grounding my analysis upon the phenomenology of technology that grew out of Martin Heidegger's (1977) essay "The Question Concerning Technology," I reasoned that the evolution of the cyborg human was one of *gradual penetration of technologies into the body*, beginning years ago with the replacement or augmentation of skeletal structures and culminating in the future with physical brain-AI interfacing. Following Heidegger, at each step in the process of technological penetration the technology would both "withdraw" from consciousness (become unconsciously present; see Ihde [1983]) and become an extension of the consciousness of the cyborg. For those readers unfamiliar with Heidegger's thinking—the so-called Heidegger's hammer analysis—a technology of any kind, when used, inevitably transforms the relationship between the individual and the real world. Give a person a hammer and the world fills with things needing pounding; give a person a gun and the world becomes filled with targets. In a subsequent paper (Laughlin 2000) I used this argument to anticipate future possibilities of AI penetration of the human brain and consciousness. In short, cyborg technologies, as with all technologies, will be *multistable*; that is, AI may be applied to uses both utopian and dystopian (Ihde 1979, 1983). Just as a hammer can build a house and bludgeon a spouse, cyborg IV technologies will be used both to control brains and to condition them in their development toward social purposes (the "ideology chip") and to set them free by guiding individuals to optimal enlightenment and post-cultural consciousness (the "guru program").

This distinction between utopian and dystopian visions of the future characterized SF in the early days of the genre. Indeed, as Lyman Sargent (1976) demonstrates, there were more than four hundred utopian novels published in English before H. G. Wells put pen to paper, and they continued to be written throughout the twentieth century. Dystopian fiction was a nineteenth century reaction to utopian visions (Lepore 2017; Babaee et al. 2015, 64), and in my estimation, the utopic-dystopic split in creative vision is another manifestation of Heideggerian multistability.

HUMANIZING SPACE

Slowly but surely we are humanizing space (Finney 1987; Olson 2018). We have sent people to the moon and have built rudimentary orbital space stations (the ISS, Mir, Tiangong 1 and 2, the Almaz and Salyut series, and Skylab) in which humans have lived and worked for longer than a year. Part of the rationale for these experiments has been the desire to learn what conditions will be necessary for establishing permanent space colonies, perhaps on the Moon, Mars, on asteroids, or in space stations located at Lagrange points (see Battaglia, Valentine, and Olson 2015). For some anthropologists, the virtual certainty that human societies will live in space in the foreseeable future presents a challenge (Rastogi 1966). The dean of extraterrestrial anthropologists, Ben Finney, has suggested an important role of anthropology in designing space colonies: "I wish to suggest two specific areas in which this cultural perspective of anthropology could be useful in working on problems of space living: (1) in cross-cultural relations in heterogenous space crews and societies; and (2) in drawing upon the cultural resources of the Earth's people for practices and institutions that might be appropriate models for space living" (1987, 190).

Anthropologists informally shifted NASA planners' thinking away from the early presumption that the best cultural and social organization of a space colony would be a military one, a hold-over from the "right stuff" orientation of early astronaut recruitment. I myself was involved with the NASA-sponsored Strategic Avionics Technology Working Group (SATWG) in the 1990s, as was my colleague Dr. Robbie Davis-Floyd (Davis-Floyd, Cox, and White 2002). I recall numerous discussions with NASA scientists, engineers, and industrial designers about likely sociocultural scenarios for successful space colonies (see Valentine, Olson, and Battaglia 2009). By that point, nobody believed that a military-style social structure would be appropriate or efficient. For one thing, the rigidity of political structure and top-down decision-making would be utterly stultifying to the creative thinking and experimentation that will be necessary in the early stages of the humanization of space. For another, the culture of a space colony must remain dynamic to adapt to the conditions of living in an artificial environment, be it in space, during a lengthy space voyage, or on another world (Smith and Davies 2012). Spacefaring human societies *must* remain flexible in their cultural worldviews, for there will be a rather mysterious aspect to "nature" other than what our cultures are adapted to on Earth (for a hypothetical and very different nature that may be confronting spacefarers, see Varughese's 1975 report on planet Xeno). This is the reason ethnographer Stefan Helmreich has suggested that an attitude of "extraterrestrial relativism" must prevail in space culture, "for extraterrestrial relativism, knowledge or truth about 'life' (or even its 'conditions') is imagined as relative to a 'nature' whose full character we do not yet know, whose outlines may lead us toward comparisons we cannot predict" (2012, 1130). Relativism and flexibility can be accentuated by recognizing that "culture" is an adaptive tool and must be dynamic to fit perhaps extreme "natures" as we encounter them off-planet (Olson 2010). As Finney noted above, making sure that the population of space farers is fully multicultural would be a fundamental requirement. One science fiction novel that nicely illustrates this kind of consideration in the planning of lengthy, multigenerational space voyages (in this case involving human clones, planned euthanasia, advanced AI, and other issues) is Marina J. Lostetter's 2017 book *Noumenon*. Neal Stephenson's 2015 novel *Seveneves* also sends a human founder population into space in a large artificial colony to wait out a devastating catastrophe on Earth. In a curious twist, Hugh Howey's *Silo* series describes life in a subterranean colony, the "silo," created to save humanity in a post-apocalyptic Earth.

As Finney suggested, there will be problems that arise that may be solved by applying the insights gained from the cross-cultural study of cultures in transition (see also Valentine, Olso, and Battaglia [2009]). Only a few years ago, for example, it would not have occurred to NASA designers that they might have to consider designing a culture that would be tolerant of more than two sexual orientations (see Oman-Reagan [2017] on the "queering" of outer space). Some social problems will be like those we already face here on Earth. Technologies will continue to develop, especially in AI and robotic labor, and this will necessitate changes in labor-related social roles and mechanisms for introducing cultural change, occupational retraining, and so forth (Hakken 2000).

Space station and colony designs have, of course, figured prominently in SF stories going all the way back to the nineteenth century. Edward Everett Hale's stories "The Brick Moon" (1869) and "Life in the Brick Moon" (1870), now available online from Project Gutenberg, take place on a space station. Neil R. Jones published a story entitled "The Jameson Satellite" (1931) in which the character lives in a one-man space station (more like a sarcophagus). Robert Heinlein's novel *Space Cadet* (1948) takes place on a space station as well. More modern treatments figure in Asimov's "The Martian Way" (1952) which takes place in a Martian colony, while Frederik Pohl's *Gateway* (1977) explores the notion of a space colony inside an asteroid, a concept given real consideration among astrobiologists today. More complex and sophisticated colonies have frequently featured in SF. The six novels of Mack Reynolds's *Lagrange Five* series depict life on massive artificial space colonies located at the Lagrange Points.

A common theme in SF is that colonization is initially motivated by something catastrophic happening on Earth (decimation of the planet, escaping tyranny, overpopulation of the planet, etc.), as in Lostetter's *Noumenon* mentioned above and in Olaf Stapledon's *Last and First Men* (1930) where Earth has become uninhabitable, driving humans into a deep space diaspora, and in Heinlein's *The Moon is a Harsh Mistress* (1966) where a colony on the Moon rebels against Earth's tyranny. One of the most sophisticated depictions of colonization on another world is found in Kim Stanley Robinson's *Mars* trilogy—*Red Mars* (1992), *Blue Mars* (1992) and *Green Mars* (1996)—which describes three phases in the terraforming and colonization of the red planet. Possibly the most ingenious artificial space colony is found in Larry Niven's controversial 1970 novel *Ringworld*, titled for the structure of the colony, which is essentially a revolving bicycle wheel one million miles wide and six hundred million miles in diameter, with a concave inner surface and sides a thousand miles high to keep the atmosphere in. It spins, producing artificial gravity. There have been endless critiques and speculation about whether such a massive engineering feat could ever really function as described.

Serious scientific thought has been given to the long-term future of efficient adaptation to resources on a planetary and interplanetary basis. Some of these scenarios would entail the construction of enormous artificial colonies and mechanisms. For instance, Russian astrophysicist Nikolai Kardashev calculated the amount of energy utilized by three levels of hypothetically advanced future civilizations in his so-called *Kardashev Scale* (Kardashev 1964, 1985). Considering that all the energy available on any planet derives from its star, there are three ideal types of civilization we might imagine:

A Type I Civilization can efficiently use and store all of the energy that reaches its home planet from its parent star.

A Type II Civilization is interplanetary and can efficiently use and store all of the energy of the home star, perhaps by utilizing space colonies and power processors that form an artificial network around a star—something like a *Dyson Sphere* (Dyson 1960).

A Type III Civilization is galaxy-wide in scope and able to efficiently use and store the energy available from the stars and other recourses of its home galaxy.

The fundament assumption for many scientists and SF writers is that advanced intelligent beings will eventually find their way off their home worlds and form a diaspora in outer space.

ANTHROPOLOGY AND FIRST CONTACT

To tell you the truth, I don't have a clue whether ETIs have surreptitiously visited us here on Earth or whether we will be contacted by aliens in the future. After all, sentient beings of any sort in the universe must confront the vastness of space and the technological challenges of crossing that immense distance. There has been some interest among anthropologists about human reactions to first contact (Vakoch and Lee 2000). There is also some physical science behind the possibility of ETI visitation (Deardorff et al. 2005), but UFO reports at the best of times are so vague, anecdotal, and imprecise that they do not appeal to the scientific mind. There are, of course, those who believe that human beings could never have produced civilization without help, and that acceleration must have come via ancient astronauts from outer space (e.g., Von Däniken 1969). Drawing upon the ethnographic work of anthropologists Marcel Griaule and Germaine Dieterlen, Robert Temple (1987 [1976]) argues in his book *The Sirius Mystery* that the stories of the Dogon people living in northwestern Mali incorporate knowledge of an alien visitation some five thousand years ago.

Science fiction has played upon the theme of first contact numerous times, and predictably the scenarios range from utopic to dystopic. Steven Spielberg's classic 1977 movie *Close Encounters of the Third Kind* presents a positive, spiritually uplifting meeting of ETIs and humanity. The story, however, barely touches upon the long-term consequences of first contact on human culture. Stanley Kubrick and Arthur C. Clark's *2001: A Space Odyssey* goes further in depicting alien influence on human evolution (the famous monoliths) and the emergence of transcendental consciousness. At the opposite dystopic extreme are the horrifying adventures of Ellen Ripley among the deadly xenomorphs in the *Alien* films, which leave the audience with a deep sense of menace and the dark view of outer space as a very dangerous place perhaps best avoided.

This alternation between utopic and dystopic memes runs throughout first contact novels. Larry Niven and Jerry Pournelle explore the chancy nature of contact in their 1974 *The Mote in God's Eye* in which the aliens (the "Moties") at first present as friendly, hospitable, and helpful, but in fact harbor a dark, violent past and disingenuous intentions. Arthur C. Clarke, ever the optimist, presents a utopian future in *Childhood's End* (1953) when alien "Overlords" take over Earth, end all warfare, and catalyze the rapid evolution of humanity into a new golden age of spiritual maturity. Along the same lines, Robert Heinlein, in his controversial classic *Stranger in a Strange Land* (1961), has his character Valentine Michael Smith, a human born and raised on Mars, return to Earth and transform human culture, presumably for the better. Of course, Heinlein also took the *Alien*-like dystopian tack in his 1959 novel *Starship Troopers*, in which aliens are basically antagonistic human-chomping bugs.

SETI AND ANTHROPOLOGY

What I can say with certainty is that people are fascinated by the possibility of interstellar contact and wonder about the impact of contact upon us Earthlings (Dick 1996, 2015; Harrison and Dick 2000). Thinking about radio communications with ETIs began back in the nineteenth century (Seifer 1996, 157). The now famous search for extraterrestrial intelligence began in earnest in 1959 with the publication of an article by Giuseppe Cocconi and Philip Morrison, followed by the Project Ozma experiments by Frank Drake (1960) and the 1961 conference on SETI convened by Drake at the National Radio Astronomy Observatory in Green Bank, West Virginia (Dick 2006; Gardner 2005, 165). It was at this conference that Drake presented the now famous equation that purports to estimate the number of communicative extraterrestrial civilizations in our home galaxy, the Milky Way (Burchell 2006).

SETI quickly became an interdisciplinary project (Harrison and Vakoch 2011; Morrison, Billingham, and Wolfe 1977) bringing together physical scientists and social scientists into fruitful dialogue (Finney

1992). As it happens, anthropology's cross-cultural perspective fit right in (Denning 2018; Stull 1977; Vakoch 2011). As Donald Tarter put it,

> cultural anthropology has always sought to explore and catalogue the diversity of human cultures. SETI seeks to explore and catalogue cultures of other intelligent beings in space. The agenda of cultural anthropology embraces certain values, namely that information about others of different cultures than our own will lead to an understanding and appreciation of the diverse behaviors of the people of planet Earth. SETI has a similar value agenda except its focus is on the cultures of extraterrestrial beings in space. (2001, 90)

While carrying out ethnographic research over the past century and a half, anthropologists have developed the view that each society's values and beliefs must be understood and evaluated within their local frame of reference. Beliefs and behaviors that appear to us to be strange (yes, "alien") make sense only when understood within a total local cultural package. This is a view in opposition to most people's natural ethnocentrism (the projection of our system of values onto other people). This is also a view commensurate with the goals of the SETI project.

Moreover, sociocultural anthropology in company with archaeology have tracked the evolutionary stages of the emergence of civilizations and eventually technocracies—a process that has occurred over a remarkably short period of time, something less than ten thousand years. What this tells us is that a sentient being that has taken millions of years to evolve a sufficiently advanced social brain can create agriculture and urban living, and a few thousand years later can become a spacefaring being in a blink of an eye, evolutionarily speaking (Denning 2011a). It does *not* tell us that intelligence is necessarily linked to technological advancement, for there are highly intelligent sentient beings right here on Earth that did not evolve clever, widget-making hands (e.g., dolphins, elephants, wolves). At the same time there are many animals that do fashion and use tools; for example, the Caledonian crow is deft at producing the right tool for the job "at beak" (van Casteren 2017).

This is a crucial point, because SETI is grounded upon the assumption that there may be ETIs out there who are technologically advanced enough to emit intentional signals by way of electromagnetic waves (Denning 2011b). We make this assumption because we humans have, for a couple of million years, used our technological prowess to adapt to, migrate around in, and explore our home planet (Finney and Jones 1986). Our natural assumption is that there are ETIs that have also relied primarily upon technological means of adaptation, wherever they dwell in the universe. This is not, in my opinion, merely an anthropocentric bias (see also Finney [1992]). As Ben Finney noted: "I think that many SETI theorists vastly overestimate the ease of comprehending extraterrestrial transmissions, and their consequent impact, because they conflate technical and cultural understanding. My experience as an anthropologist studying the contact of formerly isolated terrestrial cultures leads me to be much more alert to the difficulties of intergroup communication than many SETI advocates seem to be. Misunderstandings abound on the frontier of culture contact" (1990, 118).

Keep in mind that as of this moment, the Rongorongo script of Easter Island, the Cretan script Linear A, Mexico's Olmec script, and the Indus script from India have yet to be deciphered. Imagine the difficulty in translating symbols used by ETIs thousands of light years away. Not only that, but neighbors here on terra firma who have different languages and cultures very often misunderstand each other in serious and even violent ways (Finney and Bentley 1998). Finney (1990, 119; see also Vakoch 2008), an Oceanic ethnologist, used the analogy of the "cargo cult"—the view that if we build the right technology, the ETIs will contact us and bestow humanity with advanced knowledge that we may use to better our lot—to caution SETI enthusiasts about their naïve assumptions. The difficult challenge of understanding messages from ETIS is well known among astrobiologists engaged with SETI (Heller 2018; Vakoch 1998, 1999). Consider the difficulty we have understanding the signals of our fellow big-brained mammals here on Earth. On top of that, there is the problem of how to portray human culture(s) to ETIs at a distance (Vakoch 2008; Vakoch et al. 2011). If we are somehow able to get into an exchange—a conversation—how can we control for how our messages are interpreted? David Brin features dolphins in his brilliant 1983 book *Startide Rising* and its five sequels in the *Uplift* series. In these delightful stories, dolphins and other big-brained animals are "uplifted" in intelligence and taught to communicate with humans with whom they crew on space voyages.

Receiving messages from outer space has been a common theme in science fiction stories (see Bova and Preiss 1990), including Carl Sagan's 1985 novel and subsequent film, *Contact*, in which SETI scientists connect with an extremely advanced ETI civilization. Toward the more dystopian view of messages from ETIs, Robert Crane explored the dangers of ignoring messages from outer space in his novel *Hero's Walk* (1954). Piers Anthony, in his novel *Macroscope* (1969), depicts outer space messages that turn out to be deadly Basilisks that destroy any mind smart enough to comprehend them. And Chloe Zerwick and Harrison Brown depict a politically divisive world in their thriller *The Cassiopeia Affair* (1968), in which a scientist receives messages from ETIs and the knowledge of first contact becomes a political football.

ANTHROPOLOGY AND SPACE VOYAGING

We humans have evolved to be inherent explorers (Finney and Jones 1986). As early hominids we had our beginnings in tropical Africa, where we remained for millions of years until we advanced technologically to spread northward into Europe and Asia. From there we have spread over the planet, able to survive in the harshest of climates, as well as under water, upon mountain peaks, in the air and now out in interplanetary space. The natural extensions of these urges to expand and explore are space colonization and space voyaging. Future interplanetary space voyaging seems inevitable. At our present state of technological and scientific understanding, plans for interstellar voyages appear to be inhibited by the belief that superluminal (faster-than-light) speeds are impossible due to the limitations of relativity. However, there is some solid theoretical physics to suggest that warp speeds and wormholes are possible (Alcubierre 1994; Morris and Thorne 1988; Puthoff 1996, 2010; Visser 1995)—and not only that, but the vacuum energies of "empty" space may be tapped to fuel starships (Puthoff 1998).

The problem of getting from here to there over vast reaches of space has been solved in science fiction stories in many different ways (Nicholls 1983). Jack Williamson was one of the first to play around with superluminal speeds in his 1931 *Astounding Stories* tale "The Meteor

Girl," in which his hero manipulates spacetime to rescue his girlfriend thousands of miles away. Wormholes feature in Sagan's *Contact* (above) and numerous other novels, such as Alastair Reynolds's *House of Suns* (2008), in which two of the protagonists use a wormhole to travel to the Andromeda galaxy, and Lois McMaster Bujold's *Shards of Honor* (1986), where they enable warfare and empire, a common theme in David Weber's *Honorverse* novels as well. Another solution to the problem is travel through hyperspace (a dimension where superluminal speed limits do not apply), first used by John W. Campbell in his 1931 novel *Islands of Space*. Hyperspace features most famously in Gene Roddenberry's *Star Trek* universe but is found also in Robert Heinlein's 1953 novel *Starman Jones* and many other stories.

CULTURE AND SPACE VOYAGES

Anthropology is, of course, less interested in the physics and engineering of space flight and more interested in the sociocultural aspects of life on lengthy space voyages (Finney 1988a, 1988b). Although we have been developing a space culture for more than six decades—a period in which that culture has changed dramatically—a true space culture will only exist when we humans are permanently living in colonies and spacecraft. As space psychologist Philip Harris wrote,

> With permanent extension of human presence beyond Earth, *a true space culture will emerge, quite distinct from its terrestrial analogs.* The high frontier can become a living laboratory to promote peaceful, synergistic societies. Imagine space communities which promote cultural norms that support cooperation instead of competition; group development over excessive individualism; mutual help in place of aggressive behavior. Such a space culture has a better chance for survival and development aloft, in contrast to the 1584 "lost colony" of our English forbears at Fort Raleigh, Virginia! The hostile orbital environment requires a collaborative, regulated society to ensure the safety of the commonwealth—individuals will be regulated for safety's sake and that of their community. (1996, 401–2; emphasis added)

Anthropologists who have done ethnographic fieldwork among societies living on small islands have developed an understanding of social cooperation, technological challenges, and conflict resolution quite appropriate to predicting cultural issues arising in planning for long space voyages, small artificial space colonies, and small colonies on other worlds (see Smith and Davies 2012, chapter 6). As Finney noted,

> the exploration of the sea and the discovery and settlement of the oceanic islands is perhaps the one phase of humanity's spread over Earth that is most evocative of our future expansion into space. The adventure of exploring the unknown, the struggle to develop new technology to go where no human had ever been before, and the establishment of colonies on uninhabited shores are the obvious features of oceanic migration that make it relevant to the one about to unfold in space. (1988b, 225–26)

Finney goes on to show that the peoples who discovered and colonized Pacific islands did so not en masse but rather from one island to the next, depending upon the pattern of islands in chains. This is a process that William Keegan and Jared Diamond (1987) termed *autocatalysis*, where successful colonization of each island further along a chain encouraged exploration and colonization of the next island.

Planning for biological succession and cultural factors appropriate to living in starships is at least as important as engineering. As physical anthropologist Cameron M. Smith notes,

> if space colonization is to succeed in the long run, we must consider biology and culture as carefully as engineering. Colonization cannot be about rockets and robots alone—it will have to embrace bodies, people, families, communities and cultures. *We must begin to build an anthropology of space colonization to grapple with the fuzzy, messy, dynamic and often infuriating world of human biocultural adaption.* And we must plan this new venture while remembering the clearest fact of all regarding living things. They change through time, by evolution. (2013, 38; emphasis added)

Most space-oriented social scientists agree that the space culture of colonies and starships will be unlike the kind of laissez-faire, narcissism-tolerant culture that is in the process of decimating Gaia. Indeed, reproduction and genetic combinations will be required by any successful space-dwelling society. It will need to emphasize childrearing practices that develop social cooperation and team skills instead of dangerous and even iconoclastic self-centeredness. Nor, as I have said above, will the social structure be authoritarian, for anything like a military command structure would stultify creative problem solving.

The optimal population size of long duration, multigenerational, permanent colony ships is controversial. The question is how many people must be included in a starship to guarantee genetic viability across generations. Smith (2014) estimates at least twenty-five thousand will be required, while others suggest two thousand or even fewer. Regardless of how many folks are included as colonists, selection will not be a random sample of human genetics. This is a crucial point, for no matter the number, the population will have a founder effect (Provine 2004) on the future colony's gene pool. Let us suppose that the initial astronauts are chosen in part for their intelligence, a practice that has been in play since the inception of the space program. We know that there is a genetic basis for intelligence. Thus the gene pool aboard the colony ship will constitute a non-random selection for intelligence that will influence the genetics of future generations. Considering that there will undoubtedly be a eugenics program in place as well, one can imagine the level of average intelligence aboard the ship will gradually increase over the generations until we have colonies with an average intelligence greater than that back on Earth.

Now, if we imagine that the level of cultural complexity is correlated with level of intelligence (there is scientific evidence for this; see Laughlin [2017]), then we can see that the cultures of starship societies will be more complex, flexible, and adaptable than the average Terran culture. One can see that space cultures and Terran military or other authoritarian cultures would be incompatible, even disastrous. The enhanced flexibility of advanced intelligence will prove crucial for adapting to extraterrestrial colonies, whether they be on board a starship or on the Moon, Mars, or Europa. The impact of the founder effect could become profound as a consequence of humanizing interplanetary space, for there would likely be an autocatalyzing effect in the exploration from one successful colony to the next colonizing effort. Each exploratory step outward would draw colonists not from Earth but from the most intelligent and adventurous of the previously successful colony.

The role of the founder effect in accelerating the evolution of advanced intelligence, or other qualities, has been a theme in science fiction. Perhaps most famously, in the 1951 film *When Worlds Collide*, people are selected for their superior intelligence and placed on board a colony ship to escape the threat to Earth posed by an oncoming planet and tasked with the mission of establishing a new colony. We encounter the concept again in Ken MacLeod's recent short story "Who's Afraid of Wolf 359?," published in *The New Space Opera* anthology edited by Gardner Dozois and Jonathan Strahan, in which the hero is sent to find a lost colony on a planet around Wolf 359, a real red dwarf star found in the constellation Leo. And Robert Heinlein explored selective breeding over generations within the Howard Foundation families in *Methuselah's Children* (1958). A clear description of the process Heinlein called "forced Darwinian selection" can be found in *Time Enough for Love* (1973).

Perhaps one of the best fictional accounts of generations-long space voyages is found in James Blish's *Cities in Flight* series, which covers roughly two thousand years during which whole cities (called Okies), powered and protected by an anti-gravitational machine called a "spindizzy," escape Earth's global tyranny and form colonies in space. The series deals with politico-economic issues of various sorts as the cities evolve. Some of the features anthropologists study in virtually all societies are rites of passage (Van Gennep 1960; Turner 1969; Davis-Floyd and Laughlin 2016): rituals constructed to transform an individual's social status and role, as in coming-of-age rituals that change the status of a child into that of an adult. One of the most interesting treatments of this social process in science fiction is Alexei Panshin's 1968 novel *Rite of Passage*, which follows the adventures of a young woman named Mia Havero, who was raised on a gigantic spaceship, as she undergoes her adolescent "trial" by surviving on a colony world for a month with few supplies. After the trial, she is considered an adult aboard the starship.

Human space cultures will, like their Terran counterparts, have value systems. However, these values cannot be overly influenced by Earth cultures, or in any way be traditionally hidebound, for Terrans have value systems, especially among technocratic societies, that destroy the very ecosystems that support them (see Smith and Davies 2012, 223–33; Valentine 2016). No such value system will carry us very far in space, for values that result in intended or unintended destruction of the ecosystem will be felt immediately, not over generations, given the technical fragility of a space colony. For instance, every adult member of a space colony and of a starship, initially at least, will have to have a working knowledge of the life-support technology. Offspring will have to be schooled to fully understand their environment and what ways of thinking and acting might be harmful. Personal identities that emphasize group cohesion and social cooperation rather than laissez-faire egoism will of necessity be valued. Yet the exercise of creative intelligence within the context of cooperative teamwork will also be highly prized. Cultural rationalizations for individual greed, selfishness, and xenophobia will be eliminated in space, and rigid adherence to ideologies could well prove disastrous.

Nowhere is this progression more obvious than in identification with gender. Anthropologists have long pointed up the deleterious psychological and sociocultural effects of patriarchy. Female anthropologists since the time of Margaret Mead, Hortense Powdermaker, and Ruth Benedict in the early twentieth century have insisted that the roots of sexism be exposed in both traditional and modern cultures in order both to correct male bias in ethnographic research, and to free each individual to reach their optimal development as a human being (see Geller and Stockett 2007). This background of feminist social science had an impact upon science fiction writers, especially feminist authors like Margaret Atwood, Joanna Russ, and L. Timmel Duchamp.

Science fiction writers can be notoriously ethnocentric in the biases they depict in their stories. There was something about Robert Heinlein's stories that annoyed me for years. I finally realized that most of his characters came out of middle American rural culture and libertarian values. However, there are other more anthropologically astute writers who seem to be aware of the value systems they portray and take pains to show how those values might be realistic, given the environments of their protagonists, and open to change through time. I think Kim Stanley Robinson's picture of adaptive culture in his *Mars* series is exemplary, especially in the first novel, *Red Mars*. The hundred or so colonists are drawn from two different cultures, plus a French psychologist (alas, no anthropologist). Integral to the plot is tension between two very different value systems, one in favor of terraforming (the "green" contingent) and the other opposed to this procedure (the "red" contingent). One of the colonists, Arkady Bogdanov, takes the view that the Martian colony Underhill need not be subject to Earth's political authority or cultural traditions, for the special conditions on Mars are not understood by or acknowledged by political figures back on the home world. This political tension between Earth and space colonies will be inevitable, especially if the motivation for space exploration is mangled by capitalist values and the desire for wealth at the expense of the colonists. This theme is found in numerous science fiction stories, including Heinlein's *The Moon Is a Harsh Mistress* (1966), in which a lunar colony revolts against Earth's hegemony; James S. A. Corey's (pseudonym for Daniel Abraham and Ty Franck) *Expanse* series, in which humanity has spread throughout the solar system and there are political tensions and conflicting interests between Earth, Mars, and the outer planets (the asteroids); and Isaac Asamov's *The Martian Way* (1952), in which the interference of Earth's politics impacts the lives of a couple of men born and raised on Mars.

A CAUTIONARY NOTE

In my opinion, there is one overarching issue of which we should be cognizant as we move forward with the humanization of space. That is the role we want corporations to play in space exploration (see Olson 2018). As I write this, some of the more exciting space-related events are the launches of vehicles designed and built by private companies. Space x, Orbital Sciences, Bigelow Aerospace, Blue Origin, Virgin Galactic, and other companies are vying for government and corporate contracts for manned and unmanned flights into orbit. Elon Musk, CEO and founder of Space x, has announced serious plans for a colonizing mission to Mars. The critical question we should be asking is about *what role the people of Earth want to assign to individual governments, entrepreneurs, private enterprise projects, and corporate-industrial incen-*

tives (Valentine 2012). I word this question advisedly, for as it stands now, although there is a body of space law that may regulate human activities in outer space, these regulations are bound up in treaties that range from significant to failed. There is actually very little in the way of international regulation about what individual governments and corporations can do in space, other than statements of grand ideals. There are five treaties that various countries have signed that are of relevance and were devised under the auspices of the United Nations Committee on the Peaceful Uses of Outer Space.

> These five treaties deal with issues such as the non-appropriation of outer space by any one country, arms control, the freedom of exploration, liability for damage caused by space objects, the safety and rescue of spacecraft and astronauts, the prevention of harmful interference with space activities and the environment, the notification and registration of space activities, scientific investigation and the exploitation of natural resources in outer space and the settlement of disputes. . . . Each of the treaties stresses the notion that outer space, the activities carried out in outer space and whatever benefits might be accrued from outer space should be devoted to enhancing the well-being of all countries and humankind, with an emphasis on promoting international cooperation. (http://www.unoosa.org /oosa/en/ourwork/spacelaw/treaties.html; accessed on 7/7/18)

While it is true that the most important treaty, the Outer Space Treaty, has been signed by 107 countries and forbids any one country, much less a company, from claiming a world (moons, planets, and presumably asteroids), it also gives the individual country, and by inference a corporation, control over resources it has discovered and mined. If Corporation x flies to Mars and establishes a mining colony with an associated company town, what will be the legal, economic, and political limits on Corporation x's power over the geographical region, its resources, and the workforce providing the labor? Another question is already pressing: Does NASA have the right to capture and transport a small world, namely an asteroid, as it plans to do in the near future (David 2013)?

Science fiction stories have had a field day depicting greedy, amoral-to-downright-evil, and totally self-interested corporations in space.

Frank K. Kelly's "Famine on Mars" (1934) depicts a massive corporation, the Combine, that controls Mars and space colonies alike, and is vindictive with the Martians when they rebel. In the 1957 novel *The Stars My Destination*, Alfred Bester tells of the adventures of a marooned spacer who is abandoned by the Presteign corporation spaceship *Vorga*. After repairing his ship, he seeks revenge against the evil company. James Corey's *Leviathan Wakes* (2011) is replete with shadowy, secretive corporations. David Weber includes the nasty Manpower, Inc., which condones and profits from slavery, in his beloved *Honorverse*. Notable is the scheming, power-hungry Omni Consumer Products corporation in the *Robocop* franchise, and the Yoyodyne company in Thomas Pynchon's novels *V* (1963) and *The Crying of Lot 49* (1966). In the latter, a housewife also uncovers a secret plot by Trystero, an underground postal delivery service. And who has not encountered the ubiquitous Weyland-Yutani company, the very epitome of the evil and destructive megacorporation of the *Aliens* franchise?

Corporate involvement in space is an issue of paramount interest to extraterrestrial anthropologists. One of the most important articles yet written about conflicting values and motivations in space exploration and colonization was published in 2015 by York University anthropologist Rayna Elizabeth Slobodian. Reacting to the Dutch *Mars One* program to send colonists to Mars within a decade, Slobodian criticizes the "space nationalism" behind much of the pressure to rush to Mars. What is wrong about all this are the motivations and incentives for rash, underfunded, poorly thought out programs designed to "beat the opposition"—the opposition being other competing countries. This incentive is obviously in conflict with the spirit of the Outer Space Treaty and the kind of careful planning most likely to make space colonization succeed while eliminating as much risk to colonists' lives as possible. She also criticizes the standard rationales for space exploration, such as an innate biological drive to explore. Are we "destined" to expand into outer space? I believe we are, and for good reasons, but Slobodian raises crucial questions that should be thought through. What if, after years of industry and trillions in wealth, we discover that humans cannot in fact live permanently on any world close enough to reach? There are very good biological reasons that this might prove to be the case. Among other things there are ethological studies of groups living in extreme conditions here on Earth to consider (e.g., life at Antarctic stations [Tafforin 2009] and the Biosphere experiments [Nelson et al. 1993]) as analogs to living on Mars (see Olson 2010). In addition, Slobodian deconstructs the ideologies of those urging rapid human dispersal into space and reveals numerous scientifically unsupportable assumptions that are iffy at best, risk-wise. She suggests that "we must look at the issues fully and thoroughly before moving forward. Some space entrepreneurs want to get out there and colonize Mars as quickly as possible, but hopefully they can realize that taking the time to work through some of the previously stated consequences might be more important than adhering blindly to their ideologies" (Slobodian 2015, 102). We have an opportunity at this juncture in human history to use the exploration of space and the exploitation of interplanetary material resources (1) to energize humanity behind a single global project, (2) to spread the wealth derived from that project to all countries and to all mankind (Barker 2015), and (3) possibly to save our species from the destruction we have, in our ignorance and greed, wrought upon Gaia. Interestingly, several science fiction authors have recently explored the realistic problems facing our species on Mars. These include Andy Weir's marvelous novel *The Martian* (2011), which explores the plight of an astronaut abandoned on Mars struggling to survive until rescued, and Jonathan Maberry's children's novel *Mars One* (2017), which explores the costs to an individual kid of being a member of the Mars One project.

CONCLUSION

Anthropology and science fiction have been entangled for decades, sharing many of the same tropes, such as the role of culture in forming personal identity and the fundamental issue of how one culture is able to translate meanings from an alien culture. "Both genres encounter the problematic of cultural translation. Indeed, one might go so far as to say that both genres exist, in part, in order to explore just that problematic. Cultural translation—the idea that the modes of thought, feeling, and action of one culture are, at least approximately, translatable into those of another—is at once one of the central and one of the thorniest precepts in the discipline of anthropology" (Samuels 1996, 90).

The above reviews and reflections have, I hope, demonstrated how the two fields of interest interpenetrate and inform each other. More than that, I hope that our glimpse at anthropology's concern with artistic imagination (a cultural universal, by the way) may be translated into scientifically supportable, pragmatic planning and design programs for seeking out signals from outer space and for interpreting the meaning of communications with and anticipating the reaction of different peoples to ETIS. Moreover, I hope to see a more public and sustained engagement by anthropologists with envisioning the problems and solutions involved in well thought-out planning for our future in outer space; for instance, with programs like X-Hab (Crusan, Galica, and Gill 2018).

REFERENCES

Aiken, Jo. 2015. "Otherworldly Anthropology: Past, Present, and Future Contributions of Ethnographers to Space Exploration." In *Applied Anthropology: Unexpected Spaces, Topics and Methods*, edited by Jo Aiken. New York: Routledge, 30–44.

Alcubierre, Miguel. 1994. "The Warp Drive: Hyper-Fast Travel Within General Relativity." *Classical and Quantum Gravity* 11, no. 5: L73.

Almon, A. J. 2018. "Developing Predictive Models: Individual and Group Breakdowns in Long-Term Space Travel." *Acta Astronautica*, doi: 10.1016/j.actaastro.2018.04.036.

Babaee, Ruzbeh, Hardev Kaur Jujar Singh, Zhang Zhicheng, and Zhang Haiqing. 2015. "Critical Review on the Idea of Dystopia." *Review of European Studies* 7, no. 11: 64–76.

Backe, Emma Louise. 2015. "Aliens Among Us: Extraterrestrial Anthropology." *Geek Anthropologist*, March 20, 2015. https://thegeekanthropologist.com/2015/03/20/extraterrestrial-anthropology/.

Baird, John C. 1987. *The Inner Limits of Outer Space*. Lebanon NH: University Press of New England for Dartmouth College.

Barker, Donald C. 2015. "The Mars Imperative: Species Survival and Inspiring a Globalized Culture." *Acta Astronautica* 107: 50–69.

Battaglia, Debbora, David Valentine, and Valerie Olson. 2015. "Relational Space: An Earthly Installation." *Cultural Anthropology* 30, no. 2: 245–56.

Balch, Robert W., and David Taylor. 1977. "Seekers and Saucers: The Role of the Cultic Milieu in Joining a UFO Cult." *American Behavioral Scientist* 20, no. 6: 839–60.

Bohannan, Paul. 1990. "Anthropology and Science Fiction." CONTACT *Newsletter* 1, no. 2.

Bova, Ben, and Byron Preiss. 1990. *First Contact: The Search for Extraterrestrial Intelligence.* New York: NAL Books.

Burchell, Mark J. 2006. "W(h)ither the Drake equation?" *International Journal of Astrobiology* 5, no. 3: 243–50.

Charbonneau, David. 2008. "The Era of Comparative Exoplanetology." *Bulletin of the American Astronomical Society* 40: 250.

Clynes, Manfred, and Nathan S. Kline. 1960. "Cyborgs and Space." *Astronautics* (September): 26–27, 74–75.

Cocconi, Giuseppe, and Philip Morrison. 1959. "Searching for interstellar communications." *Nature* 184, no. 4690: 844–46.

Collins, Samuel Gerald. 2003. "Sail On! Sail On!: Anthropology, Science Fiction, and the Enticing Future," *Science Fiction Studies* 30, no. 2: 180–98.
———. 2004. "Scientifically Valid and Artistically True: Chad Oliver, Anthropology, and Anthropological SF." *Science Fiction Studies* 31: 243–63.

Connors, Mary M., Albert A. Harrison, and Faren R. Akins. 1999. *Living Aloft, Human Requirements for Extended Spaceflight.* Washington DC: NASA, Ames Research Center.

Cook, Ryan J. 1999. "'God's Descending in Clouds (Flying Saucers):' Anthropological Approaches to UFOs in the Religious Register." *American Anthropological Association Annual Conference*, Special session on UFOs and religion, 20 November 1999.

Crowe, Michael J. 1997. "A History of the Extraterrestrial Life Debate." *Zygon* 32, no. 2: 147–62.

David, Leonard. 2013. "Is NASA's Plan to Lasso an Asteroid Really Legal?" *Space.Com.* August 30, 2013. https://www.space.com/22605-nasa-asteroid-capture-mission-legal-issues.html.

Davis-Floyd, Robbie E., Ken Cox, and Frank White. 2002. *Space Stories: Oral Histories from the Pioneers of the American Space Program.* Self-published, Amazon Digital Services. Kindle.

Davis-Floyd, Robbie E., and Charles D. Laughlin. 2016. *The Power of Ritual.* Brisbane: Daily Grail.

Deardorff, James, Bernard Haisch, Bruce Maccabee, and Hal E. Puthoff. 2005. "Inflation-Theory Implications for Extraterrestrial Visitation." *Journal of the British Interplanetary Society* 58: 43–50.

Denning, Kathryn. 2011a. "Ten Thousand Revolutions: Conjectures About Civilizations." *Acta Astronautica* 68, no. 3/4: 381–88.

———. 2011b. "Being Technological." *Acta Astronautica* 68, no. 3/4: 372–80.

———. 2018. "How Humans Matter Now: The Relevances of Anthropology and Archaeology for the New SETI." SETI Institute March 14–16 Workshop, Mountain View CA. https://daiworkshop.seti.org/sites/default/files/workshop-2018/Denning%20-%20How%20Humans%20Matter%20Now%20-%20The%20Relevance%20of%20Anthropology%20and%20Archaeology%20for.pdf.

Dick, Steven J. 1996. *The Biological Universe: The Twentieth Century Extraterrestrial Life Debate and the Limits of Science.* Cambridge: Cambridge University Press.

———. 2006. "Anthropology and the Search for Extraterrestrial Intelligence: An Historical View." *Anthropology Today* 22, no. 2: 3–7.

Dick, Steven J., ed. 2015. *The Impact of Discovering Life Beyond Earth.* Cambridge: Cambridge University Press.

Dobbert, Marion Lundy. 2000. "Anticipatory Anthropology and World Peace: A View from 2050." *Futures* 32, no. 8: 793–807.

Drake, Frank. 1960. "How Can We Detect Radio Transmissions from Distant Planetary Systems?" *Sky and Telescope* 19: 140–43.

Dunn, Thomas, and Richard Erlich, eds. 1982. *The Mechanical God: Machines in Science Fiction.* New York: Greenwood Press.

Dyson, Freemann J. 1960. "Search for Artificial Stellar Sources of Infra-Red Radiation." *Science* 131, no. 3414: 1667–68.

Finney, Ben R. 1987. "Anthropology and the Humanization of Space." *Acta Astronautica* 15, no. 3: 189–94.

———. 1988a. "Will Space Change Humanity?" In *Frontiers and Space Conquest/Frontières et Conquête Spatiale*, edited by J. Schneider and M. Léger-Orine. New York: Springer, 155–72.

———. 1988b. "Solar System Colonization and Interstellar Migration." *Acta Astronautica* 18: 225–30.

———. 1990. "The Impact of Contact." *Acta Astronautica* 21, no. 2: 117–21.

———. 1992. "SETI and the Two Terrestrial Cultures." *Acta Astronautica* 26, no. 3/4: 263–65.

Finney, Ben, and Jerry Bentley. 1998. "A Tale of Two Analogues: Learning at a Distance from the Ancient Greeks and Maya and the Problem of Deciphering Extraterrestrial Radio Transmissions." *Acta Astronautica* 42, no. 10–12: 691–96.

Finney, Ben R., and Eric M. Jones, eds. 1986. *Interstellar Migration and the Human Experience*. Berkeley: University of California Press.

Funaro, Jim. 1994. "The Evolution of COTI: A Personal Memoir." *Contact: Cultures of the Imagination (COTI)*, http://www.contact-conference.com/c02.html.

Gardner, Martin. 2005. *The New Ambidextrous Universe: Symmetry and Asymmetry from Mirror Reflections to Superstrings*. New York: Courier Corporation.

Geller, Pamela L. and Miranda K. Stockett, eds. 2007. *Feminist Anthropology: Past, Present and Future*. Philadelphia: University of Pennsylvania Press.

Hakken, David. 2000. "Resocialing Work? Anticipatory Anthropology of the Labor Process." *Futures* 32, no. 8: 767–75.

Haraway, Donna. (1985) 1991. "A Cyborg Manifesto: Science, Technology, and Socialist-Feminism in the Late Twentieth Century." In *Simians, Cyborgs and Women: The Reinvention of Nature*, edited by Donna J. Haraway. New York: Free Association Books, 149–81.

Harris, Philip R. 1986. "The Influence of Culture on Space Developments." *Systems Research and Behavioral Science* 31, no.1: 12–28.

———. 1989. "Behavioral Science Space Contributions." *Systems Research and Behavioral Science* 34, no. 3: 207–27.

Harrison, Albert A. 2002. *After Contact: The Human Response to Extraterrestrial Life*. New York: Basic Books.

Harrison, Albert A., and Steven J. Dick. 2000. "Contact: Long-Term Implications for Humanity." In *When SETI Succeeds: The Impact of High-Information Contact, edited by Allen Tough*. Bellevue WA: Foundation for the Future, 7–31.

Harrison, Albert A., and Alan C. Elms. 1990. "Psychology and the Search for Extraterrestrial Intelligence." *Systems Research and Behavioral Science* 35, no. 3: 207–18.

Harrison, Albert A., and Douglas A. Vakoch. 2011. "The Search for Extraterrestrial Intelligence as an Interdisciplinary Effort." In *Civilizations Beyond Earth*, edited by Douglas A. Vakoch and Albert A. Harrison, 1–30. New York: Berghahn.

Heidegger, Martin. 1977. "The Question Concerning Technology." In *Basic Writings*, translated by D. Krell. New York: Harper and Row.

Heller, René. 2018. "Decryption of Messages from Extraterrestrial Intelligence Using the Power of Social Media—The SETI Decrypt Chal-

lenge." *International Journal of Astrobiology.* https://doi.org/10.1017
/S1473550417000568

Helmreich, Stefan. 2009. *Alien Ocean: Anthropological Voyages in Microbial
Seas.* Berkeley: University of California Press.

Helmreich, Stefan. 2012. "Extraterrestrial Relativism." In *Anthropological
Quarterly* 85, no. 4: 1125–39.

Herzing, Denise L. 2010. "SETI Meets a Social Intelligence: Dolphins as a
Model for Real-Time Interaction and Communication with a Sentient
Species." *Acta Astronautica* 67, no. 11/12: 1451–54.

Hough, Peter A. 1991. *Looking for the Aliens: A Psychological, Imaginative,
and Scientific Investigation.* London: Blandford.

Ihde, Don. 1979. *Technics and Praxis.* Dordrecht: Reidel.

———. 1983. *Existential Technics.* Albany: State University of New York Press.

Kardashev, Nikolai S. 1964. "Transmission of Information by Extraterrestrial Civilizations." *Soviet Astronomy* 8: 217.

———. 1985. "On the Inevitability and the Possible Structures of Super-
civilizations." *The Search for Extraterrestrial Life: Recent Developments;
Proceedings of the Symposium, Boston, MA, June 18–21, 1984* (A86–38126
17–88). Dordrecht, D. Reidel Publishing Co., 497–504.

Keegan, William F., and Jared M. Diamond. 1987. "Colonization of Islands
by Humans: A Biogeographical Perspective." *Advances in Archaeological
Method and Theory* 10: 49–92.

Kirksey, Stefan, and Stefan Helmreich. 2010. "The Emergence of Multispecies Ethnography." *Cultural Anthropology* 25, no. 4: 545–76.

Kosek, Jake. 2010. "Ecologies of Empire: On the New Uses of the Honey-
bee." *Cultural Anthropology* 25, no. 4: 650–78.

Laughlin, Charles D. 1997. "The Evolution of Cyborg Consciousness."
Anthropology of Consciousness 8, no. 4: 144–59.

———. 2000. "The Cyborg, the Ideology Chip and the Guru Program:
The Implications of Cyborg Technologies for the Development of
Human Consciousness." *Foresight* 2, no. 3: 291–312.

———. 2017. "Conceptual Systems Theory: A Neglected Perspective for
the Anthropology of Consciousness" *Anthropology of Consciousness* 28,
no. 1: 31–68.

Laughlin, Charles D., and Sheila Richardson. 1986. "The Future of Human
Consciousness." *Futures: The Journal of Forecasting and Planning* 18, no. 3:
401–19.

Lepore, Jill. 2017. "A Golden Age for Dystopian Fiction." *New Yorker,* June 5 & 12. https://www.newyorker.com/magazine/2017/06/05/a-golden-age-for-dystopian-fiction.

Maruyama, Magoroh, and Arthur M. Harkins, eds. 1975. *Cultures Beyond the Earth.* New York: Vintage Books.

Mason, Carol, ed. 1974. *Anthropology through Science Fiction.* New York: St. Martin's Press.

McGee, Ben W. 2010. "A Call for Proactive Xenoarchaeological Guidelines—Scientific, Policy and Socio-Political Considerations." *Space Policy* 26, no. 4: 209–13.

Mead, Margaret. 1978. "The Contribution of Anthropology to the Science of the Future." In *Cultures of the Future,* edited by Margoroh Maruyama and Arthur Harkins, 3–6. Chicago IL: Mouton.

Morris, Michael S., and Kip S. Thorne. 1988. "Wormholes in Spacetime and Their Use for Interstellar Travel: A Tool for Teaching General Relativity." *American Journal of Physics* 56, no. 5: 395–412.

Morrison, Philip, John Billingham, and John Wolfe, eds. 1977. *The Search for Extraterrestrial Intelligence.* Washington DC: NASA.

Nelson, Mark, Tony L. Burgess, Abigail Alling, Norberto Alvarez-Romo, William F. Dempster, Roy L. Walford, and John P. Allen. 1993. "Using a Closed Ecological System to Study Earth's Biosphere." *BioScience* 43, no. 4: 225–36.

Nicholls, Peter. 1983. *The Science in Science Fiction.* New York: Knopf.

Nuttall, Mark. 2012. "Tipping Points and the Human World: Living with Change and Thinking About the Future." *Ambio* 41, no. 1: 96–105.

Olson, Valerie A. 2010. "The Ecobiopolitics of Space Biomedicine." *Medical Anthropology* 29, no. 2: 170–93.

———. 2018. *Into the Extreme: US Environmental Systems and Politics beyond Earth.* Minneapolis: University of Minnesota Press.

Oman-Reagan, Michael P. 2017. "Queering Outer Space." *SocArXiv,* Open Science Framework. Manuscript submitted January 22, 2017. https://osf.io/preprints/socarxiv/mpyk6/.

Pass, Jim. 2009. "Pioneers on the Astrosociological Frontier: Introduction to the First Symposium on Astrosociology." *AIP Conference Proceedings* 1103, no. 1: 375–83.

———. 2011. "Examining the Definition of Astrosociology." *Astropolitics* 9, no. 1: 6–27.

Provine, William B. 2004. "Ernst Mayr: Genetics and Speciation." *Genetics* 167, no. 3: 1041–46.

Puthoff, Harold E. 1996. "SETI, the Velocity-of-Light Limitation, and the Alcubierre Warp Drive: An Integrating Overview." *Physics Essays* 9: 156–58.

——. 1998. "Can the Vacuum Be Engineered for Spaceflight Applications? Overview of Theory and Experiments." *Journal of Scientific Exploration* 12, no. 1: 295–302.

——. 2010. "Advanced Space Propulsion Based on Vacuum (Spacetime Metric) Engineering." *Journal of the British Interplanetary Society* 63: 82–89.

Rastogi, P. N. 1966. "Existential Phenomenology and Sociology: A Critical Note." *Kansas Journal of Sociology* 2, no. 3: 107–12.

Reiss, Diana. 1990. "The Dolphin: An Alien Intelligence." *First Contact: The Search for Extraterrestrial Intelligence*, edited by Ben Bova and Byron Preiss, 31–40. Byron Preiss Visual Publications.

Russell, Dale A. 1981. "Speculations on the Evolution of Intelligence in Multicellular Organisms." NASA *Conference Publication* 2156: 259.

Samuels, David. 1996. "'These Are the Stories that the Dogs Tell': Discourses of Identity and Difference in Ethnography and Science Fiction." *Cultural Anthropology* 11, no. 1: 88–118.

Sargent, Lyman Tower. 1976. "Themes in Utopian Fiction in English Before Wells." *Science Fiction Studies* 3, no. 3: 275–82.

Seifer, Marc J. 1996. "Martian Fever (1895–1896)." *Wizard: The Life and Times of Nikola Tesla: Biography of a Genius*, edited by Marc Seifer, 152–57. Secaucus NJ: Carol.

Sisson, R. D. 1977. "Extraterrestrial Anthropology: A Model Social and Family Structure." Master's thesis, San Diego State University.

Slobodian, Rayna Elizabeth. 2015. "Selling Space Colonization and Immortality: A Psychosocial, Anthropological Critique of the Rush to Colonize Mars." *Acta Astronautica* 113: 89–104.

Slusser, George Edgar, and Eric S. Rabkin, eds. 1987. *Aliens: The Anthropology of Science Fiction*. Carbondale IL: SIU Press.

Smith, Cameron M. 2013. "Starship Humanity." *Scientific American* 308, no. 1: 38–43.

——. 2014. "Estimation of a Genetically Viable Population for Multigenerational Interstellar Voyaging: Review and Data for Project Hyperion." *Acta Astronautica* 97: 16–29.

Smith, Cameron M., and Evan T. Davies. 2012. *Emigrating Beyond Earth: Human Adaptation and Space Colonization*. New York: Springer.

Smith, Valene L. 2000. "Space Tourism: The 21st Century 'Frontier.'" *Tourism Recreation Research* 25, no. 3: 5–15.

Stover, Leon E. 1973. "Anthropology and Science Fiction." *Current Anthropology* 14, no. 4: 471–74.

Stover, Leon E., and Harry Harrison, eds. 1972. *Apeman, Spaceman*. New York: Penguin Books.

Stull, Mark A. 1977. "Cultural Evolution." In *The Search for Extraterrestrial Intelligence*, edited by Philip Morrison, John Billingham, and John Wolfe, 49–52. Washington DC: NASA.

Sullivan, Woodruff T., and John Baross, eds. 2007. *Planets and Life: The Emerging Science of Astrobiology*. Cambridge: Cambridge University Press.

Tafforin, Carole. 2009. "Life at the Franco-Italian Concordia Station in Antarctica for a Voyage to Mars: Ethological Study and Anthropological Perspectives." *Antrocom* 5, no. 1: 67–72.

Tarter, Donald E. 2011. "Can SETI Fulfill the Value Agenda of Cultural Anthropology?" In *Civilizations Beyond Earth*, edited by Douglas A. Vakoch and Albert A. Harrison, 87–101. New York: Berghahn.

Temple, Robert K. G. 1987[1976]. *The Sirius Mystery: Was Earth Visited by Intelligent Beings from a Planet in the System of the Star of Sirius*. Rochester VT: Destiny Books.

Textor, Robert B. 1985. "Anticipatory Anthropology and the Telemicroelectronic Revolution: A Preliminary Report from Silicon Valley." *Anthropology & Education Quarterly* 16, no. 1: 3–30.

———. 1999. "Why Anticipatory Anthropology." *General Anthropology* 6, no. 1: 1–4.

———. 2009. "Practicing Anticipatory Anthropology with Austrian National Leaders." *Anthropology News* 50, no. 1: 21–22.

Todd, Peter M., and Geoffrey F. Miller. 2017. "The Evolutionary Psychology of Extraterrestrial Intelligence: Are There Universal Adaptations in Search, Aversion, and Signaling?" *Biological Theory* 13, no. 2: 131–41.

Traphagan, John W. 2015. "Equating Culture, Civilization, and Moral Development in Imagining Extraterrestrial Intelligence: Anthropocentric Assumptions?" In *The Impact of Discovering Life Beyond Earth*, edited by Steven J. Dick, 127–42. Cambridge: Cambridge University Press.

Turner, Victor. 1969. *The Ritual Process: Structure and Anti-Structure*. Chicago IL: Aldine.

Vakoch, Douglas A. 1998. "Constructing Messages to Extraterrestrials: An Exosemiotic Perspective." *Acta Astronautica* 42, no. 10–12: 697–704.

———. 1999. "The View from a Distant Star: Challenges of Interstellar Message-Making." *Mercury* 28: 26.

———. 2008. "Representing Culture in Interstellar Messages." *Acta Astronautica* 63, no. 5/6: 657–64.

Vakoch, Douglas A., ed. 2011. *Communication with Extraterrestrial Intelligence*. Albany: State University of New York Press.

Valentine, David. 2012. "Exit Strategy: Profit, Cosmology, and the Future of Humans in Space." *Anthropological Quarterly* 5, no. 4: 1045–67.

———. 2016. "Atmosphere: Context, Detachment, and the View From above Earth." *American Ethnologist* 43, no. 3: 511–24.

Valentine, David, Valerie A. Olson, and Debbora Battaglia. "Encountering the future: Anthropology and outer space." *Anthropology News* 50, no. 9: 11–15.

van Casteren, Adam. 2017. "Tool Use: Crows Craft the Right Tool for the Job." *Current Biology* 27, no. 24: R1314–R1316.

Van Gennep, A. 1960. *The Rites of Passage*. Chicago IL: University of Chicago Press.

Varughese, Shirley Ann. 1975. "The Planet Xeno." In *Cultures Beyond the Earth: The Role of Anthropology in Outer Space*, edited by Magoroh Maruyama and Arthur M. Harkins, 129–66. New York: Vintage Books USA.

Visser, Matt. 1995. *Lorentzian Wormholes: From Einstein to Hawking*. New York: AIP Press.

Von Däniken, Erich. 1969. *Chariots of the Gods*. New York: Bantam.

Wescott, R. W. 1975. "Toward an Extraterrestrial Anthropology." In *Cultures Beyond the Earth: The Role of Anthropology in Outer Space*, edited by Magoroh Maruyama and Arthur M. Harkins, 12–26. New York: Vintage Books USA.

9

Genres of Memory

Reading Anthropology's History through Ursula
K. Le Guin's Science Fiction and Contemporary
Native American Oral Tradition

When history of anthropology first emerged as a field of specialization in the 1960s, a divide depending on whether that history was written by anthropologists or historians seemed almost inevitable. At one extreme, George W. Stocking, Jr., posed a dichotomy between the historian's method of "historicism" and the "presentism" or Whig history practiced by anthropologists (Stocking 1968). By implication the latter had no clear method beyond expediency in framing the contemporary work of the author. Stocking's dichotomy seemed accurate in the years between the seminal Social Science Research Council conference on the subject in 1962 and the publication of Stocking's collection of his own methodological vignettes, which contrasted starkly with the partisan character of prominent critiques of anthropology's past by Leslie White and Marvin Harris in particular. The collection was also a (remarkably successful) effort to showcase Stocking's own work from the 1960s as an exemplar of how to do history of anthropology properly.

But there was an alternative from the beginning. In the first volume of the *Journal of the History of the Behavioral Sciences, published* in 1965, elder statesman A. Irving Hallowell proposed treating the history of anthropology "as an anthropological problem," applying the methodology of the fieldworking ethnographer to the discipline itself. Dell Hymes (1962) framed the disciplinary binary in terms of tables turned, with anthropologists as the uncomfortable subjects of study and the truths they took for granted questioned by historians whose interpretations failed to acknowledge the authoritative character of what Franz Boas (1911) called "the native point of view."

Stocking, Hallowell, and Hymes all converged in Philadelphia at different points in my own undergraduate and graduate education during the 1960s. Each of them influenced my appreciation of how to do history of anthropology and why it mattered, though they were not in the same place at the same time nor did they necessarily influence one another.[1] My trajectory was punctuated by Thomas Kuhn's claim in *The Structure of Scientific Revolutions* (1962) that the social sciences are "pre-paradigmatic" because new theories do not displace old ones, which produces an implicit recursive potential in parallel continuities alongside the revolutions. In any case, a fledgling historian of anthropology had to take a stand. The following assumptions have persisted for five decades (Darnell 2001): anthropologists can learn the historicist method; many anthropologists have long been diligent archival scholars bringing temporal depth to the otherwise synchronic snapshots of fieldwork; anthropological audiences are acutely interested in the verisimilitude of ethnographic detail alongside interpretation; oral history, whether in fieldwork or among disciplinary colleagues, is an important source of evidence; and the emic perspective is crucial to understanding how practitioners create and sustain their discipline(s) as they understand them.

Until relatively recently, few historians were trained to seek out or trust the historical accuracy of materials from oral traditions or to respect the authority of knowledge keepers with personal responsibility to pass on what had come to them from teachers over successive generations. In their fieldwork, anthropologists take for granted that accurate histories will include the standpoint of the teller or teacher, especially where oral tradition remains a major source of transmitting cultural practices and values. What really happened in the past is inaccessible to any single observer at the time and in retrospect. It follows that such histories are partial, subject to multiple interpretations, and are ideally based on convergent evidence from multiple sources, including the archive.

Since the 1960s, anthropologists have come to recognize that their ethnographies are dependent on the standpoints of both observer and observed (Clifford and Marcus 1986). Although there were certainly precursors to experimental ethnographies, during the final decades of the twentieth century anthropology as a whole became more reflexive about the nature of the signature disciplinary method of participant-observation fieldwork, the dialogic engagement of the observer, and facile assumptions about the presumed audience. Outside the discipline, in contrast, emphasis on the rhetorical structure of ethnographic writing led many cultural theorists who had never done fieldwork to conclude that it was merely rhetorical and thus to occlude the authority and validity attributed to the fieldwork experience by anthropologists acknowledging their own intuition based on the very real evidence of their situated role as ethnographers.

What most puzzles me is that the postmodernist revolution did not carry over into the way we anthropologists think about the history of anthropology. Stocking changed his mind about the impermeability of a barrier based on initial disciplinary socialization and acknowledged excellent work by historians, anthropologists, literary scholars, and occasionally even members of the groups or cultures studied. In the years since his early dichotomous formulation, moreover, many historians also have moved beyond historicism versus presentism. It is increasingly difficult to distinguish an author's discipline of original training based on the published product. And yet Stocking's binary distinction is still widely cited without nuance or acknowledgment of the change in Stocking's own position as both the field and his experience of it changed.[2]

In contrast to anthropology's mainstream, history of anthropology has been assumed static, and the positivist standard of objectivity has maintained its credibility in disciplinary history. *Histories of Anthropology Annual* has challenged this rigidity and attempted to deconstruct the boundaries between written and oral history; history and histories; the dialogic and emergent character of all histories; the necessity of choosing between alternative interpretations; and, of course, the inevitability that our finest histories—regardless of disciplinary authorship—inevitably will be replaced by other histories for which our own provide fodder. Both sides have learned that the method of historicism, the insistence on seeing things in their own terms as they were in their own times prior to judgment, is compatible with presentism in the sense that topics of no contemporary interest are unlikely to be studied or their studies widely read. This chapter addresses the question of the conditions under which the history of anthropology might build and sustain an audience reflexive about its past in relation to contemporary practice.

A PARABLE OF MEMORY AND HISTORY

This chapter employs a case study of genre bending, the contingency of memory, and its relevance to exploring the assumptions that underlie writing the history of anthropology in an anthropological vein.[3] The science fiction of Ursula K. Le Guin has been proudly cited by anthropologists who claim her as one of their own because she was the daughter of Alfred L. Kroeber, among the most prominent of the first-generation Boasians. Her speculative exploration of the consequences of discontent with contemporary society ranged across issues including gender, shamanism, social engineering, and ecology. Surprisingly little has been said, however, about the most explicitly anthropological of her novels. *Always Coming Home* (1985) is a complex and difficult book that did not sell well or attract critical acclaim. But its subject is precisely the one at stake here: the nature of history and how anthropologists think about the accessibility of the past in relation to our capacity to know it. Le Guin's narrative structure and methodology are deeply ethnographic. The novel, described in the frontispiece blurb as a work of magical realism, may also be read as a reflection on the ecology and social organization of California Indians as she experienced their worlds from childhood on.

Anthropologists rarely venture beyond Kroeber as an influence on Le Guin's writing. Her mother, Theodora Krakow Kroeber (Quinn), however, merits equal consideration. She was a folklorist and lyrical translator of her husband's more austere anthropological science for a public audience. It was "Krakie," for example, who highlighted the plight of Ishi, the last of the Yahi tribe (Kroeber 1961), and her daughter Ursula who returned to challenge the ethnographic methodology of anthropological preservation and interpretation in fictional form. The subtitle *A Novel* highlights the exercise of imagination and invites Readers to join in.[4]

The surface structure of *Always Coming Home* may puzzle readers who, at least in 1985, may have expected a single plot line and identifiable dramatis personae.[5] The novel's backbone is formed by three segments of narrative told by a woman whose final name was Stone Telling about different times in her life. The woman reflects on different parts of her experience away from the home territory of the Kesh, a future people living in the space once occupied by California Indians. The continuity of the land provides Le Guin with a bridge to the world of Stone Telling in the Valley of the Kesh, a.k.a. home, and enables her to muse on the sustainability of the Indigenous way of life on the land and the unsustainable trajectory of her own society. Briefer narratives, poems, and drawings by other members of Kesh society are interspersed. There is a glossary of the Kesh language and about two hundred pages of ethnographic appendices that provide the context necessary to understand a narrative that is distributed across multiple voices. This chapter focuses on the voice of Pandora, Le Guin's sometime alter ego, an outsider to the world of the post-apocalyptic Kesh and the consequences of their contact with the invading warrior society of the Condors.

ARCHAEOLOGY AND TIME DEPTH

Le Guin's method for "an archaeology of the future" bends the conventions of English grammar as well as the familiar time divisions of a distinct past, present and future: "The people in this book might be going to have lived a long, long time from now in Northern California" (Le Guin 1985, unnumbered front matter), "The difficulty of translation from a language that doesn't yet exist is considerable, but there's no need to exaggerate it. . . . The fact that it [the literature of the future] hasn't yet been written, the mere absence of a text to translate, doesn't make all that much difference. What was and what may be lie, like children whose faces we cannot see, in the arms of silence. All we ever have is here, now."

Because the people of the Valley "walked lightly" on the land (3), as do the ones she seeks in the future, conventional archaeology can recover little of the past and nothing of those to come; they will speak for themselves in the narratives that follow. The only "practical" archaeology, in Le Guin's view, has nothing to do with digging. The archaeologist holding artifacts in her hand has only glimpses of "the dead or the unborn" (4) that she seeks. Nonetheless, the material realities of the archaeologist's artifacts as they emerge from the earth have a powerful impact:

> What does she [the Archaeologist] get besides cut hands? Bits, chunks, fragments, shards. Pieces of the Valley, lifesize. Not at a distance, but in the hand, to be felt and held and heard. Not intellectual but mental. Not spiritual but heavy. A piece of madrone wood, a piece of obsidian. A piece of blue clay. Even if the bowl is broken (and the bowl is broken),[6] from the clay and the making and the firing and the pattern, even if the pattern is incomplete (and the pattern is incomplete), let the mind draw its energy. Let the heart complete the pattern. (53)

Here Le Guin evokes Ruth Benedict's epigraph to *Patterns of Culture* (1934), in which the broken culture of the Digger Indians of California was condensed in a metaphoric equation to a broken piece of pottery. The literal experience of the archaeologist simultaneously evokes a larger one that requires an exercise of imagination. The life to which Le Guin seeks to attune herself is invisible and intangible to ordinary sight. "You take your child or grandchild in your arms, a young baby, not a year old yet, and go down into the wild oats in the field below the barn. Stand under the oak, on the last slope of the hill, facing the creek. Stand quietly. Perhaps the baby will see something, or hear a voice, or speak to somebody there, somebody from home" (5). Le Guin counters the limitations of archaeology by taking the land itself, the Valley, as her constant; the traces of those who lived and will live on it in the future allow her to extrapolate what might have happened but leave room for alternative futures that depend on the actions of her Readers.

PANDORA'S QUANDARIES

Le Guin's voice shades into Pandora's in this framing prologue. Like mythological figures across time and space, Pandora has a single characteristic attribute: she is always "worrying" about something. Pandora rejects the value of looking at a culture, past or future, through a telescope from a distance, with "everything under control" (53). Pre-existing categories from her world, which is our world, are useless. Rather, she closes her eyes and focuses all of her senses to perceive fragments of wood, obsidian, and clay at a "mental" rather than "intel-lectual" level. These customary data of the archaeologist speak beyond their materiality. Although the pattern is incomplete, she pleads with the Reader to "let the mind draw its energy. Let the heart complete the pattern" (53). Imagination has the power to lay bare the essence of things, revealing a pattern between and beyond their static forms when restricted to a single time-space continuum. Objects encased in a museum were once the "belongings" of real people, in the idiom many contemporary Indigenous peoples use to express the capacity of what is left behind to speak to descendants and other receptive lis-teners across time. Grounding in space enables movement across time.

This is the way the storytelling process works in Native American oral traditions. For example, in *The Truth about Stories* (2003), Thomas King emphasizes the repetition of stories that builds deeper meaning over the course of the lifecycle. The child first hears stories literally, and gradually learns to respond to their cautionary wisdom based on the experience of the teller, usually a grandparent. Those who become transmitters of stories in this more figurative sense evoke their wisdoms indirectly, leaving to the listener interpretive responsibility for both (re-)telling and acting in everyday life. In a similar vein, Paul Radin, a maverick among first-generation Boasian anthropologists, used stories, life histories, and ongoing dialogues to argue that the questions of phi-losophy were universal and that his interlocutors were the philosophers of their societies (Radin [1927] 1957). In contrast to the characteris-tic Boasian method of historical reconstruction based on evidence of contact and borrowing of traits and story motifs among neighboring peoples, Radin (1933) went on to redefine history, to the extent that it could be known, as limited to what had been transmitted through generations in oral tradition. The distant past, beyond the memory of particular people, receded into revered but non-specific tradition. Oral tradition is immanent in the experience of those who live it through stories and cultural practices; its ongoing relevance is more important than its temporal depth. Not much came of this argument at the time

Radin made it, but it resonates with Le Guin's instincts for the malleability of history as a subject for ongoing reflection and emergence.

Pandora addresses the Reader at intervals with her worries and clarifies her understanding of her role in terms of the mythological forbear who shares her name, in the process raising the Reader also to mythological resonance. Pandora explains that she knew "what would come out of the box Prometheus left" (148) but still chose to open it. Prometheus is "Foresight, Fire-Giver, the Great Civilizer" (148). From his distant position at the height of Olympian power, he called it hope. Pandora is, after all, married to his brother, Hindsight, and has her own ideas about war, plague, and famine. Hope, to Pandora, is a tale told by the powerful or their unquestioning spokespersons; it is the tale we have inherited. But Pandora also has much in common with Albert Camus's Sisyphus. Although she does not really expect her or Prometheus's optimism to prove justified, she persists doggedly. "But I won't mind," she continues "if the box is empty, if all that's in it is some room, some time. Time to look forward, surely; time to look back; and room, room enough to look around" (148). This is the moral for our present time. The Reader is left by this prologue to wonder why "room" and "time" are the desiderata of a possible different future for us that might even stretch back (or forward, depending on the standpoint from which one looks) to create a different past for the Kesh.

Pandora tasks herself with teaching us, contemporary Readers, how to look. So she "finds a way into the Valley through the Scrub Oak" (239). It is an object lesson in the qualitative method, arising from intuition and the rhizomatic character of experience and experiencing beings. The scrub oak has no useful purpose and it sits on a ridge with no "overall shape," "center" or "symmetry" (239). But its roots lie deep in the earth. Each scrub oak is slightly different from the others, yet like the individual members of a society they share an essential property of scrub oak-ness. There are a lot of them, "but the numbers are wrong. They are in error. You don't count scrub oaks. When you can count them, something has gone wrong. It is innumerable. It is not accidentally but essentially messy" (240). Pandora insists that the scrub oak, "the wilderness," has nothing to do with the observer. It simply is. "The civilized mind's reaction to it is imprecise, fortuitous and full of risk. There are no shortcuts. All the analogies run in one direction, our direction" (41). It would do "infinite good" if we could imagine all the other scrub oaks, "even for a moment" (41). But to do this would require experiencing them in all their diversity; "deeply, beyond the surface" (41); over time, in that space.

The effectiveness of this strategy draws on a way of understanding metaphor and metonymy that Le Guin would have known well from her experience of California Indians. This is in contrast to a literary mode more familiar to potential Readers, in which metaphors identify the literal with the symbolic and the literal fades into the background. Le Guin tells us that the scrub oak is concrete and literal; it shares properties with the Kesh people of the Valley. The literal and the figurative move interchangeably in the imaginative mode of Indigenous storytelling. The people of the Valley are not separable across time from the continuity of the scrub oak, which shares their combination of individuality and multiplicity. It is a reciprocal relationship among parts of a whole in a space-time continuum.

Pandora offers to take the Reader to the Valley but cautions that one cannot simply see it and think "that's it" (339). When the Reader wants to stop, Pandora cajoles them to rest and then go on, because "it is a long way yet" (339). The need to establish dialogue with the Valley and its peoples in relation to the land leads Pandora to postpone in infinite regress the eagerness of the Reader to impose closure and retreat to the safety of a view from afar. Pandora speaks from the lessons of her own journey, as a self-appointed guide, a moralist determined to engage the Reader in creative dialogue. "I cannot go without you" (339); a solitary journey, like scrub oak-ness, would have no purpose.

Pandora's periodic interventions in the text are never juxtaposed. They are interspersed with other events, actors, and genres for the recording of experience. Her positions shift depending on context. If there is a constant, it is that she stands apart from the experience of the Kesh and invites the Reader to decide what it all means. The most extensive of Pandora's interventions concerns the significance of history and grounds it in the time frame of oral tradition. Once the names are no longer remembered by living people, the details cease to matter. Adopting the view of the society from which she came in her dialogue with the Archivist, who is also a mythological cipher more than a developed personality, Pandora exposes the alternative understandings of history that separate her from the Kesh and moves them into a frame of mutual conversation.

DIALOGUE BETWEEN PANDORA AND THE ARCHIVIST

Pandora's moralizing contrasts the Valley, with its robust oral tradition, and her own society's obsession for record keeping. It is an object lesson in what matters to whom and for how long. She converses with the Archivist of the Madrone Lodge (madrone is a kind of wood found in the Valley). The Archivist is the keeper of records that have little to do with the everyday life experience of the Kesh (314). The Archivist explains that people bring things there "when they get very old" and are seen as "venerable" and thus not to be lightly discarded (314). Pandora asks how the Archivist decides "what to keep and what to throw away" (314). "It's difficult . . . arbitrary, unjust and exciting," replies the Archivist. Every few years it is necessary to cull the records of the heyimas (local clan-like groups). Annual "destruction ceremonies" are held at the Lodge. "They're secret. Members only. A kind of orgy. A fit of housecleaning—the nesting instinct, the collecting drive. Turned inside out, reversed, unhoarding" (315).

The Archivist explains that "the City of the Mind" does the culling, removing the burden of worry from the people. "They want a copy of everything. We give them some" (315). This, of course, entails a process of selection. The Archivist appears serene as she explains, "Books no one reads go; books people read go after a while. But they all go. Books are mortal. They die. A book is an act; it takes place in time, not just in space. It is not information but relation" (315). Pandora is horrified. She protests that electronic storage would not take up space. She realizes, and the Reader now understands for the first time, the conditions under which the Kesh can retain their innocence and their sense that their world is static and predictable (at least until the appearance of ripples of disruption from the events chronicled by Stone Telling, whose time with the Condor reveals that aggression and violence are present also among the Kesh).

The City of the Mind is a computer that preserves much of the so-called civilization that preceded the Apocalypse. It removes the burden of the distant past from people going about their daily affairs and regulates the balance in the Valley, acting as a presumptively objective hand behind the scenes. This insulation from a traumatic past allows the Kesh to rebuild a life somewhat like the one of the Valley's first peoples, the California Indians as Le Guin knew them. But there is a fly in the ointment, in the removal of the possibility of "two-eyed seeing" in the idiom of many contemporary Indigenous peoples of the Americas. Removing the burden of selecting what is to be transmitted and why eliminates the necessity for reflexivity that is the common essence of history and memory. The dialectic between Pandora and the Archivist restores dynamism to the ethnographic encounter.

Pandora argues that "information storage and retrieval" is a value, because the passing on of information from one generation to the next is "the central act of human culture" (315). Her initial outburst appears to be an ethnocentric judgment without evidence or reflection, presumably mirroring the reaction of the Reader she hopes to lead to an alternative view of history and preservation. For Le Guin, as for Pandora, there is intrinsic value to history in the sense of making information about the past available to anyone who wants or needs it. Academic life shares with the literary canon an attunement to this position. We protect our venerable records, books, and other artifacts, albeit by keeping them out of use and separate from everyday life, at a distance. We have special institutions devoted to the task: libraries, archives, museums, art galleries, perhaps even classrooms with smart technologies to preserve the very process of recording and remembering so it will be available for further application, perhaps of reflection.[7]

The Archivist's reply to Pandora captures our attention precisely because it upends our cherished but usually unexamined assumptions and priorities. "Tangible or intangible. Either you keep a thing or you give. We find it safer to give it.... Keeping grows" (315). It outgrows the bounds of keeping track of what is kept, whereas "giving flows" (315). The Archivist proposes that giving is more complex because it requires "discrimination," a more disciplined intelligence: "Disciplined people come here, Oak Lodge people [each Lodge has characteristic skills and responsibilities], historians, learned people, scribes and reciters and writers, they're always here" (315). By implication, ordinary people do not want the burden of responsibility for deciding what to keep and what to discard. The Archivist challenges Pandora by reversing her question. "What if I asked you if you had considered the danger of storing up information as you do in your society?" (315). She elaborates:

> Who controls the storage and the retrieval? To what extent is the material here for anyone who wants and needs it and to what extent is it "there" only for those who have the information that it is there, the education to obtain that information, and the power to get that education? . . . How much information is available to ordinary non-government, non-military, non-specialist, non-rich people? What does "classified" mean? What do shredders shred? What does money buy? In a state, even a democracy, where power is hierarchic, how can you prevent the storage of information from becoming yet another source of power to the powerful—another piston in the great machine? (315–16)

At the start of this exchange, Pandora accuses the Archivist of being a luddite, while the Archivist sees Pandora as a utopian idealist. The positions are polar opposites. The Archivist, accustomed to a society based on oral tradition (though the Kesh are literate) among people who know one another well beyond the context of any single debate, tries to mediate the impasse. She assures Pandora that she does value machines; a machine that is part of her life is like "an old friend." But her examples (a washing machine, an office printing press, a poem valued because it was written by a deceased community member who was a dear friend) all serve to disengage machine-ness from the system of information manipulation she has just attributed to Pandora's society and by extension to Pandora's status as an outsider historian looking at the Kesh through an alien lens.

The Archivist believes that she is not rigid in her principles of selection. She makes exceptions based on personal relationships and contemporary concerns. "When Mines died last year, I printed this poem of his, thirty copies, for people to take home and give to the heyimas (local clan groups), here this is the last copy" (315). There is no reason to save it any longer. Pandora retorts, rather feebly, that lack of censorship, free public libraries, and computer media make a difference, but admits, "I don't know. It keeps getting harder" (315). The Archivist "worries," usually Pandora's job, and apologizes for making her sad. The relational response flows naturally from an oral culture grounded in face-to-face relations.

Pandora and the Archivist reconcile their positions and find common ground by agreeing tacitly that a critique of both civilizations might be in order. They exit singing together. The book's final section, consisting of Le Guin's Acknowledgments, is titled "Pandora no longer worrying" (506) and asserts by implication that Le Guin's text has been woven from dialogue and that her companions in that journey began an ongoing conversation that the Reader is now invited to join.

The challenge to the Reader was posed earlier in a poem that now fits into a larger reflection on memory and history across time—a reflection that exudes worry about the more general influence that Pandora as an outsider might have on the Kesh: could her presence change their history? Pandora is worrying "with agitation" (147):

Have I burned all the libraries of Babel?
Was it I that burned them?
If they burn, it will be all of us that burned them.

In any case, the texts sent away for archiving remain on shelves "and electronic brains" (315). The Archivist continues: "Nothing is lost, nothing is forgotten, and everything is in little bits. But you know, even if we don't burn it, we can't take it with us. Many as we are, there's still too much to carry. It's a dead weight . . . [to] bear the load of civilization forward into the future" (315). Indeed, in one sense it was Pandora who killed the babies, the people who might have been born in the Valley, presumably making her complicit in the apocalypse, because they were too "weak" to "complete the task" (315) of preserving and sorting through all that information. Does she, because she sees the consequences, hold greater responsibility for not changing the course of history in her time? Does telling her tale mitigate the guilt? Or is that a by-product of other reasons she is driven to tell the story and to enlist others in its lack of ending, of closure? Pandora has suffered something of a crisis of conscience. The tension between foresight and hindsight as a result of her encounters in the Valley leave a residue, a burden of responsibility that she chooses to share with the Reader.

The apologetic tone is the crux of the matter: "Listen, I tried to give them time, that's all, honestly. I can't give them history. I don't know how—but I can give them time. . . . All I did was open the box Prometheus left with me. I knew what would come out of it" (135). The Kesh did not suffer the population explosion that strained the resources of Pandora's society beyond sustainability. There were few of them and they trod lightly on the land, attuned to its animals, plants, and wilderness, moving with the Valley's changing states. "You may have noticed that the real difference between us and the Valley, the big difference, is quite a small thing really. There are not too many of them" (135). So space or location becomes "room" and time becomes the lens by means of which Le Guin, via Pandora, dissolves the barriers between past, present, and future into shifting standpoints and potential crossovers. This might produce a dialogue in which the essential things that Pandora knows can emerge in ongoing dialogue with the Reader. But it all depends on the Reader. Perhaps another future is still possible if Readers also see seemingly inevitable disasters with no viable way forward and act upon what they have seen.

IMPLICATIONS FOR WRITING THE
HISTORY OF ANTHROPOLOGY

Most formats preserving the information (primary data) on which our histories are constructed are neither interactive nor dialogic. In *The Dialogic Emergence of Culture* the late Dennis Tedlock argued that culture does not exist until it comes into being as a result of dialogue. Such a description can never be definitive or replicated by different interlocutors on other occasions and in other contexts. We can evaluate it, however, insofar as we are given access to the standpoint of the interviewer. In Tedlock's framing essay, he charges that anthropologists know all this, but, when they write their ethnographies, they privilege one voice in the dialogue to the exclusion of the other. The dialogic process is circumscribed even though ethnographers know better. Either the ethnographer paraphrases what the consultant said, with an occasional brief quotation, or the consultant tells the story in their own words with little or no intervention from the ethnographer. Both strategies imply an aspiration to objectivity that is alien to the ethnographic imagination as it is engaged during fieldwork. On one hand, the urge to produce "scientific" and authoritative discourse is deeply engrained in professional socialization and there is little preparation for the messier relationalities experienced "in the field." On the other hand, the urge to remove the realities of everyday experience in favor of generalizing a larger pattern is also part of socialization in the mainstream North American culture shared by most practicing anthropologists until quite recently. A logical hypocrisy is entailed in the perceived contradiction between what constitutes an adequate report from another place (or time, in the case of the archival historian) and the particularity of the experience whereby that information was obtained and interpreted.

What would it take to redefine science and the scientific method in terms more appropriate to dialogue and intersubjectivity? Can our reflexive processes of memory bridge the gap between the ontological worlds from which we come and those we hope to understand? There are at least three terms to the relation: the participant-observer, the interlocutor, and the audience who must understand without the benefit of having been there. To the extent that this is possible, constant vigilance is needed to avoid falling back into familiar habits of thought and feeling.

Le Guin's challenge, based on the ethnographic particularism of her novel, is to open up a contemporary dialogue about alternative futures for the Kesh and their valley. At a more fundamental level, however, we are challenged to rethink the way we write our own histories. The experience of the Kesh as explicated by the Archivist should teach us to claim equal but different values for qualitative methods and from-the-ground-up ethnography building from everyday experience to large interpretative consequences. Historians and literary critics over recent decades have turned to histories of marginalized voices and recorded the everyday lives of the victims of ever-tightening hegemonic authority.

Anthropology as a discipline is at least as well situated as history or literature to redefine the terms of the historicist debate. For example, we can talk about communities rather than populations; about reliability when new data does not surprise; about the cross-cutting intersectionality of age, gender, class, ethnicity, occupation, education, and more on an empirical basis as they manifest in particular cases; and about validity when evidence is internally consistent and there is convergent evidence from multiple sources. We can argue that knowledge of the particular is transportable (i.e., generalizable) even though in other cases the variables may be somewhat different and combined in unique ways. The causes and effects arising from human action make sense of correlations based on a more distanced quantitative approach and bring the past they describe to life for the public record, public audiences, and public policy.

NOTES

1. The genealogy of influence is personal and does not reflect how these matters came together for any other participant. Evidence from oral tradition must always be evaluated relative to what the speaker knew at the time or learned later and projected back into the original experience. Memories change over time and hindsight modifies the accessible past. I owe much of my understanding of these issues to conversations with the late Stephen O. Murray.
2. Although my own choices have not been Stocking's, the myopic retrospective assessment of his work illustrates the blind spot in theorizing the history of anthropology that I address in this chapter.
3. An earlier version of this chapter was delivered as a plenary lecture to an interdisciplinary graduate conference on theory at the University of Western Ontario in March 2019. In that context I deployed Le Guin's metaphor of "coming home" to envision recovering the things one might claim to know for certain in the aftermath of a lobotomy. As Pandora did, I "worried" the ability to distinguish essential from incidental bits of knowledge, using events from my own career as illustrative material. This chapter transposes the argument to the process and value of preserving the past for the writing of anthropology's history.
4. The Reader is elevated to rhetorical stature, parallel to and facilitating Le Guin's myth-parable structure in the figure of Pandora.
5. I read *Always Coming Home* very differently today than I did at the time of its publication or when I first taught it a few years later. This

makes sense given what I argue Le Guin is up to here. She was acutely attuned to directions of change in literature as well as anthropology. Scientific revolutions emerge from a general social milieu and are rarely restricted to single disciplines.

6. When it comes to our personal records, memories and reflections, most of us want to believe that they will be preserved, that our own identities will somehow live on through them, all under the happy assumption that others in the future will care enough to access the records we so diligently preserve.

7. As Boas argued in "The Study of Geography" in 1887, different methods are needed for the historical sciences, but they are equally rigorous and therefore scientific.

REFERENCES

Benedict, Ruth. 1934. *Patterns of Culture*. Boston MA: Houghton Mifflin.
Boas, Franz. 1887. "The Study of Geography." *Science* 9: 137–41.
———. 1911. *The Mind of Primitive Man*. New York: Macmillan.
Clifford, James and George Marcus, eds. 1986. *Writing Culture: The Poetics and Politics of Ethnography*. Berkeley: University of California Press.
Darnell, Regna. 2001. *Invisible Genealogies: A History of Americanist Anthropology*. Lincoln: University of Nebraska Press.
Hallowell, A. Irving. 1965. "The History of Anthropology as an Anthropological Problem." *Journal of the History of the Behavioral Sciences* 1: 24–38.
Hymes, Dell. 1962. "On Studying the History of Anthropology." *Kroeber Anthropological Society Papers* 26: 81–86.
King, Thomas. 2003. *The Truth about Stories*. Toronto ON: House of Anansi Press.
Kroeber, Theodora. 1961. *Ishi in Two Worlds: A Biography of the Last Wild Indian in North America*. Berkeley: University of California Press.
Kuhn, Thomas. 1962. *The Structure of Scientific Revolutions*. Chicago IL: Phoenix.
Le Guin, Ursula. 1985. *Always Coming Home: A Novel*. New York: Harper & Row.
Radin, Paul. 1933. *The Method and Theory of Ethnology*. New York: McGraw-Hill.
———. (1927) 1957. *Primitive Man as a Philosopher*. New York: Dover.
Stocking, George W. 1968. *Race, Culture and Evolution: Essays in the History of Anthropology*. New York: Free Press.
Tedlock, Dennis and Bruce Mannheim, eds. 1995. *The Dialogic Emergence of Culture*. Urbana: University of Illinois Press.

10

A Public Anthropology of Transition

Vintilă Mihăilescu (1951–2020) was a leading Romanian cultural anthropologist and highly regarded public intellectual. A widely published researcher, he was a professor at the National University of Political Studies and Public Administration in Bucharest. This article prefaces the English translation-to-be of his volume *A Public Anthropology of Translation*, a synthetic presentation by an attentive and reflexive observer of more than two decades of cultural-anthropological study of the Romanian society during its transition from communism (formally deceased in December 1989) to less tentative forms of capitalism. Written from the ground up, this text is an engaging, alertly written, and often humor-laden take on phenomena not too familiar to the North American reader.

Any and every object, if properly studied, will bring with it the whole of (its) society.

—André-Georges Haudricourt

Anthropology is translation.

—All the anthropologists I respect

This work brings together in narrative form a selection of my articles that appeared in the Bucharest cultural journal *Dilema Veche* (*The Old Dilemma*) over a twenty-year period, and which were published, again selectively, in four successive volumes by Polirom Publishing House. The last two of these bore the subtitle "Notes on Public Anthropology" in order to highlight the fact that these pieces are the product of an anthropological reading of post-communist daily life, though translated for a wider public. With this in view, all the texts depend on humor and irony; at times they verge on being anecdotal and, on the face of it, without real value. On the other hand, although references are generally made to Romanian society, they are wherever possible presented in the context of the whole sweep of history and compared with other similar or contrasting situations in today's world. As its subtitle suggests, this book is not necessarily *about* Romania but only written *in* Romania; its topics and the interpretations given of them cover a far wider sociocultural area (and in fact one version of the subtitle was "Recent Tales from Rumelia"). Furthermore, all articles touching on subjects of general interest are handled in such a way as to make a clear connection between their starting points in anecdote and anthropological interpretations that are much more comprehensive in nature. This is the point of the quotation from André-Georges Haudricourt that I have chosen as a motto for the entire volume.

The pieces are arranged as a series of stories in the style of *The Arabian Nights*, but they are also grouped in accordance with a made-up dialectic: *thesis, antithesis, synthesis*, with intercalated *parentheses*.

The *thesis* is made up of texts that confer a kind of genius loci. This is achieved by their having a species of oral fixation on food, but (also) via references to the givens and implications of an "oral society," with implicit reference to Freud's oral stage. And the chapter does in fact close with a psychoanalytical dialogue on this topic.

The *antithesis* brings together texts about the ruptures, discontinuities, and tensions caused by the fall of communism and the real changes that have taken place during the so-called transition period. The chapter opens with the suggestion that, in fact, this "second Europeanization" has involved two transitions, one to capitalism and the market economy in the towns and cities, and the other, by omission, to feudalism and a subsistence economy in rural areas, with the divide between "the two Romanias" being thus accentuated. It goes on to investigate some contradictions in the social reality of this world of "posts": post-communist, post-peasant, post-industrial, post-religious (and yet it is the most religious society in Europe), with a state that is both faux-minimal and only on paper socially responsible, and in which the pace of economic development is matched by that of the increase in poverty.

The *parenthesis* brings together some pieces that could be regarded as belonging to "the anthropology of the everyday," since they convey an atmosphere, mood, and happenings that have local but also often general human significance.

The *synthesis*, besides outlining the degree to which and manner in which globalization has been taking place in a society in transition, also provides an opportunity for critical reflection on postmodernity in general. It deals with such major European (and sometimes global) trends as those that have affected family structure and intergenerational relations, the postmodern cult of the body, the quest for authenticity, the appearance of "neo-tribes," alterations in the human-animal relationship, and so forth. To be precise, it is in fact a discussion of the relations between freedom, transparency, and control, along with the emergence of a phenomenon that could be termed assisted individualism (or hedonism).

The *epilogue* is a confession of faith that advances a categorical imperative developed from the Hegelian paradigm of the struggle for recognition: *don't despise!* The entire work has in fact been written in this spirit, involving an effort to understand even what is hard to accept.

1. THESIS: GENIUS LOCI

The day was December 22nd, 1989, there was still plenty of shooting in Bucharest, and news about more people being killed in the Revolution kept coming in from all over the country. Yet among the flying bullets everyone was trying to buy themselves a tree and a pig. Christmas was around the corner, that Christmas Day when the Ceaușescus were to be executed. The Romanians entered post-communism with a religious festival that trod death underfoot.

The Pig's Progress (in a Time of Transition)

SONG XIX

There's a fine smell of sarmale over the Carpathians
a smell that makes you want to die
that makes you long to stretch yourself out over the Carpathians
like a breeze that blows for aye.[1]

—Ion Nicolescu

Do you have a problem with others? Do sociology! Do you have a problem with yourself? Do psychology! And if you have a problem with both yourself and others, do anthropology! I am an anthropologist.

More apropos, for the past twenty years I have been writing a weekly column entitled "Socio-to-and-fro" (*Socio hai-hui*) in the leading Romanian cultural magazine, *Dilema Veche*. Week in and week out, out come my attempts at answering the problems and dilemmas posed by Romania's (and, yeah, the rest of the world's) transition to globalization. And so a collection of about one thousand and one splinters came into being, piling up in a *sui generis Halima*. All through this period my chosen topics have changed from one week to the next and have ranged over the ideas' four winds. Enigmatically, however, my wandering splinters have had the habit of coming home from time to time, as if led by some sort of to-and-frolic moves, to visit their families—other splinters related to them by blood or simply by alliance. Of all these, the pig splinters, if I may so term them, were the most constant and over time came to compose the most numerous family. For I have been the chronicler of festive *sarmale* for twenty years and have followed in great detail the progress of the pig into pork and into its derivatives, which are more material but no less splintery than their financial counterparts. Why, I have even written in the most academic terms possible on "Problems Encountered in the Deconstruction of Sarmale," on "The Legal Pig and the Real Pig," and so on and so forth, tracing to the best of my ability the long and winding road of the identitary pig, all the way from cosmogony to food safety. This is where my story starts: with the ground-pork-filled *sarma*, Romania's national dish.

Before I begin, I should forewarn you that, although it is Balkan, that is, Persian, that is, circum-Mediterranean, with distant cousins to be found as far away as Kazakhstan, as we learned recently, the sarma is the national dish of Romanians, indeed the unmistakable stamp of Romanian identity. Here, in brief, is the sarma's recent history, as portrayed in a number of texts kept here in their original forms (albeit translated into English).

Prologue: There's a Smell of Sarmale over the Carpathians

Every Christmas I would write a befittingly festive splinter, and came to realize that, if they were lined up in chronological order, sarma after sarma, as it were, these splinters would provide a unique picture of our far-reaching transition. Because, believe it or not, not even the sarma is what it used to be, and its story is our shifty story, too.

The first splinter is a song of the sarma, an aesthetic-gustatory relishing of the good things in life that sends patriotic shivers down the spine: *There's a smell of sarmale over the Carpathians!* You can smell them in the house, where love for one's wife and love for one's wider family blend together in the steam of the sarmale's love for life. What could be more uplifting? And at the same time this first splinter is an almost true-to-nature text, a screen onto which is projected what's happening along the highways and byways of our native land.

Year in, year out I felt *sarmalic*—meaning that I was a good Romanian, always at peace with myself and with life—during the suspended time represented by major festivals. In fact I enjoyed them wholeheartedly and tried—without overdoing it—to provide them with a more chic cultural cushioning.

At the same time, these were also good years of education-focused festivals belonging to the Learn Romanian Ethnology by Eating series, which I had designed for my masters' students in anthropology, whom I would regularly invite to my home for New Year's. The two or three days of intensive teaching and learning would always be brought to a natural and apotheotic close with a giblets sour soup (*ciorbă de potroace*) in which the uninitiated would just as invariably start looking for giblets to the delight of those in the know. In this way the time-honored yet measured atmosphere of the celebration was passed on, yielding me a teacher's satisfaction. However, after some ten years all this came to a natural end; I stopped inviting them, not that they would have come any longer. The Internet and its holiday-time emoticons had come to replace the giblets in the soup.

The first meta-*sarmaliciteme* that hit the market were the fireworks. I was in a small town hugely overshadowed by the mountains the year it first happened, where I witnessed an unprecedented visual extravaganza that went on for hours on end: it rained rainbows over the Carpathians! The following year I had gotten used to this spectacle; after another couple of years it had become less intense—or perhaps I was no longer regarding it as something out of the ordinary. The attack of festive-consumerist bulimia had passed. Last year the fireworks reappeared, but now on a different level of the spiral of history: not so many as before, but far more elaborate, with a proud middle-class whiff about them.

Toward the end of the 1990s I was struck by a first transformation, social in nature for the moment, among city-dwellers. Christmas was no longer a purely familial celebration. *Relatives* were increasingly being joined (or even replaced) by *friends*, and these friends were more and more often selected from among one's work colleagues. The questions "Whose son or daughter are you? Where do you belong in the family?" were slowly but surely mutating into "Where do you work?"

I think it was at Christmas 1999 that there occurred a cataclysmic event that, at that time, left me at a loss: a former student, who had been converted a few years previously in India, cooked us some delicious vegetarian dishes. Say what: me, eating green stuff at Christmastime?! I felt I really must go to church to light a candle for all my forbears and ancestors who had doubtless spent the festive season turning in their graves, appalled by such treachery on the part of their unworthy successor. However, the year after that, feeling I needed to take a closer look at the eating habits of my fellow citizens, I set my students as homework the task of giving a "thick" (to use the jargon of the profession) ethnographic description of their Christmas meal or meals. It was then that I learned that the pig was no longer king but merely a kind of constitutional president whose scope and prerogatives had been severely curtailed. The turkey had already put in an appearance, there were some "corporate" families in which catering companies were used, and I even discovered two cases among my students' parents in which Chinese food (pork gong bao, for example) had been ordered in for Christmas dinner. At about the same period, my own children—in other regards well trained in the gastronomic identity of the nation and free of nutritional sectarianisms—began to give rather long, hard looks at pork dishes and to prefer something "lighter." We were, no doubt, well on the way to betraying our country, our sarmale, and our nation . . .

The moment came for the pig-to-pork to join the EU. This was perhaps the first time since the Revolution that the Romanians felt that their world had been shaken to its foundations, and Eurosceptic horror was born. "If the EU means I can't raise pigs any more, then I no longer want to be in Europe!" was the succinct comment, for the mass media, to a countryman stunned by the news that from now on the pig was no longer to be slaughtered, but humanely stunned. But all the same, the minister of agriculture attempted to make the case for the change: "Isn't it tidier; isn't it nicer?" The general public grunted a decided *no*. Along with my colleagues from *Cațavencu*[2] magazine I therefore lost no time in devoting a porkshop to this national drama and tracing the entire semantic journey of the pig all the way from cosmogony to bioethics. Even we were scared when we realized how much we could find out about ourselves if we shifted our gaze from the fit-to-eat pig to the fit-to-think-about pig, as Lévi-Strauss would have said!

In parallel with this, Christmas was increasingly becoming a kind of pretext, a sort of license for shopping and entertainment spread throughout an ever longer and more thoroughly commercialized month for giving presents. This was why for two or three successive years I wrote about window displays, retail figures, consumerism, and other replacements for Christmas. Journalists, too, in their interviews, were beginning to move away from "Tell us how Romanians celebrate Christmas" toward "We would like your expert opinion here: are any features of the old Romanian way of celebrating the festive season still practiced?"

As for the present day, how is the pig doing now, and what else does it have to tell us about ourselves and our world?

Well now, in the first place, we gather from the statistics that where today's adolescents are concerned, sarmale have practically disappeared from their lists of favorite dishes, and pork is bad for your health. We gather (if we want to) that *pig business is big business* and we understand (if we can) why agriculture and country people look as they do. And if we were also to see the way in which pigs are reared in these mega-combines that have appeared in Romania, as in other countries, we would be in danger of becoming a nation of vegetarians. Not to mention the stories I heard not long ago from a leading specialist in the European food industry, who explained to me with a wealth of detail just what the relationship is between our processed meat products and actual meat. But it would be better for me not to tell you ...

Just as whatever perishes has to be reborn, so it is with the pig. Even if we must give up raising pigs at home, the "traditional" fairs have become full of pork products "just like Mum makes at home." Where our country people have gone abroad to work these pork products have followed them and are now traveling all over Europe by truck. Facebook is full of "Mum, Mum, send us some fat bacon!" and the coaches that travel the highways of Europe, headed for Rome, Brussels, or London, bear with them food parcels sent by the old folks at home. And when the emigrants come home for Christmas they gather round the pig; it's a kind of equivalent of the Spanish *matanza didáctica*, changing the standard way in which a group celebrates and consumes food into a festive mise-en-scène of the group itself. It is not so much that the family meets around the pig as that the pig unites the family. More than that, although the Romanian pig has kind of disappeared, some people have managed to bring back to life nice (i.e., imported from Hungary) Mangalița pork, that source of good cholesterol. And, to make everyone happy, given that pizza has replaced sarmale, even pizza with a religious offering of pork has made its appearance. You've got to hand it to us—we're a tough and ingenious people!

However, let's also investigate some of the significant details of this "Pig's Progress," starting from the zero hour when Romania joined the EU.

First Story: The Pig According to Law, the Real Pig

First there was the news that Romania was being integrated into Europe; straight after this the pig crisis erupted. A rumor began to spread throughout the country (in fact, to be fair to the pig, the EU generally was and remained for a long time more a rumor than anything else): that the EU was ill-disposed to the Romanian porker. What precise plans it had was not known, with the result that the reports started to expand and to impinge on our newspapers and TV screens. *What have their lordships got against my pig?*—was the puzzled reaction of one countryman caught on the TV cameras. Just so—what do they want to do with our national pig?

The only more specific information we had concerned a new obligation to use "euthanasia," which, arriving as it did just on the eve of St Ignatius's day, when every man Jack of the Romanians had his knife to his pig's throat, set many people thinking. However, taken in itself, this requirement contained a generous dose of hypocrisy, with the consequence that it was not very convincing. Next we started hearing that the Europeans were going to stop us using parts of the freshly killed pig for edible offerings (*pomana porcului*), that Christian culinary deed so dear to our hearts. Coming as it did without the underlying medical explanation, namely that, where pork is concerned, any of its parts eaten immediately after the animal is slaughtered is slightly toxic, this ban too seemed ridiculous. Then there came the minister of agriculture's memorable comparison between the Romanian pig and the Spanish bull, which had the world making jokes at our expense. But in fact, if we restore it to its original context, this comparison to one of the best-known cases of an exception from EU legislation being made on grounds of cultural specifics was highly relevant and potentially strategically useful. But as it was, the phenomenon of scraps of information being passed on in a haphazard way from mouth to mouth made it impossible for people to form anything like a coherent picture of the situation, which, taken as a whole, was connected with what even our prime minister had admitted in public to be the trickiest aspect of the negotiations: agriculture. Except that the Romanian government didn't really attempt to negotiate this area but instead said, "No problem—we'll do it!," in response to almost everything Brussels demanded. It even said yes on points where it had been told in words of one syllable that it could say no provided it explained why. Stun pigs? By all means, we'll do it—no problem, the Romanian government rushed to respond, even though point 18 of European Council Regulation 1099/2009 on the protection of animals at the point when they are killed contains a clear provision that "it is important that potential for exceptions being made from the stunning of animals before slaughter should be upheld, so that each member state has a measure of subsidiarity. Thus, this regulation makes provision for freedom of religion and for people's right to express their religion or convictions by means of adherence to a religious denomination, teaching, practices and the performance of rituals." So subsidiarity is kindly disposed toward us and does not force us to turn an integral identity festival into an illegal act.

But let's not panic; as in so many other cases, no one proved weak enough to follow the EU legislation—no pig was stunned—one reason being that there were no facilities for doing so. But the idea persisted that slaughtering pigs in the way we Romanians do it is cruel and barbaric, whereas they, the people in civilized countries, are much more... civilized. From the perspective of European norms on the subject, "the traditional method of killing the Christmas pig can be regarded as barbaric," as a leading Bucharest daily claimed (Sabău 2011).

So, are the Romanians barbarians? What a pigsty of an idea!

My mind takes me back to various merciful scenes connected with the fate of pigs. I recall my mother, for example, having to kill the ritual Christmas pig on her own in an apartment building in Bucharest. To make things easier, she decided to challenge the pig to a *corrida* in the stairwell of the block using a scarf soaked in chloroform. After a few minutes, the pig grunted angelically, rolled its eyes up, and settled down with its legs in the air. So did the guests who, a few hours later, ate some of the offering of the anaesthetized pig. Some other tender-hearted people once tried to gas their pig to economize on effort. They stuck a pipe in its mouth, turned on the gas, and waited. For some unfathomable reason, the pig seemed to like this, with the result that, after a few minutes, it happily departed this life for the pigs' paradise. The shock came when they started burning its hair; full of gas as it was, the pig blew up.

But these are minor individual aberrations, departures from the collective norm. If you ask anyone in the country why they kill their pig the way they do, they'll shrug their shoulders and reply, "That's the way it's done round here." Or, more specifically, "That's the custom!" The pig is killed not the way each person fancies doing it, but according to the custom. And this *custom* is neither more nor less than the cosmic order, a shared vision about the world and life in which both man and pig have their place. Indeed, this is a vision that requires a man to ask the pig's forgiveness and then to make an offering of it in an almost Christian way in order not to disturb the custom or order of the world. There is a *purpose* in the collective activities carried out so frenetically by Romanians over Christmas and New Year, that is, a meaning legitimized in and through a vision of the world. And there are *norms* that

228   *Mihăilescu*

go with these ritual activities: It's not just anyone who is entitled to slaughter the pig, and above all it can't be done just anyhow. Any deed that replaced ritual violence with personal cruelty would instantly be sanctioned by the community. The pig is therefore an *institution*, more precisely a component element of that complex of codified actions of a group that generally constitute an institution. The pig's progress or transition is thus in its turn an institutional transition.

Here we need to turn to Mary Douglas and her book *How Institutions Think*. "A convention is institutionalized," she says, "when, in reply to the question, 'Why do you do it like that?' [. . .] the final answer refers to the way the planets are fixed in the sky or the way that plants or humans or animals naturally behave" (Douglas 1986, 46–47). After this she goes on to explain that "for a convention to become a legitimate institution there has to be a parallel cognitive convention to support it"—what Douglas calls "conviction." Institutions therefore have power to the extent that the *conventions* with which they operate in their ongoing transactions are founded on—and thus legitimized by—higher-order cognitive convictions. So it is too with the institution of the pig: current pig-killing practices are established by ritualized conventions that in their turn are legitimized by the conviction that there exists an order uniting pigs, man, and the universe. A number of festive pig customs, beginning with the offering of the pig (which in the north of Romania is called God's vapor), thus establish the correspondences between the vital organs of the pig and the elements of which the universe is composed. There is therefore nothing "barbaric" in the institution of the pig. This does not mean, however, either that the custom of slaughtering the pig is good in itself or that it has to be preserved unchanged; it means that it is not an act of cruelty but a sacrifice that has a purpose of its own as an institution.

But this story of the pig has a far more comprehensive and profound moral: What is the point of changing this institution and how could it be achieved?

Any change such as that involved in joining the EU involves the modification of institutions. But changing them cannot be limited to their legal framework or to imposing norms of social interaction. It requires, in addition, a cognitive legitimization that cannot be achieved except by a link being made with "the way in which the planets, human beings and animals naturally behave," that is, a conviction, a transcendence of the conventional, as André Petitat called it; in short, a *meta-social vision* of the world and of life. The traditional institution of the pig will truly change into the EU institution of food safety only when and to the extent to which the traditional view of plants, human beings, and animals changes in a similar way, giving a new meaning to new methods of killing a pig and to new relationships between people. Mind you, here the pig is a mere metonym.

In short, institutional codifications need to have a point for those who are meant to be taking part in the functioning of the institutions concerned. Only thus are "the common good" and the carrying out of collective actions possible. And for these things to happen, institutions need to be coherent, stable, and transparent, in order that individuals may, in time, find a point in belonging to them. Of course, institutions can constrain people to conform to them by keeping the letter of the law. But they cannot really function merely by imposing legal conventions without also proposing moral convictions. If they try to do so, there is a risk that the slightly bookish distinction between *society according to law* and *real society* may become the schizoid way in which society operates from day to day: sometimes according to the conventions, sometimes following convictions.

The way in which the pig's progress has taken place in Romania casts light on another moral of the fable, too: the nourishing of lawlessness. The reason is a simple one: the legislator passes a law about stunning, even though it wasn't necessarily needed (or not in that form), and the citizens might put it into practice, but don't understand why—nor have they the means to do so. Furthermore, even the government doesn't particularly believe in this law, and the citizens don't particularly conform to it, unless they are sanctioned for not doing so. Well now, this being the situation, actual social behavior ends up conforming to that old folk principle: "we'll see ..."

At present the pig isn't sacrificed very often anymore, but neither is it generally stunned; most often, it is butchered ...

The transition had been in place for some time and the world already looked different. For me, however, the story I'm about to tell you got stuck in my mind as if it had been the first one I wrote after 1990, a kind of inaugural moment of change. Even now I do not know why I called it the fish tank of transition. But in one sense I felt in my element in that villa belonging to a nouveau riche family, while on the other hand it was as if I were in a shop window, disorientated and embarrassed about the situation I was in.

First Story: We and They, or the Fish Tank of Transition

When we didn't really know where we were going to go on holiday—or how we were going to afford one—lo and behold, a childhood friend who had become a successful businessman rang to ask if we'd like to stay for a week, just us, in his seaside villa. What a lucky strike![3] So we found ourselves in an apartment just like in the pictures, right on the waterfront, with a façade made of sliding glass doors. After some minutes of amazement, we swiftly went and bought a pack of good cigarettes and a bottle of vintage wine—*noblesse oblige*, what the hell!—and stretched ourselves out in armchairs at the entrance to the veranda. The sea expanded before us at our feet; the wind rustled the tree leaves lightly and ruffled the white curtains; the first stars began to show in the sky. We sipped our vintage wine from cut-glass goblets, up there, in enjoyment, while a few meters in front of us and below us people thronged the promenade. We were already in a different world.

Somewhat later, we too went down to the seafront and walked leisurely up and down. We passed in front of other villas, with other people savoring their drinks in other crystal goblets. A group of youngsters were listening to music on the radio of an open-top Porsche and drinking beer. *Who knows what their parents are,* my wife thought aloud, with some acerbity. *Conceited parvenus!* I spat out bitterly. Then I realized that the passers-by who were looking at us from below would have said the same thing. *But we are totally innocent . . .*—my wife read my thoughts. After which we went up again, into our world, to finish our wine, watching those below as if through a glass. Sidelong glances and ill-natured mutterings would tell us as explicitly as could be what they were thinking about us, if we wanted to know.

The next day we went to collect our child from a camp being held in another Romanian seaside resort. A one-star hotel and a damp room in which there was no running water except down the walls from a pipe that had been broken for God knows how long, with mosquitoes all over the ceiling and a light bulb that had been waiting for days to be replaced. *Little do they care about us! Scoundrels, the lot of them!* the lady in charge of the camp complained. I didn't know who "they" were, but I was inclined, spontaneously and sincerely, to fully agree with her. We are clearly the victims of parvenus and scoundrels.

How fortunate that we were able to return home, up there, to the glass veranda, and open another bottle of vintage wine. I gazed at the wide sea and sank into the deep stillness of the twilight in my crystal glass. From time to time I caught from somewhere below the curious glances of the people strolling on the front, mumbling isolated words that only they could fathom.

I feel that I am in a fish tank: they on one side, we on the other. But if I think about it for a little while, I find I can no longer say for sure which of us is "they" and which is "we." I am aware of the existence of the fish tank, but do I know which side of the glass I am on?

Honestly, do *you*?

3. PARENTHESIS: FEELINGS, ACTIONS, AND KINDS OF HUMOR

In which I will be talking, purely and simply and without hermeneutical pretensions, about precisely what it says in the title: feelings, actions, and kinds of humor that have shaped me one way or another over these twenty years and change.

First Story: The Story of the Hubble-Bubble Pipe

The musician, hailing from our part of the world, takes his leave of the public on the train that connects Charles de Gaulle Airport to Paris, but not before playing a medley of tunes drawn from the folklore of the Paris metro. Then, from the platform, laughing and waving his hand, he lets off a short, sonorous "train wheel sound," the jingle that in Romania precedes station announcements. And so I enter Paris as if I had just gotten off the train in a Romanian province town.

There's a surprise waiting for me at the hotel: even though everything had been paid for in advance, the receptionist, who speaks broken French, sends me to a different hotel, as this one is being repainted. But I have no complaints, as I end up in the Rue des Abbesses in the heart of Montparnasse. What more could I have asked for? A small and somewhat dodgy hotel, where my room boasts neither table nor chair, but where the Bohemian atmosphere of old Paris lies at my feet. I open the window and stand there looking out for a while, letting my eyes rest on memories. Then I go down to drink a just-arrived beer at the nearest bistro, following a ritual that is now in my blood. Around me there are many foreigners—a lot of English is being spoken, and some Italian. Two Maghrebians are taking with the *patron* at the bar. My beer is so small and so horrifically expensive that it almost takes away my wish to keep sampling the Paris bistro atmosphere. I knew it would be like this from the last time I'd passed through Paris, but I still can't get used to it. You know, in my time . . .

I am in Montparnasse, I know these places, but it's hard for me to grasp the fact that I'm no longer in Bucharest. I recall the joke about the Buddhist priests who arrived in New York and stayed in the airport for several days with their eyes staring into the void. When a cop asked them what was going on, one of them explained, "Our bodies got here too quickly, by plane; now we're waiting for our souls to catch up with them!" So I go back to the hotel and apply myself to my work. Late at night I open the window again and look out at the bustle in the street. In my own attempt to contact my soul I set up my hubble-bubble on the windowsill and allow the fragrant smoke to calm me. But before even ten minutes have passed I hear hammering on the door and angry voices shouting in the corridor, "Open the door, you're smoking, you're smoking, open up right now!" Now, I have never stolen in my life, but I guess I'd have felt the same had I been caught holding up a bank. I swiftly put out of sight all I can and shout in my turn, "Just coming, wait a moment!" But I'm still speaking when the door slams against the wall and in the doorway I see the two American women who are staying in the next room, accompanied by a blasé police officer and the receptionist. "He's smoking!" One of the Americans points her finger at me and the whole bunch of them comes into my little room to carry out a search. The blood rushes to my head. I hurl myself towards the English-speaking dragon, seize her by the collar and yell in her face, "Madam, I'm not smoking, I'm taking drugs!" She calms down at once, mutters an apologetic "Oh, sorry!" and the two of them depart to their own room in embarrassment. Smoking is a public offence, while taking drugs is a private matter. "They said you were smoking . . . ," the policeman says in his turn, and then he too leaves, with a shrug of the shoulders. So, I am left on my own in my little room in Montparnasse, overwhelmed by my sin and by a bewilderment as old as time: *Comment peut-on être étranger?*

After an hour or so I go out for a walk. The bars are closed now, and the bustle has died down. I go down towards Pigalle, where I can still find places that are open and full of people. I ask the Chinese behind the bar for a *pastis*. He appears to be the boss (I learn later that many Chinese have taken over late-night bars in the area). But the combination of Chinese and *pastis* doesn't suit me, I don't know why, something seems out of place, so I return to the hotel and try to get into the bed. For the whole of the rest of my time in Paris, no matter where I went, I felt guilty and had the feeling I was being followed. Until I chanced upon Belleville, always a more working-class neighborhood and currently strongly African and Arab, and went into a hubble-bubble den perched on a heated and covered outdoor deck. After an hour or so my soul was back in place. The reason: not so much an excellent pipe as a rediscovered sociability. Different, exotic, almost unintelligible, but evident in the movements and the sound of voices, with a power to enfold you, overcome you, and make you feel good. "Alternative Parises," retorted a female friend, smiling.

Late at night I catch the last metro and go home to Montparnasse. It's Saturday evening so the street is still full of people. It holds no attraction for me, however, so I go up to my room, open the window, and look from that distance at the people enjoying the charm of Montparnasse. Then I turn on my laptop and let Aznavour lullaby me with *La Bohème* on YouTube.

Ça voulait dire on a vingt ans...

It's quite a recent concert. Aznavour, in black and smiling, keeps folding and unfolding a huge white handkerchief. Then, with a touch of pathos, he lets it fall on the otherwise empty stage.

Ça ne veut plus rien dire du tout...

I'm tired. I close the window, turn off the laptop, and go to bed.

4. SYNTHESIS: ASSISTED HEDONISM

The Sixth Story: The Audit Culture

The round table discussion on "the social sciences and those who finance them," which a colleague of mine ran at the annual conference of the Anthropological Association, brought to light an issue that should have had behind it—in Romania, too—hundreds of discussion sessions and dozens of well-researched volumes. It does not have them. The "audit culture," which is in fact its broader context, is not however (merely) a frustration felt more or less intensely by a few visionary university teachers, but something that concerns all of us wherever we are. And it is not a simple matter of the "I like it/I don't like it" kind.

But can one seriously talk about an audit culture?

Apparently one can. Here are the main arguments for its existence:

It has an institutionalized language or, perhaps more accurately, an idiom of its own, Anglo-Saxon in origin, a fact also reflected in the phenomenon of the "translation services" offered by "consultants" who, from Brussels to Bucharest, are paid to translate the thoughts of the beneficiaries into the terminology of the financiers;

It has a set of norms of good practice, with rules for the inclusions and exclusions that derive from them, and for systems for checking and sanctioning. The tangible expressions of these norms are the template and the "verification rituals" described by Michael Power;

The fetishization of the template also expresses the ideology of this culture that puts its confidence in procedures rather than in people: *in template we trust!*

Finally, this entire structure of ideas is given legitimacy by a set
of values founded on a new universalist creed: *accountability*.
A democratic free market society has to be efficient in a way
that is transparent to everyone, and with this in view it has to
be constantly quantifiable in a rational way. In fact, the responsibility to demonstrate transparency shifts from the state to the
institutions it finances. In Romania we have POSDRU. I am still
at a loss regarding this acronym's meaning, but I do know that
this institution, which is part of the Ministry of Education, dis-
tributes monies for research projects. Over the past few days I
have signed the twelve full boxes of files of a POSDRU interim
progress report, while a colleague of mine was tearing his hair
out trying to discover the tax code for pretzels, without which
we could not claim reimbursement for the refreshments served
at a conference. I have yet to hear what the government did
with the money allocated under the contract . . .

However, this "culture" also has some distinctive features of its
own. In the first place, it is, most likely, the first-ever culture that
is artificial rather than organic, because it is generated not by the
social life of a local population but by a trans-local bureaucratic
elite. This also accounts for the tensions and contradictions that
arise between this new imperial-oligarchic culture and national
cultures. Take, for example, the case, brilliantly argued by one
of my female colleagues, of the national folklore archive. As an
essential government tool of Romanian policy and identity, this
institution and its work of "providing knowledge of society"
continue to be funded by the state. Yet there is something of a
mismatch between its modus operandi and the creativity and
efficiency criteria of the audit system: it just does not fit any of
the available templates. And for this reason the state, trapped
as it is by the obligations imposed by its agreement to conform
to the international audit culture, has effectively abandoned it,
expressing regrets that are merely formal in nature.

For many post-socialist countries, and certainly for Romania, this
process of conforming to the audit culture has been salutary. The sys-

tems of education and research had come out of communism delegitimized. That being so, the criteria for transparent evaluation developed in the "civilized world" were the ideal instrument for overhauling the system: university staff had to provide a justification for their positions—and many no longer had any way of doing so. But it was also an opportunity, legitimate up to a point, for some academics to (also) use this instrument for self-advancement, so that they changed from "plain" university teachers to the new system's managerial leaders: we are the bringers of the audit! What occurred was a kind of a second *trahison des clercs*, that betrayal of intellectuals that is indispensable to the logic of the system, which could not have been put into place without support from inside: the proponents of audit began to hunt down their competitors by introducing into the national validation norms certain criteria that only they knew and favored.

Leaving aside the opportunities and cases of opportunism, what have we ended up with? As yet we are not fully aware, because we have not yet devoted the necessary time and energy to thinking it through, except on the occasions and to the extent to which we have been personally affected by it in one way or another. All the same, even taking a very small step back from the day-to-day amusing aspects of the matter can make it possible for us to discern a number of constant features.

In the first place, the university is no longer invested with *authority* but with *utility* (of a market kind, with applicability value, so to speak), and is directly dependent on this. The autonomy it has extends only to administering resources within the limits of the funding allocated to it, and this also fixes its intellectual priorities. More than that, given that the university is in fact funded not *by* the market but only *for* the market, as is the situation in Romania, it is not the market's *needs* but only its *opinions* that are the decisive factor. In this case, therefore, it is not so much its relationship to the market that is the issue as the impossibility of there being a genuine strategic relationship to it. And, last but not least, university teachers (and intellectuals in general) are trapped in a multifaceted velvet marginalization. As (still) citizens of a nation, they are in danger of waking up to find themselves in a peripheral zone, and of being valued—and paid—in line with the ranking of that zone. This comment is particularly relevant to the humanities and social sciences, which are (still) chiefly focused on their own nations; a good specialist on the romantic poet Eminescu or on common-ownership villages will be but a marginal figure in the world of the audit. In addition, they need to work for nothing in order to be paid. For peer-reviewed publications, the work done by a teacher is not paid (in the worst-case scenario, they even have to pay for it themselves), but this is how you accumulate "points" that count toward being "eligible" to be a "manager" of well-paid projects. The "pedagogical vocation" becomes out-of-date and student-centered education a simple legitimizing rhetoric—or even private enterprise. In the end the whole system flows from and justifies itself by institutionalized mistrust. Prestige becomes each day's rating, and competence has to be justified on a daily basis. No one is above the audit—which, however, also means that every teacher has to be able to combat, constantly and in audit terms, an unspoken presumption that they are operating on false pretenses.

I am audited, *ergo cogito* . . .

Do you still remember the "fish tank of transition"? Well, I feel rather like that right now: am I in the system or outside it, privileged subject or suspect object?

The Seventh Story: The Wretchedness of Rational Choices

A few days ago, at an academic event, I met a fellow member of the honorable guild of anthropologists with whom I had not spoken for a long time. Or, to be more precise, we had spoken to each other but not discussed anything since the 1990s, when we had both been at the beginning of the "new road," caught up in grand projects and critical of the waste of money that was a characteristic feature of the enthusiasm of those days. "I could have done three spells of fieldwork with my students for the money that's been thrown away on hotels and meals," I feel I used to exclaim in disgust on every such occasion. But we were convinced that things would sort themselves out and that everything would become better and more efficient. Weighing it up, I have concluded that things have become worse and more inefficient, and that it is still impossible to hold discussions about world poverty anywhere except in five-star hotels. The only difference is that (as in Brel's *Les Notaires*) it is now we who are the people who initiate and manage more and more projects of this kind, costing more and more money, and who ask ourselves, when they are over, what has become of it. And where is all the knowledge that—after such exhausting effort—we have produced?

"How did we get here?" my old friend wondered aloud at one point in our conversation in purely professional puzzlement, with no trace of the pathetic or of that depression-with-a-whiff-of-masochism that has been so fashionable recently. The transition passed us by (or the transition ran off us like water off a duck's back) without us realizing what was happening to us, how we were becoming different people but not the ones we had dreamed of being. We distanced ourselves from communism, we got closer to the West, we opened relations with the inter-war period, and, it goes without saying, we criticized the government for not distancing itself sufficiently from communism, for not getting close enough to the West, and for the fact that things were not like they had been between the wars. And so our minds were always somewhere other than where we were; we were obsessed by what we had missed but were failing to see what had happened to us. And even more sadly, this happened to *us*, specialists in social sciences that we were—people who carefully deconstruct all the mystifying phenomena that come our way and lay bare hidden mechanisms and processes; we forgot to ask ourselves how and why we were a naïve part of these phenomena. If we want to know who we are and what we are doing, we have to consult our agendas, but we no longer have time to wonder what is hidden behind them. We have lived through the transition only to become a subject of study for the next generation, just as communism has become a particular preoccupation for today's young people . . .

From this sprang a more disturbing question: How is it that we have managed, via our free rational choices, to increasingly box ourselves into a life that we did not actually want? Because we did not want to move from research to research management, or to be running, in a free and rational way, after more and more constraints. And our dreams did not involve having to learn another wooden language. Worse than that, the old one, that of communism, was one we had all managed to learn, whereas for the POSDRUghese and Brusselsese of today we have to pay expert translators who, after pocketing their fees, explain to us that we'd be dead without them (a project under-manager even explained to me at one point that without his help I wouldn't even be capable of completing a doctoral thesis; I initially took offence, then held my peace and continued to pay him out of the money allocated to the project for which I, to the best of my ability, was the coordinator). Nor, again, did we dream that the dreadful communist soy salami would be replaced by the posh vegetarian soy without salami, or that, if we were good children, we would have the right—and the opportunity—to buy free-range eggs complete with their traditional-product markup. Just as no Romanian was expecting, after a lifetime's work, to have the democratic right to a pension that would scarcely cover his utility bills. We did a calculation of how much money we two would be retiring on, at the height of our professional glory, and were appalled. And the tale of non-expectations that had come true went on late into the night . . .

And all this has come about as a consequence of our free and rational decisions. Because that's what they're called—rational choices—or at least that's how the economists who rule the world explain it to us, maybe only in order to pander to our vanity or to conceal the irrationality of the story.

In a way, it really did happen like that: we chose, by putting one foot in front of the other, to arrive here, somewhere we didn't want to be and don't like being, even though we fought hard to get here. So how is it possible for each person's rational choices to have the effect of boxing in the lives of everyone? How is it possible that these choices, being free (for they are "free"!), should synergize in such a way as to increase the number of freely-consented-to constraints? More than that, in our cases at least—mine and my colleague's—we made good choices, seemingly, that is—we "succeeded," we ended up in the best possible positions, we are among the winners.

So, what have we won? We looked at each other and smiled. We decided that whoever found the answer first should make a note of it in their agenda.

NOTES

Text translated from the Romanian by Dorothy and Stuart Elford and edited by Călin-Andrei Mihăilescu.

1. From the poem "Song XIX" by Ion Nicolescu, *Mioriţiada*, p. 74. Bucharest: Cartea românească, 1973. Translation by the author.
2. *Caţavencu* was, in the 1990s and 2000s, the leading political satire magazine, much prized by the Romanian public.
3. In the original, "La barza chioară face Dumnezeu cuib," literally, "God gifts nests to one-eyed storks."

REFERENCES

Douglas, Mary. 1986. *How Institutions Think*. Syracuse NY: Syracuse University Press.
Cristina Sabău. 2011. "Tăierea porcului. Tradiţii de Ignat." December 19, 2011. https://timponline.ro/povestea-porcului-traditii-de-ignat/.

1. (*left to right*) Stephen O. Murray, Regna Darnell, Matthew Bokovoy, and Keelung Hong in San Jose, California, November 2018. Photo courtesy Keelung Hong.

STEPHEN O. MURRAY, WENDY LEEDS-HURWITZ,
REGNA DARNELL, NATHAN DAWTHORNE,
AND ROBERT OPPENHEIM

11

An Interview with Stephen O. Murray on Stephen O. Murray as Historian of Anthropology (and More)

Stephen O. Murray (1950–2019) trained as a sociologist at the University of Toronto and anthropologist at the University of California, Berkeley, and worked as an independent scholar for most of his professional life. He published two dozen books and numerous articles, book chapters, notes, and comments, as well as thousands of book and film reviews. He pursued two major research strands: first, the history of the social sciences (specifically anthropology, sociology, and linguistics), and second, homosexuality across geographic and historic locations. The best known of his books in the first strand were *Group Formation in Social Science* (1983), *Theory Groups in the Study of Language in North America* (1994), and *American Sociolinguistics* (1998), and in the second strand, *American Gay* (1996a) and *Homosexualities* (2000). Those who want a more complete picture of Steve's life than that evident from this summary and what follows should consult the obituary published in the *San Francisco Chronicle* (*San Francisco Chronicle* 2019).

What follows has two major parts. The first is a synthesis of Steve's research into theory groups, prepared at his request (details below). The second is a collaborative interview based on email correspondence during the last weeks of Steve's life. He is listed as first author since he was well aware of the intent of the project and fully invested in its success. Each of the other authors provides a brief introduction to their own role. It is our feeling that this novel approach to an interview should prove more revealing than the standard one-on-one effort.

Brief Introductions of the Authors and Their Roles

For Wendy Leeds-Hurwitz (WLH), this chapter has its genesis in Steve's request for a synthesis of my prior reviews of his books on theory groups, which he wanted for a projected final volume of otherwise scattered works. It did not, in the end, get completed prior to his death in August 2019. When we met in San Francisco in March 2019, Steve said that I had done a better job of concisely explaining his ideas on theory groups than he had, and so he wanted to use what I had said in his book. We are honoring that request by including the summary here.

Regna Darnell (RD) had been thinking for some time about adding a regular feature to each Histories of Anthropology Annual (HOAA) volume interviewing someone for whom history of anthropology (HoA) has been a major specialization over a substantial portion of their career. Steve's precarious health bounced him to the top of that list, particularly given how strongly Steve felt about consolidating his work from a remarkably diverse range of publication venues and ensuring his input to a succession plan for his editorial work on the University of Nebraska Press Critical Studies in the History of Anthropology (CSHOA) series. HoA is an inherently interdisciplinary field and requires, in addition to its own theories and methodologies, one or more substantive areas of anthropological, historical, and ethnographic specialization. Steve's work could be consolidated equally plausibly in relation to an audience of linguistic anthropologists, language and communication specialists, comparative sociologists, and students of homosexuality in cross-cultural settings (especially Latin American, Asian, and contemporary North American). The methodologies that crossed these commitments, however, at least in the view of these historians of anthropology, were grounded in Steve's commitment to evidence-based history of science through archives, interviews, and extensive reviews and commentaries. Nathan Dawthorne joined the attempt to complete this interview after Steve's death because he wondered about how the work on homosexuality fit with the historical and comparative perspectives discussed by RD and WLH. Robert Oppenheim documents Steve's assessment of his hopes for CSHOA and HOAA in expressing the reasoning underlying Steve's choice of Rob to succeed him. Steve remains the primary author of his own interview and the rest of us are simply using his previously published words to fill in gaps that he was unable to complete, a perspective that has helped us to sort out how this interview differs from the conventional interview of a senior scholar.

By distributing coauthorship of this inaugural interview among five voices, we attempt to adapt to the contingencies that precluded a more conventional interview process in order to more effectively reflect the complexity of the interview subject. Each of us knew Steve in different contexts. I (RD) am often startled when learning from a new medium or review how much I have yet to learn about people I thought I knew well, professionally and personally. How a scholar reflects back upon their own work is itself a statement contributing to, though not constituting, the interpretation of that work at a given point in time. As we acknowledge that history is a moving target and histories change as fields of discourse and events in the world reframe them for new generations, it is particularly poignant to capture what may seem quite obvious today but will inevitably recede and evade the understanding of successive generations unless documented in its own terms. That is one intent of the interview feature; the other is to highlight models of best practice in HoA regardless of the discipline from which its knowledge arises.

PART 1: STEPHEN MURRAY ON THEORY GROUPS

WLH: After previously corresponding, I first met Steve in 1984 at the Edward Sapir Centenary Conference in Ottawa, Canada, where we both presented papers. After that he often served the important role as first reader on any of my publications overlapping with his interests. In addition to having many informal conversations over the years, and periodic visits, we've traded the roles of author and editor: with Regna Darnell he coedited the series at the University of Nebraska Press in which I published a book (Leeds-Hurwitz 2004), and later he wrote a chapter for a book I edited (Murray 2010). Attentive readers can discover that we have thanked each other in multiple lists of acknowledgments. One of the areas in which our work overlapped concerns his research into theory groups, a major topic in his oeuvre and one on which he published three books. The fact that he was both inside the ethnography of communication theory group he chose as his primary case study (as a student of Keith Basso at Arizona and William Samarin at Toronto, as well as a postdoc with John Gumperz at the University of California, Berkeley) and outside it (he did not hold a university position, and was primarily a sociologist rather than a linguist) presumably accounts for his ability to observe and comment with such insight on this and other theory groups.

Scholars often assume that the best ideas just naturally rise to the top, but in fact ideas have no physical existence and thus cannot stand on their own as if they were pieces of furniture left in place when the carpenter leaves the room. Instead, as a type of thought, ideas exist only through the continued attention of people. And so new ideas must be adopted and supported by people who claim them—if not, they disappear. One early strand of Steve's work examines the necessary requirements for groups of people to share ideas, promoting one over another, and analyzes the circumstances required for a good idea to be taken up by a group.

Steve actually published three versions of his investigations on this topic, so it's worth taking a moment to sort them out. The first version (1983) was his doctoral dissertation published as a paperback. The second version (1994) was substantially revised, updated, and expanded (with much new material carefully integrated into the original study), published as an expensive hardcover. This is the edition most often cited, and the version of greatest value to scholars with research interests in sociolinguistics, given that they will most appreciate the considerable detail provided. The third version (1998) was a streamlined paperback, more reasonably priced and less intimidating, absent half the case studies to permit a clear focus on the main strands of the argument yet still incorporating later publications; this is the version most accessible to most people.[1] His project to understand theory groups has a great deal to offer not only the few fascinated by the history of American sociolinguistics (the specific case study examined at length), but also the much larger cohort of scholars interested in the process by which new ideas do or do not come to be accepted. To my mind, that should be nearly everyone.

As a sociologist, Steve was primarily interested in the people who compose a research group, not solely in their ideas: he carefully documented the connections among researchers, information generally omitted from more traditional histories of ideas, which often take this for granted and omit discussion. Briefly, his approach asks why some good ideas lead to the development of theory groups (that is, a cohesive, overlapping set of people who maintain, expand, and share those ideas), while others do not. What are the critical factors, and in what ways are they related? Steve focused on the communication of ideas within groups because "changes in science are made by groups, not by the automatic breeding of ideas by other ideas, nor by single individuals, however brilliant their thoughts and research" (Murray 1983, 389). He formalized, expanded, and tested the concept of theory groups initially proposed by Griffith and Mullins (1972), using data drawn from sociolinguistics and its predecessor, anthropological linguistics. The initial data emphasize the ethnography of speaking (later known as the ethnography of communication—see Leeds-Hurwitz [1984] for explanation of the shift from speaking to communication—and abbreviated as EOC or EC, depending on where and when practitioners studied). Even in the first book, the boundaries drawn around the EOC group rapidly expanded to include antecedents of that group and then other contemporary groups. In the process of testing his hypothesis, Steve made it clear that he thoroughly understood the broader history of research on language in the United States.

Steve framed his analysis with a summary of related research in the sociology of science; this serves as a short introduction to the topic and is likely to be especially useful to EOC practitioners unfamiliar with that part of the story. The model he tests has two main parts. In the first, he hypothesizes that three factors are essential to the establishment of coherent scientific groups: good ideas, intellectual leadership, and organizational leadership. Each of these is proposed as necessary, but not sufficient, for the formation of a group. The second part, drawing on Kuhn (1962), considers the factors that determine whether the rhetoric of a group will be revolutionary or will stress continuities from preceding research. Here Steve hypothesizes that choice of rhetoric depends on three characteristics: the academic "eliteness" of group members (specifically the universities that grant their degrees, and those in which they teach), their professional age (whether students or faculty), and their access to recognition (primarily evaluated through publication).

Regarding the first part of the model, Steve found intellectual and organizational leadership to be critical to the formation of groups, with the presence of good ideas as a necessary but not sufficient factor. Intellectual leadership together with good ideas also proves insufficient, something many readers may find surprising. The most interesting of his conclusions concerns the second part of the model: the conditions required to produce a rhetoric of revolution versus one of continuity. His case studies demonstrated that no groups whose participants were primarily faculty members used revolutionary rhetoric, and that "eliteness" is not essential—but that perceived blockage of access to publication is. (Whether a blockage exists in reality turns out to be irrelevant, in a nice example of social construction.) Additionally, he found that group coherence is both an indicator of the success of the group and a characteristic of revolutionary groups. Finally, dispersal of the group is not necessarily destructive, especially when this occurs due to students moving around the country to obtain faculty positions and begin their own research centers, because ideas are portable and, when this happens, they just gain a new and larger audience. Steve found no link between the claim to novelty and the real novelty of ideas, and concluded that "the fate of ideas can be considered as depending on social processes rather than the intrinsic merit of ideas" (1994, 490).

EOC provides the most extensive case study supplied. Because the majority of the early members were still alive at the time of the initial investigation, far more information was available than for studies of groups in earlier decades. Steve took advantage of the opportunity by contacting all those actively involved in the first or second generation of researchers. Their stories supplement more publicly available material (such as acknowledgment patterns) to make history come alive. In this way Steve documented the gradual development of a coordinated research group from an initial informal gathering made up of junior faculty, tying in all of the related outgrowths—from the Center for

Applied Linguistics to the Social Science Research Council's Socio-linguistics Committee.

Steve stressed that leadership in an interdisciplinary group such as this one must be especially strong, given that education and professional socialization, as well as later advancement and prestige, are in large part determined within, rather than across, disciplines; and he found such leadership abundant in this particular case. His analysis of EOC led to consideration of rhetorical style, since a shift in paradigmatic assumptions occurred simultaneously with a rhetoric of continuity. This apparent contradiction worked because the shift in assumptions was intragenerational (against transformational grammar), rather than intergenerational, the argument being for a return to the original intent of the prior generation of researchers.

Overall, Steve presented an unusually clear synthesis of large amounts of material in an easily readable form. He had a specific sociological agenda to pursue, but in the process of testing his model he presented more than enough material to satisfy those more interested in the study of linguistics (and ideas) than sociology (and people). Any of his three books on this topic introduce beginners to the field of sociolinguistics more completely than standard textbooks ever could, even when combined with the stories one hears as a graduate student. I wish even one of his books had been available when I was in graduate school; it would have helped immensely in the scramble that a new student goes through to understand the connections between various schools of thought and the people involved. At the same time, his work can serve as a resource for researchers in one part of linguistics who want to learn about the rest of the field. More broadly, anyone who works with ideas in any discipline is likely to be fascinated by Steve's investigation of what it takes for an idea to grow into a school of thought.

PART 2: INTERVIEWS WITH STEVE MURRAY

In the days immediately before he died, Steve had several email exchanges with WLH, RD, and ND. We were each coming up with a list of questions, and due to lack of time sent all three lists to him separately. The fact that Steve spent time in his last days answering these questions says a great deal about how important it was to him to put his ideas on the record. That the answers get shorter and shorter is only a reflection of the lack of time remaining, not the significance of the questions or answers to him.

Questions from Wendy Leeds-Hurwitz

WLH: Who were the most important intellectual influences on your work?

SOM: Regna Darnell influenced me early and often. We met at Canadian sociology and anthropology meetings held at the University of New Brunswick in 1976, though we had corresponded earlier, when I started my dissertation work on the history of anthropological linguistics. In 1979 she defended my dissertation to a committee of sociologists who had not read it or even glanced over it (my real committee was all on sabbatical), something I was too naïve to have considered a possibility. Dennis Magill, the chair of my committee (and of the sociology graduate program at Toronto) was there, but apparently did not take on explaining and defending what I'd done, though he had worked closely with me and definitely had read multiple drafts of the dissertation.

The third member of my committee (who did not show up for my defense), Africanist missionary and linguist William J. Samarin, taught me a lot in a weekly reading course. It was Keith Basso, back at the University of Arizona, in a seminar with only three students, who introduced me to fascination with the ethnography of speaking (and cognitive anthropology) and some classic works, such as Stanley Newman's article on Zuni sacred and secular slang. Newman was a student of Edward Sapir. Keith and Dell Hymes, as well as Sapir's biographer (Regna) stoked my interest in Sapir's ideas (and failures to connect with Chicago sociologists other than William F. Ogburn).

I was excited by the work John Gumperz was doing during the 1970s on interethnic (mis)communication, and he agreed to take me on as a postdoc, though he spent the first year I was in Berkeley at Princeton. Eventually, I was disappointed in the failure of an ethnology of communication to develop, and disappointed that we Gumperzologists did not compare our data.

Veering back to Tucson, I was one of the few graduate students of Robert Nisbet there, because he gave up on teaching Arizona sociology graduate students, whom he found ignorant in general, and in particular in regard to the history of sociological theory. He sent me to Toronto to work with Lewis Feuer, whom I once saw in the departmental office picking up mail, but never met before he moved on to the University of Virginia (Nisbet had moved on to become an Albert Schweitzer Professor at Columbia).

And Keelung Hong schooled me in the American neocolonialist social science work on Taiwan that became the subject of our two books (Hong and Murray 2005; Murray and Hong 1994) and various articles (Murray and Hong 1988, 1991).

WLH: Did whether they were your actual teachers make a difference? Or is just the writing sufficient?

SOM: I was influenced by reading the work of Thomas Kuhn, Robert Merton, Irving Hallowell, Anthony Wallace, Norma Diamond, Robert Mullins, Margaret Hodgen, Dell Hymes et al., and also had a fairly extensive correspondence with Hymes, but the difference between studying with and reading definitely matters!

WLH: Divide your publications into a few major strands and talk about what you've accomplished in each research area.

SOM: I sometimes say that I'm a Mesoamericanist who drifted (to Taiwan and points father east). I did not expect to live into this millennium and worked hard to finish what I saw as my work: on *Latin American Male Homosexualities* in the 1995 New Mexico book of that title, then on Anglo North American homosexualities in the 1996 University of Chicago Press book, *American Gay*. I redid my dissertation as *Theory Groups in the Study of Language in North America* (and my original more limited conception for it as *American Sociolinguistics* (both Amsterdam: John Benjamins). I sought the aid of Will Roscoe to finish *African Homosexualities* (retitled by St. Martin's Press, over my objections, as *Boy Wives and Female Husbands*) and *Islamic Homosexualities* (NYU Press). The protease revolution saved me and I was able to complete my other summa, this one of social organizations of homosexual relations in *Homosexualities* in 2000. I think that establishing that homosexuality is not "un-African" was an important contribution, along with complicating the conception of Latin American homosexualities beyond strict gender binaries. Alas, my correctives to the histories of North American homosexualities have gone largely unheeded.

WLH: You've worked in multiple research areas, not just one. Do you see your work in these areas as separate or interrelated?

SOM: I'd say interrelated, not least in that the historical subject area in which I worked, anthropological linguistics, is also the area of some substantive (if uncollected) empirical work. Also, my historical work seems to me to be work on the boundaries of disciplines as they have been organized in Anglo North America, particularly the ones dividing anthropology from sociology and anthropology from psychology.

WLH: What advice do you wish someone had given you at the start of your academic career?

SOM: Learn a trade that pays (the classic one for leaving the mind free to do other work is plumbing). I have never had an academic job, let alone an academic career, and see the positions available for free thought about any kind of history becoming even scarcer!

WLH: Email and social media and digital publications make it easier to connect with other people now than when you started publishing. Do you find it easy to make new connections with scholars as a result, or do you think it's more useful as a way to maintain connections with those you already know?

SOM: I think that it is easier to make new connections with scholars than before the Internet era and [digital media are] useful as a way to maintain connections with those whom I already know, but it is difficult to get the attention it takes to lay out historical patterns (as I received in ages past from elders) from people accustomed to dashing off tweets and emails. The Internet makes it easier to send drafts quickly to multiple people. Alas, this has not led to more or more thoughtful responses.

WLH: What new project would you start now, if you had the time?

SOM: Rather than doing new research, I'd like to consolidate what I've done—that is, collect heretofore uncollected works that are spread over a range of journals and books.

WLH: What's an answer in need of a question?

SOM: I think that we can no more recover the past than we can enter into the full native sense of cultures other than those in which we were raised. Again, searching across time is similar to reaching across space or across social/cultural distances within a place to so-called "subcultures." Nonetheless, I think that these ultimately impossible goals are ones we should reach for and try to approximate. I do not approve of jettisoning attempts at sympathetic understanding of other cultures or of other anthropologies. Berating those who came before us for not seeing things the way we see them is equivalent to berating other peoples for not doing things the way we do them, or patronizing them for what seems to me similarities to "our way" the "right way" or the way we should be in some imagined future, or the way we were in some imagined golden past age.

Questions from Regna Darnell

RD: Steve did a pretty good job above describing how we met and found that we shared a view of HoA and believed it has or at least should have some center of gravity as a specialization within anthropology. I was impressed when he first approached me with written questions for his dissertation research, and by how thoroughly prepared he was to frame the answers beyond any one individual's response. Linguistic anthropologists, however, were not eager to respond to someone they did not know, so I found myself introducing Steve and vouching for the importance of his work; many of my friends agreed to talk to him. The CASCA (Canadian Anthropology Society) meeting where we first met in person demonstrated how productive his persistence could be. Steve's description of his dissertation defense is also accurate. I did not report to him in any detail the foibles of an unprepared though not antagonistic examination committee; their concept of sociology simply did not include the kind of work Steve was doing. So I explained it to them (as I have found myself doing on several other occasions). We stayed in close touch on multiple issues, bouncing ideas off of each other, often debating whether the Chicago sociologists beat Boas and the anthropologists to the interesting insights of cross-cultural and subcultural ethnography. That seemed to me a reflection of his training in sociology as opposed to my own in anthropology. I associated him with the Chicago school of sociology and was less aware of his own recognition of ties to linguistic anthropology, particularly in its University of Pennsylvania version, which at different times included Hallowell, Wallace, Hymes, and Darnell. When the University of Nebraska Press invited me to develop the Critical Studies in History of Anthropology (CSHOA) series, beginning with my own book *Invisible Genealogies* in 2001, I wanted to work with a coeditor and Steve was the person I wanted. Fortunately, he agreed, so for roughly twenty years we have been in very regular contact, not always in agreement, but always able to see the rationale in the other's position and to defer to it if peer reviewers agreed. It was usually clear who was most enthusiastic about a given project and they would do the first draft of the series editors' introduction. Then it would change substantially on second draft by the other of us. We kept each other on our toes. Some of it was a difference between sociology and anthropology, but each of us had an idiosyncratic take on the discipline of our initial training. I have intervened in some of Steve's responses, trying to minimize my own position while still conveying the flavor of the conversation if we had been able to sit and talk.

RD: How did you come to see history of anthropology (and linguistics) as the core of your work?

SOM: Is it?

RD: Or is it myopic that it has always seemed so to me?

SOM: I don't ponder what is the core or whether there is a core. I was interested by Keith and others in questions of language in society. Wendy is well off having a discipline, communication, to [support her] interest in historical work. History of sociology has failed, despite the influence of Merton and exemplars from him and from Nicholas Mullins.

RD: Would you say then that HoA has some hope of not being a failed enterprise? Or is the verdict still out? Has HoA also failed (like history of sociology and linguistic anthropology) to realize its comparative potentials?

RD: How has your training in sociology been part of the method and theory you bring to HoA?

SOM: It taught me some quantitative methods that I use when there are phenomena to count and as a reminder of the ubiquity of variance even within a culture or society.

RD: Steve did teach me how to count. Quantitative methods weren't part of my own training and I started out in medieval English alongside anthropology. Sometimes it really does make sense to count the forms variability takes even though my own instincts are to model variability in terms of patterns that cross ethnographic particulars and combine in specific ways that depend on context and require nuanced ethnography to document.

RD: Does this relate to ethnography of contemporary communities versus the ones anthropologists usually study?

SOM: It shouldn't. Finding myself in Arizona interested me in Huichol, Pima, Tohono O'odham, Apache, Navajo, though being in Ontario didn't have a similar effect.

RD: Yes, in principle one could study anything anthropologically, but it's harder to study one's own culture of origin, especially for those who have chosen to leave it largely behind. And without the potential effects of defamiliarization to enhance reflexivity.

RD: When I first met you in the mid 1970s, you already wanted to focus on oral history with living people who could tell you things that were not in the archival records. How do you see the relation between that work and the archival and library work you had already done?

SOM: Triangulation. Dating is very unreliable in memory, but it is important to see what our informants see as important in their professional socialization and practice even if they misremember the order. (There is *way* too little about what fieldworkers do when they do fieldwork, though there's more available than when I was starting out in the mid-1970s. I'd like finer analysis of how ethnography [oral history, etc.] is done, less about promulgation of results and theories.)

RD: Steve applies this triangulation to studying anthropologists as part of understanding their history. There is probably more to be said about how that differs from "the field" more conventionally defined by fieldwork as a disciplinary credential.

RD: How do you assess the reliability of evidence from interviews? Is this different from how you assess the reliability of archival evidence?

SOM: Triangulation with other data and plausibility of what is "remembered" and how it is remembered.

RD: Who gets to decide what's plausible? Isn't it kind of arrogant to assume you know that? (In various writings, Steve remained skeptical about memory and meticulously documented the inaccuracy of remembered dates, locations, and meetings of colleagues who saw themselves within a particular anthropological tradition.)

RD: Do you think of interpreting the archive as fieldwork? Is that different in kind from fieldwork face-to-face with living subjects?

SOM: [No response.]

RD: How has your understanding of what HoA is or ought to be changed over your career?

SOM: See the last chapter in the Nebraska history book.

RD: Having done so, I note that he explicitly addressed this question (Murray 2018, 284–87). He proposes five principles of doing HoA well: Studying with someone does not automatically mean that they do the same things or belong to the same school of thought; dates are slippery and often misremembered, with texts often written (and circulated) long before they are published; older texts use the same words in different ways than we use them today, leading to inaccurate presentist judgments; geographic proximity is not correlated with contact or mutual influence in any direct or necessary way; "schools" of thought are "possibly useful fictions, not explanations" that often mask gradual changes and shifts in individual positions over a "life-course." He argues that we have been too quick to apply "etic" labels and missed the actual process, the social organization. His search for a "dialogue of interpretation" often provoked "combative" responses that he did not avoid because they clarified what could be known about the past, by triangulation rather than single sources. He was explicit that this credo for the history of anthropology provides some guidelines for reaching partial truths that will in turn be replaced by other partial truths in a process that involves both continuity and revolution. Doing the history of anthropology is an "experience of questioning 'just-so' stories about intellectual connections in the past to offer some suggestions about how not to do the history of a field" (2018, 273).

RD: Yours is an interdisciplinary approach to your scholarship (with possible implications for activism?). Do the disciplines matter at all in terms of the audience you want to speak to or your own sense of interesting questions?

SOM: Perhaps I should have attended to that better, but selling myself is not one of my specialties. I scoff at the view that one just has to do good work and that it will be recognized. I am not sufficiently aware of who my audience might be.

RD: I extrapolate that you want to consolidate your work so it is accessible as a body to multiple potential audiences, not just those in HoA. There is a sense in which you did not practice what you preach in analyzing the foibles of others. Most of us don't think in terms of consolidating audiences or places of publication. And yet we develop arguments over a series of conferences and articles but cannot take for granted that readers of one piece will have a context for it in terms of your other work.

RD: Your cross-cultural evidence from as many societies as can be documented has not been explicitly HoA? Is that the ethnography part of EOC carried over into HoA?

SOM: I am comparativist in the Max Weber and Émile Durkheim traditions. In my view, Boas was fishing for counterexamples with which to trash this or that theory, not pursuing any genuinely comparativist program. I think he was a theorist in his time, though you want to make him a transcendental theorist, which would have made his skin crawl (but which Sapir found a more comfortable fit; who denies that Sapir was a theorist? No one). Weber's development of ideal types is nearly antithetical to Boas's delight in throwing away bathwaters, baby and all.

RD: Steve and I agreed to disagree about Boas's importance. In terms of Steve's frequent emphasis on organizational vs. intellectual leadership, there is no question that Boas excelled at the former and Sapir, about whom Steve and I were in greater agreement, at the latter. I don't think we should practice anthropology as Boas did, but I do think there is continuity between the paths he doggedly cleared and the opportunities to move to where we are now. I don't think I'm making him a "transcendental theorist" (whatever that is) but am pretty certain I never convinced Steve of that. This is the way our conversations went, whether by email or face-to-face. [An observation without a question.]

SOM: Irving Zeitlin, who was chair of the sociology department that granted my PhD, often urged looking for "the rational kernel" in programs of research he largely rejected. We students were amused when this came back on a midterm as looking for "the rational coronel," not least in being a confusion of levels of analysis.

RD: Is it all part of the same question(s) of widest possible comparison to you?

SOM: Sure.

RD: Dumb question I guess if it gets a one-word answer.

RD: What does it mean to do HoA in a methodologically rigorous way?

SOM: GS [George Stocking] would have said to be sure the dates are right, that what I say happened in 1918 (for example) did happen then. He was less concerned about getting the people who were there then (say in Berkeley in 1918) to understand what they thought they were doing as they did [it] (ultimately [an] impossible achievement but a useful aim).

RD: That is, the social organizations and the networks. Steve was fascinated by acknowledgements and citations. I, too, always start there.

RD: What does the "critical" in "critical studies" mean to you?

SOM: Not accepting that anyone ever was doing what they claimed to be doing or thought they were doing. Or in having the influences as self-imputed. Eliminating what is impossible is a major step to making sense (moving on to what happened when).

RD: Steve's work abounds with examples of debunking rewritten histories from memories of participants—for example, his critique of Chomsky's insistence that he was barred from publication by the establishment against which he claimed to rebel, or his detailed documentation of Carlos Castaneda's library construction of his so-called ethnography of a fictitious Yaqui shaman, or his extended critique of Derek Freeman's ahistorical methodology in his attacks on Margaret Mead that he published after her death.

I would phrase this in terms of reflexivity in the doing of HoA. Or is that just anthropological rather than sociological language addressing the same issue?

RD: What about organizing principles that have sometimes organized parts of the HOAA series, like biography/life history, national tradition, geographical/cultural area?

SOM: If they illuminate a perspective (the pragmatist's answer).

RD: Fair enough—besides, they are all interrelated anyway. These days we call it intersectionality.

RD: Who are your favorite exemplars of doing HoA well? Are they the same people who have been your mentors?

SOM: Robert Oppenheim. I wish there was more work focused on a particular fieldsite as studied by multiple researchers, as well as on theory groups.

RD: [See below for further discussion by and about RO.]

RD: Do you think interviews like this ought to ask the same questions of every subject so they are comparable, or is it preferable to think about the particular position of any and every historian of anthropology?

SOM: Some comparison is good.

RD: Or do you mean comparability?

SOM: I have been very disappointed that there is no more systematic knowledge about language in society now than there was in 1975.

RD: What would it mean to be systematic? About what? Variability? Comparison?

Questions from Nathan Dawthorne

ND: As an emerging scholar I never met Stephen, and only got to know tales of him through Regna as I ploughed away on my doctoral research with male sex workers. Despite her wish for us to connect, other priorities kept me at a distance—shoulda, coulda, woulda. Admittedly, I never thoroughly engaged with any of Stephen's work, nor dug deep into the annals of "queer" anthropology despite having *Out in the Field* and *Out in Theory* (Lewin and Leap 1996, 2002) in my pile of books to read. Hearing Regna reflect on her old friend again as issues of mortality and history coalesced, with the urgency of dissertation writing long past, I have been able to take a few moments to ponder those I consider my anthropological "queer forebears." It was by chance that, as Regna was putting her final questions to Stephen, I asked if I could satisfy my curiosity; it turns out that my questions largely reflected my own positionality as a gay academic dealing with a marginalized population.

Did Stephen feel as alienated as I do (in life, institutionally, in anthropology)? What were the struggles he faced as a gay man in academia? To what degree was his work on cross-cultural homosexualities marginalized (at all stages of the process)? How did his sexual identity affect his anthropological work beyond his focus on the homosexual male?

Although I was largely ignorant of what he may have written on these issues, these are the questions (less clearly presented) that I had the audacity to ask Stephen on his literal death bed. Unfortunately, we couldn't have any further dialogue, so I have been left with more questions as I try to fill in the blanks. Though his responses seem curt they were more layered than they first appear and certainly far from unkind, especially when all is considered. To continue the conversation, I present some of what I have found in his work (as much as possible in his own words) as if these were his actual responses to my questions.

ND: I'd like to hear about the challenges you have faced as a queer anthropologist (situated within HoA but also biographically).

SOM: I have never accepted the label, still less the self-designation of "queer." I consider it derogatory, and have not and never will apply it to myself or my work. I am an empirical and empiricist gay social scientist.

SOM IN PRINT: "My own society . . . continues to imperil me for being gay. . . . From the time I was an undergraduate and throughout my foreshortened adult life, I have . . . [not found] any utopia for sexual nonconformists. . . . I don't like how either my natal society or the scholarly disciplines in which I have been involved denigrate and marginalize homosexuality and those for whom open avowal of homosexual orientation is a defining part of self (i.e., an *identity*)." (Murray 1996a, 1)

"Articles by openly gay men about male homosexuality anywhere in the world did not appear in the pages of the official journals of American anthropological societies across the twentieth century. . . . The record of institutional support for lesbigay anthropologists into the 1990s is even more dismal, with the American Anthropological Association lagging far behind other American disciplinary associations . . . [and] even blanker . . . in regard both to the study of homosexualities and the protection of lesbian and gay anthropologists and those of whatever sexual orientation who study homosexualities from discrimination in the US in general and within American anthropology in particular." (Murray 2017)

ND: What institutional barriers did you face due to your sexuality? Or your focus on homosexuality?

SOM IN PRINT: In *Pieces for a History of Gay Studies* (2017) Stephen reports being advised to not undertake research in gay studies and one of his professors had scribbled on one of his projects, "We are not interested in your lifestyle." It was this institutional environment with which gay men wanting to do gay studies had to contend. "Some gay men doing gay studies beyond the fringes of academia, who persisted in writing about homosexualities in various cultures without any research funding, managed to publish books which, then, were not reviewed in anthropology journals, or, in a few instances, were reviewed by lesbians hostile to male sexualities." (Murray 2017)

ND: If you don't accept the label queer in any form, what are your thoughts on queer identity as a fuck you to hetero- and gender normativities? As a methodology or theory?

SOM IN PRINT: "Despite flirting with transgression, rejecting 'minoritizing logic' and making everyone 'queer' to some extent, academics who sometimes engage in same-sex sex have challenged the basis of organizing by those defining themselves by differences in sexual object choice. There are no more "homosexuals," and those who continue to define themselves as gay (or as lesbian) are treated as relics who can safely be ignored in a post-gay world (not that discrimination has disappeared or that 'queer' has been drained of its venomous connotations of effeminacy assumed to correlate with receptivity to rape of effeminate males who "really want it" when they resist providing sexual service to those who have not heard that everyone is queer . . .)." (Murray 2017)

"Many retrospective studies [on the gay liberation movement] . . . heavily romanticize everything unconventional as instances of 'resistance' to heteronormative patriarchy . . . [Instead] there were congregations of homosexual male Americans who despised drag and effeminacy and wanted to hang out with gender-conforming (i.e., masculine-acting and straight-appearing) peers." (Murray 2017)

"Descriptive studies done during the 1970s seem forgotten, and their authors (dismissed as naïve 'essentialists') have been lost to the lesbigay studies that have emerged with (mostly groundless) pretensions of being 'theoretical.'" (Murray 1996a, 8–9)

"The more recent jettisoning of 'lesbian and gay' for 'queer' has further marginalized homosexuality as a focus for interpretation (let alone research . . .)." (Murray, 2017)

ND: In what ways do you feel your queerness has affected the way you practice anthropology, if at all?

SOM: Being gay has contributed to my skepticism about authority and authorities.

SOM IN PRINT: "The analytical bent and interest in alternative social, cultural, and sexual organizations that motivated me to undertake graduate work in sociology, anthropology, and linguistics definitely also underlay attempts to understand my own sexuality and various social organizations of male homosexuality." (Murray 1996b, 236)

ND: What brought you to anthropology?

SOM: What "brought me" was the sort of estrangement from one's own natal culture similar to what Lévi-Strauss wrote about in *Tristes Tropiques* (1992) and which I immediately recognized with an interest in trying to make sense of other sociocultural relationships over time.

ND: Have you ever written your coming-out story? Activism stories? How did the HIV epidemic impact you?

SOM: "My practice" is and has been to listen to what marginalized subjects say about their selves and the cultures in which they feel estranged.

ND: I suspect his lack of direct response on these questions were because the answers can be found elsewhere, not that they were irrelevant.

SOM IN PRINT: Indeed, his coming-out story in many ways was his work. As he says in his chapter "Male Homosexuality in Guatemala," "Research and life are not distinctly compartmentalized for me" (Murray 1996b, 236). It was his early days in Mexico and Guatemala where, seemingly clueless regarding the subtle—and sometimes not so subtle—ways men signaled their interest in each other, Stephen learned how to do so in the pursuit of sexual connection. Here he was immersing himself in the field with the natural conversations and other observations from his encounters that became the basis for his work in the 1970s. It was also at this time that Stephen came to Toronto as the city was experiencing a gay de-assimilation and "pioneer work on homosexuality was . . . sought out by gay academics stimulated by the gay liberation movement in the early 1970s" (Murray 2017). This is when he seemed to come to terms with the idea of doing the "gay work" he had been discouraged from as a graduate student in sociology.

As for the HIV epidemic, Stephen wrote about its effect on American society in *American Gay* (Murray 1996a), but I was unaware of his HIV status at the time of my questioning. He discussed his status and sexual orientation in an interview with Manuel Fernández-Alemany in a blog post he published two weeks before his death (Murray 2019).

Concluding Comments by Rob Oppenheim and Regna Darnell

RD: In November 2018 Steve initiated a meeting in San Jose during the American Anthropological Association meetings to discuss succession planning with me and Matt Bokovoy from the University of Nebraska Press; the photo that heads this interview was taken by Keelung Hong at that time. We were to discuss who might take over Steve's coeditorship of CSHOA and also to some extent his role with HOAA, on whose editorial board he had served from the beginning. Steve's health appeared to be stabilizing at that time, and we agreed that inviting Rob Oppenheim, his only proposed replacement, was a good plan. Steve intended to stay on as a third coeditor for at least a year and we proceeded with the press on that basis. The invitation to Rob occasioned further discussion on Steve's thoughts for the series and for HoA more generally. It thus seems a fitting closure for this interview.

RO: I never met Steve in person—and unfortunately that remained the case even as my potential succession of him as coeditor of the CSHOA series was being discussed. My first encounter with him was through his work, and it illustrates how many sides there were to his career. As an anthropologist teaching about Korea in an Asian studies department, notably one with a strong Taiwan studies component, I had been interested in the question of different ways in which area and theory interact in the making of anthropologies (and histories). As if to prove the point, this led me to see Steve first through his collaboration with Keelung Hong and the critical history of American anthropologists "looking through" Taiwan that they developed (e.g., Murray and Hong 1998; Hong and Murray 2005). These writings featured in several courses of mine, and when it came time for me to try to publish my own take on the issue, Steve's coeditorship of CSHOA helped influence me toward the Nebraska series. In reading and commenting on the manuscript, Steve was trenchant, good at rooting out my excesses, and at times very, very funny.

I didn't know about the preliminary discussions that Steve, Regna Darnell, and Matt Bokovoy had had about the CSHOA succession. On January 27, 2019, I received an email from Steve in which he matter-of-factly noted the resurgence of his illness and his decision to step down, and then sought to gauge my interest. Over a few exchanges, we discussed several perspectives that we share; he wrote that he has tried to "advocate for publication of research about anthropologies beyond those on Native North America" and stated his aversion to "biographical hagiographies" (SOM to RO January 27, 2019). In reading a draft of this memorial interview, I've discovered a few others—we both have had more time for Max Weber, for instance, than most East Asianists, for whom Weber (or Weber via Parsons) tends to be associated solely with the worst sort of religion-produces-economic development (or not) theorizing.

The transition of roles barely seemed to be happening, and then it was done. Steve wrote Regna and me on August 19, just over a week before his death, saying that he "was expecting to be around for more of a transition" (SOM to RD and RO, August 19, 2019). At about the same time, he did some final work for CSHOA, and I my first, in adding to Regna's draft of the series editors' introduction for Grażyna Kubica-Heller's forthcoming book on Marie Czaplicka. It was a project Steve had strongly endorsed, and one I was thus happy to get started with.

RD: The story was much the same behind the scenes. Steve was eager to maintain interest in Asia and more generally in ethnographic approaches within an areal framework as the most likely to produce "critical studies" in HoA. He "did not approve," a characteristic phrase, of hagiographies, especially when the biographical subject was not framed relative to a network of interacting scholars in a specific time and place.

NOTE

1. I (WLH) published a book review of each of these books, for very different audiences (Leeds-Hurwitz 1987, 1996, 2002), and have drawn heavily on those sources for this part of the text.

REFERENCES

Darnell, R. 2001. *Invisible Genealogies: A History of Americanist Anthropology*. Lincoln: University of Nebraska Press.

Griffith, B. C., and N. C. Mullins. 1972. "Coherent Social Groups in Scientific Change." *Science* 177, 959–64.

Hong, K., and S. O. Murray. 2005. *Looking through Taiwan: American Anthropologists' Collusion with Ethnic Domination*. Lincoln: University of Nebraska Press.

Kuhn, T. 1962. *The Structure of Scientific Revolutions*. Chicago IL: University of Chicago Press.

Leeds-Hurwitz, W. 1984. "On the Relationship of the 'Ethnography of Speaking' to the 'Ethnography of Communication.' *Papers in Linguistics* 17, no. 1: 7–32.

———. 1987. "Review of Stephen O. Murray, *Group Formation in Social Science*." *Language* 63, no. 3: 668–71.

————. 1996. "Review of Stephen O. Murray, *Theory Groups in the Study of Language in North America.*" *Communication Theory* 6, no. 1: 104–7.

————. 2002. "Review of Stephen O. Murray, *American Sociolinguistics: Theories and Theory Groups.*" *Journal of the History of the Behavioral Sciences* 38, no. 2: 195–96.

————. 2004. *Rolling in Ditches with Shamans: Jaime de Angulo and the Professionalization of American Anthropology.* Lincoln: University of Nebraska Press.

Lévi-Strauss, C. (1975) 1992. *Tristes tropiques.* Translated by J. Weightman and D. Weightman. New York: Penguin.

Lewin, E., and W. Leap, eds. 1996. *Out in the Field: Reflections of Lesbian and Gay Anthropologists.* Chicago: University of Illinois Press.

————. 2002. *Out in Theory: The Emergence of Lesbian and Gay Anthropology.* Chicago: University of Illinois Press.

Murray, S. O. 1983. *Group Formation in Social Science.* Edmonton AB: Linguistic Research.

————. 1994. *Theory Groups and the Study of Language in North America: A Social History.* Amsterdam: John Benjamins.

————. 1995. *Latin American Male Homosexualities.* Albuquerque: University of New Mexico Press.

————. 1996a. *American Gay.* Chicago IL: University of Chicago Press.

————. 1996b. "Male Homosexuality in Guatemala: Possible Insights and Certain Confusions from Sleeping with Natives." In *Out in the Field: Reflections of Lesbian and Gay Anthropologists,* edited by E. Lewin and W. Leap. Chicago: University of Illinois Press, 236–60.

————. 1998. *American Sociolinguistics: Theorists and Theory Groups.* Amsterdam: John Benjamins.

————. 2000. *Homosexualities.* Chicago IL: University of Chicago Press.

————. 2010. "Interactional sociolinguistics at Berkeley. In *The Social History of Language and Social Interaction Research: People, Places, Ideas,* edited by W. Leeds-Hurwitz. Cresskill NJ: Hampton Press, 97–126.

————. 2017. *Pieces for a History of Gay Studies.* San Francisco CA: El Instituto Obregon. E-book.

————. 2018. *American Anthropology and Company: Historical Explorations.* Lincoln: University of Nebraska Press.

————. 2019. "On *Homosexualities.*" *The Tangent Group* (blog), Homosexual Information Center, Inc. August 13, 2019. tangentgroup.org/on-homosexualities.

Murray, S. O., and K. Hong. 1988. "Taiwan, China, and the 'Objectivity' of Dictatorial Elites." *American Anthropologist* 90, no. 4: 976–78.

———. 1991. "American Anthropologists Looking through Taiwanese Culture." *Dialectical Anthropology* 16, no. 3–4: 273–99.

———. 1994. *Taiwanese Culture, Taiwanese Society: A Critical Review of Social Science Research Done on Taiwan.* Lanham MD: University Press of America.

Murray, S. O., and W. Roscoe, eds. 1997. *Islamic Homosexualities: Culture, History, and Literature.* New York: New York University Press.

Murray, S. O., and W. Roscoe. 1998. *Boy-wives and Female Husbands: Studies of African Homosexualities.* New York: St. Martin's Press.

San Francisco Chronicle. 2019. Stephen O. Murray: 1950–2019. *San Francisco Chronicle*, September 29, 2019. https://www.legacy.com/obituaries /sfgate/obituary.aspx?n=stephen-o-murray&pid=193983043.

CONTRIBUTORS

Nicholas Barron, Department of Anthropology, University of New Mexico;
email: nbarron@unm.edu

Regna Darnell, Department of Anthropology, Western University, emerita;
email: rdarnell@uwo.ca

Nathan Dawthorne, Department of Anthropology, Western University;
email: ndawthor@uwo.ca

North de Pencier, MD, Faculty of Medicine, University of Toronto, email:
nddepencier@gmail.com

Frederic W. Gleach, Department of Anthropology, Cornell University;
email: fwg1@cornell.edu

Geoffrey Gray, The School of Historical and Philosophical Inquiry,
University of Queensland; email: g.gray1@uq.edu.au

Charles D. Laughlin, Department of Sociology and Anthropology,
Carleton University (emeritus); email: cdlaughlin@gmail.com

Wendy Leeds-Hurwitz, Center for Intercultural Dialogue; Communication
Department, University of Wisconsin-Parkside (emerita); email:
wendy.leeds.hurwitz@gmail.com

Herbert S. Lewis, Department of Anthropology, University of Wisconsin
(emeritus); email: hslewis@wisc.edu

Gerald McKinley, Department of Pathology and Laboratory Medicine,
Department of Anthropology, Schulich Interfaculty Program in
Public Health, Schulich School of Medicine and Dentistry, Western
University; email: gerald.mckinley@schulich.uwo.ca

Vintilă Mihăilescu, (late) Department of Sociology, National University of
Political Studies and Public Administration in Bucharest

Robert Oppenheim, Department of Asian Studies, University of Texas,
Austin; email: rmo@austin.utexas.edu

David C. Posthumus, Department of Anthropology and Sociology,
University of South Dakota; email: David.Posthumus@usd.edu

Ian Puppe, Department of Anthropology, Indigenous Studies Program, Western University; email: ipuppe@uwo.ca

Joshua Smith, Department of World Languages and Cultures, Iowa State University; email: josmith@iastate.edu

Adrian Tanner, Department of Anthropology, Memorial University; email: atanner@mun.ca

www.ingramcontent.com/pod-product-compliance
Lightning Source LLC
Chambersburg PA
CBHW032345280326
41935CB00008B/459